The Promise of Social Marketing

T0361966

Social marketing is an exciting new field of study that promises much to help alleviate many dilemmas of the human condition. It may be associated with any social project undertaken where human interests (short and long term) override commercial ones. *The Promise of Social Marketing* examines the potential of this new field to help address effectively local and global issues that most nations are grappling with. It clarifies the history, philosophies, disciplines and techniques associated with best practice and highlights the need to engage with this field to help develop it further, so as to benefit humanity as a whole.

There is an ongoing debate about the nature of marketing and whether it is able to fulfill or adapt to both commercial and social objectives. The unifying view is that marketing is a tool that can be used for individual, organizational or social benefits, and the aim of this book is to introduce the reader to an approach that is developing into a promising and rich new science, currently known as Social Marketing. It is a tool that brings hope to improving the world for good.

The book guides the reader, step by step, demonstrating how this promising area can be applied to aims as diverse as HIV/AIDS prevention, responsible (global) citizenship, conflict resolution or the promotion of a worthwhile education. It will be of interest to not only those who study marketing, management, business ethics, education and public policy but anybody who's interest is in improving the human condition.

Dr Chahid Fourali has backgrounds in psychology, education and marketing and has published extensively in all three areas. He led the consultation with the UK Government to set up the Marketing and Sales Standards Setting Body, which he then led for eight years, as well as, the development of three sets of world-class national occupational standards (in Marketing, Sales and Social Marketing) that were supported by many internationally recognized marketing/business gurus. These standards are now the basis for all nationally recognized qualifications in the UK in the three professional areas.

Dr Fourali is Senior Lecturer in Management at the London Metropolitan Business School and is examiner/subject expert for Cambridge University and University of Hertfordshire. He achieved Fellowship or professional membership status from several international organisations including FRSA, FCIM and BABCP (Psychotherapy).

The Promise of Social Marketing

A Powerful Tool for Changing the World for Good

Chahid Fourali

Routledge
Taylor & Francis Group

LONDON AND NEW YORK

First published 2016 by Routledge

2 Park Square, Milton Park, Abingdon, Oxfordshire OX14 4RN
52 Vanderbilt Avenue, New York, NY 10017

Routledge is an imprint of the Taylor & Francis Group, an informa business

First issued in paperback 2020

British Library Cataloguing in Publication Data
A catalogue record for this book is available from the British Library

Library of Congress Cataloguing in Publication Data
A catalog record for this book is available from the Library of Congress

ISBN: 978-1-4724-1685-8 (hbk)
ISBN: 978-0-367-59628-6 (pbk)

Typeset in Times New Roman
by Out of House Publishing

To my mother and the memory of my father, the archetypal loving parents.

Contents

Figures and Tables

Figures

Tables

Acknowledgements

This book may not have been written was it not for the support from many friends and family members (some are both!). Among these, I would like to register my gratitude to the many wonderful people whom I was lucky to meet and benefit from their kindness. Although there are too many to list, I would like to particularly mention the following:

- My sister, Souhila (technically Wensiya, who clearly lives up to her name).
- My brother Hourouf Eddine for his dedication to the family and being such an inexhaustible source of support.
- My Tarik Enasr, for his inspiration and dedication to preserving the memory of our father.
- Karima, for her valued companionship.
- Elzbieta, for being a trusted partner and a savvy professional advisor.
- Samih and Nour, I know your patients will be in responsible hands.
- Karim, wherever you are, I wish you the best of happiness.
- Hiba, a valuable gift to a worthy mother.
- Professor Malcolm McDonald for his wise words, support and reviewing an earlier draft of this book.
- Professor Jeff French for his thorough advice when reviewing an earlier draft of this book. His support is not new as his contribution, while at the helm of the National Social Marketing Centre, was instrumental in helping develop the new UK national standards of social marketing.
- Professor Philip Kotler for his kind support during the development of the first UK national standards of social marketing.
- Professor Gerald Hasting for his kind support in helping develop the first UK national standards of social marketing and, together with Dr Christine Domegan, for allowing the use of their case study on the truckers' eating habits in Ireland.
- All national and international contributors (many of whom friends and colleagues) that helped the development of the world-class marketing and social marketing competence standards, thereby helping to prepare the ground for this book.
- Kristina Abbotts, from Gower, for her helpful advice and support.

- Last but not least, my gratitude to Dr Fitz Taylor who, despite his departure from this world, remains a powerful influence for good on many of his students (and consequently, their students).

As with all acknowledgements, one always tends to miss or overlook the important contributions of some key influences. I would therefore like to apologize for any such oversight.

Finally, whilst the primary dedication is directed to my parents, Halima and Mouloud Fourali, by the same token, the book is also dedicated to all parents devoted to nurturing their children with a humane and just perspective, despite the countless obstacles facing them, thereby helping to create a fairer world that ultimately benefits all the children. This is implied by the qualifiers 'the archetypal parents'. The devotion to such goals must be unrelenting as the challenges are continuous and success is often mixed with failures.

Preface

There are countless books telling us about what is wrong with the world. These range from destructive attitudes within our societies such as 'if you are not wealthy, you are nothing' to extended descriptions about why there is so much injustice in the world (war, economic hardships, discriminations, etc.). Being aware of such problems in the world is important but what seems to be lacking are solutions. Additionally, such solutions should work. At times we are provided with a detailed analysis about various problems in the world and, in broad terms, what should happen to re-establish the balance. However, what tends to be generally missing is 'how do we implement a programme that can lead to a change that establishes a fair society that is at ease with itself?' This is the purpose of this book. It is to introduce a new proven approach, with practical advice and examples, about how to make the world a better place. The method, which is known as social marketing (SM), may as well be known as 'social cause methodology' or 'science', given the confusion the word 'marketing' can induce in the reader, as will be seen later. This new method, its benefits and associated evidence, will be demonstrated throughout the pages of this book. We believe that anybody who thinks there is something wrong with the world should take time to get to know this method as it can be a powerful addition to his or her 'good will armamentarium', thereby offering real opportunities to make a difference.

While this approach benefits from the insights achieved through studying the powerful techniques of marketing (widely demonstrated in the world of business), its approach and philosophy are very different. Hence it is important to differentiate this discipline from general marketing but also from other potentially misleading meanings, as explained later. Indeed, while marketing's interest is commercial viability and profitability, SM's primary concern is human welfare.

A reader may also inadvertently infer that this book is about how companies can maximize benefits through commitment to corporate social responsibility (CSR). Although this CSR is an important field that has its advocates for the long-term health (and viability) of a company (e.g., Davidson, 2002), its perspective would still be ultimately concerned with a company's commercial success rather than how to address human ills as a primary focus.

Other readers not acquainted with the concept of social marketing may also consider two other associations. One is that this is about the use of 'social media' and how they may help improve our society. Perhaps even the ideas of WikiLeaks, YouTube and Facebook come to mind, and how much they did to expose so-called 'honest politicians'. Perhaps a more accurate interpretation of the word 'social', in the sense of 'using marketing knowledge for social good', may lead to feelings of irritation, since 'marketing' and 'social good' have long been relegated to the depth of our psyche under the label 'arch-enemies' and, consequently, cannot be seen as mutually compatible! The latter interpretation has no shortage of supporters as marketing, for many readers, is the source of many evils: corruption of society, 'affluenza', unhealthy behaviour and destructive educational practices to mention just a few. All these are seen as emanating from irresponsible people intent on maximizing profit even at the price of destroying our local and global communities.

The two concepts, 'social' and 'marketing' may also attract a view about the nature of human beings and their dependence on marketing, and associated capitalist society, in maximizing their happiness. Indeed, since the dawn of humanity and throughout their lives humans, individually and as part of communities, have continuously asked the question: how do we reconcile our specific needs with those of others who share our world? As demonstrated in several disciplines of study, there are always advocates reflecting different positions in the spectrum of positions located between the polar opposites. Take psychology, where a century ago Freud argued about the need to stave off the extremes of both opposites (in the form of the id, the king of unbridled desires, and the super ego, the king of total restraint) by a 'reality' conscious entity he called the ego. In a similar vein, consider the work of Adam Smith that argued for encouraging 'rational' self-interest in helping develop a nation's economy. Clearly the question was considered because of genuine interest in doing good (or at least not hurting others), while others asked it because of what some psychologists termed 'enlightened self-interest' (or wise selfishness). Irrespective of the advocated reasons, one may argue that most big issues may go back to human societies' need to strike the right balance between individuals, groups and the wider needs of our global community. Indeed, some of the problems that used to be clearly circumscribed to certain parts of the world are becoming more and more global in that any dissension anywhere in the world may affect the very balance that many well-intentioned educators, politicians and community leaders are constantly trying to maintain, taking into consideration as many needs as possible. At times when there is an imbalance for a protracted period, this may lead people to take matters into their hands. Consider recent events such as the Arab Spring, WikiLeaks, the 'Big Society'[1] and the 'Occupy Wall Street' movements. Such recent events seem to also suggest that our societies are no longer happy with handing over completely their responsibilities to an abstract entity, a government, that assures them it is there to meet their every need. They are also increasingly more demanding in the sense that 'absence of war' (be that cold war or otherwise) is not an ideal state but rather a prerequisite state to something better.

Indeed grievances are countless and so are the solutions. Some of those solutions have been labelled too radical. However, according to some (e.g., Fukuyama, 1992), the recent past has clearly indicated that there are not many options left for running any national economy except through a liberal marketing/capitalist philosophy. Nevertheless, even if it is assumed that some form of capitalism is the future, clearly there is a need to ensure that the form of capitalism that wins the day is more socially responsible than the current one that allows huge gaps in the 'economic means' scale. This position would be supported by Piketty (2013) who recently launched a scathing attack on those who claim that governments/international bodies are powerless when it comes to regulating capitalism abuses:

> We are told constantly that states can't do anything, that it's impossible to regulate the Cayman Islands and the other tax havens because they are too powerful, and all of a sudden we send a million soldiers 10,000 km from home to allow the emir of Kuwait to keep his oil.
>
> (Piketty, in Chassany, 2015)

This may be a caricature of the event, and the current Middle Eastern situation, ironically, shows that the international interventions in the Middle East (or, some would say, the way they were carried out) appear to have been a big mistake. Nevertheless, what the statement illustrates is that if world governments are genuinely concerned about the ill-effects of a particular situation, with potential global consequences, they can find the will and resolve to take action to make the world a better place. The only proviso that could be made for such intervention would be that the action has been taken primarily as a result of genuine concern for fellow humans after weighing up the consequences of inaction.

Indeed any concept (or ideology) can be positioned in a continuum including the word 'capitalism'. At one end there is the cold capitalism whose proponents argue that society's leaders should not temper with market transactions if they want it to succeed and, eventually, maximize welfare to everybody. At the other end there is the kind and caring capitalism (if this is not a contradiction in terms) where the primary purpose of all businesses is to serve and support the society within which they operate or, using another more fashionable expression in business circles, '*noblesse oblige*'. In-between these opposites, there is the capitalism that is continuously balancing the needs of either end to ensure the needs of businesses are taken into account while keeping in mind the pervasiveness of the benefits accrued to all society's members.

Now, given the demise of communism as we knew it and the widespread adoption of marketing/capitalist philosophy, is there still a chance of addressing society's ills effectively?

This book's contention is an emphatic 'yes'. It offers social marketing, for lack of a better name as explained later, as a promising new field that, if adopted fully and objectively, would become the engine for social change in a market (or any reasonably liberal) economy. Not only that, but it can be in many ways the conscience of the market society that while operating from within this model can still offer 'radical' changes that will keep improving the welfare of all members of society (and perhaps help mitigate against the internal contradictions referred to by social theorists) to help create a society that is both economically and socially viable. In our sense, the word 'market' in 'market society' does not only refer to products and services whose aim is to make a profit. Rather, 'market' could refer to a market of ideas of social welfare, inclusion and justice that wins support and becomes a potent social force that, in turn, commercial marketing needs to notice for its own survival.

My Influences Regarding This Topic

Before proceeding further, I would like to state the reasons for my interest in this discipline. Perhaps two key influences have been most prominent in this interest: my father and my early studies. Let's start with the influence of my father.

I am very proud of my father despite the ambivalence of his presence in my life. My father died in the war of liberation that took place in Algeria following a revolt that started in November 1954. His ultimate sacrifice was honoured and a street was named after him following the Algerian independence in 1962. The ambivalence of his presence was reflected through his physical absence, as he joined the struggle for independence while I was too young to remember him. The departure of my dad did not mean 'out of sight out of mind'. In fact, his presence was continuous and his memory was preserved by my mother, a most loyal wife and companion. Not least among the family memory was the recurrent story reflected in our family's names. To understand this aspect I will, chronologically, list the names of all brothers, including one that passed away at a very young age, and a sister:

Souhila
Nour Eddine (died when he was two)
Hourouf Eddine
Chahid Elhak
Tarik Enasr

All the names above were allocated or agreed to by my father except for one: that of my sister Souhila (her later adopted name) whom my father registered as 'Mensiya' (meaning 'most deserving' or 'forgotten'). Perhaps the reader may consider this name as very unkind if we adopt the negative interpretation of the word 'Mensiya', which, of course, may also mean 'most deserving' since a person whose needs are not recognized may deserve most attention.

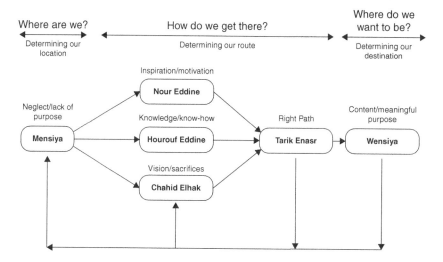

Figure 0.1 The Fourali name framework: a unique purposeful appellation

Additionally, my father recognized the plight and servitude of Algeria and its indigenous population early on in his life and was always looking for opportunities to help the movement of liberation. He devised a scheme to reflect the situation of Algeria, a country he very much loved, and its way forward, as shown in Figure 0.1. The difference is that the scheme was not written down in published papers. That would be too dangerous to do. He devised a different strategy. He was aware of the potential of names in reflecting and disseminating messages. So he took this idea to a fine art. He instructed my mother about what name she should register for each one of us including the name of my sister, their first-born, Mensiya. He explained that when Algeria will be freed, her name should be changed to 'Wensiya' after changing just the first letter of her name. The name Wensiya means 'great female companion'. Note that apart from one name, Nour Eddine, all the other instructed names were improvised by my father. Arguably he accepted the suggestion of Nour Eddine, as the name for his first son, because it matched his message of liberation scheme. Consider the above diagram.

The diagram reflects a purposeful scheme describing a strategy for the liberation from the yoke of servitude. We may call it a 'name consilience model' as it reflects convergence of the various names to a single purpose; or the 'name symphony model' to highlight the synchronicity and mutual dependence between the purposes of the various names (the musical instruments) to provide the required symphony (the solution message). The model starts with an assessment of a situation, qualified as a state of neglect (Mensiya) compared to where Algeria should be (Wensiya, a state of comfort and ease). Such assessment therefore calls for planning and action to bring about the sought-for state. The plan is a three-pronged approach reflected in each of the subsequent names:

- Step 1: the adoption of inspiring sacred values to guide or enlighten our way. This is represented by the name Nour Eddine, meaning literally 'light of the way'. Eddine comes from the root word 'Din', which can mean 'religion' or 'way of life'.
- Step 2: the design of clear guidance as to what to do in our chosen way of life written in a language that is compatible with the chosen way of life. This is represented in the name Hourouf Eddine, meaning literally the 'letters (or language) of the chosen way'. This seems to focus on the need for a clear description of purpose and process. Additionally the issue of language and its influence on the psychology and culture of a people will be taken up later.
- Step 3: Readiness to offer a clear vision supported by evidence and dedication to achieving it. This is represented by the name Chahid Elhak, literally meaning 'witness' or 'martyr for the cause of truth'.

The next stage is to determine what constitutes a victorious route (Tarik Enasr). This stage mediates between the previous, situation analysis stage, and the next, targeted outcome stage, to identify what would constitute a programme of actions that lead to success. However it also means that such programme once started should not be left to 'its own devices' to run by itself, as we know that even with the best of will, the best programmes can be diverted from their original aims as a result of many factors, not least individual errors or wilful manipulation based on selected individuals' or groups' invested interest. Hence, based on fair and mutually agreed institutions, it would be possible to establish the right structure that could independently advise on the direction of the programmes of changes that would progressively, but surely, lead to an Algeria at ease with itself, other nations and the broader environment (Wensiya).

The model is also iterative in that if there is any problem at the later stages, this may be reviewed by reconsidering the previous stages. The model clearly does not go into the details of meanings and sub-steps but rather provides a broad guide for a concerted, integrative approach that would need to determine the specific details of each stage. If the process of determining the specific details is trustworthy and inclusive (supported by right values) it should not be too difficult to agree a common way to which the whole nation could subscribe.

Some may wonder why so much symbolism in the names. The answer is that during the war of liberation in Algeria – where it is estimated about 1.5 million Algerians died as a result of a brutal colonization – any sign that could arouse suspicion could mean torture or even capital punishment.

The above model should not only be restricted to the Algerian context. It can serve all movements of liberation at individual or group levels.

Such a scheme has inspired me throughout my life, although originally the full logic of it was not clear to me. Thanks to my mother, I feel I have now managed to understand the picture. Nevertheless, it is possible that the full meaning is yet to be reached, as the designer of this scheme, my father, is unfortunately no longer around.

Hence, my father's approach was not just about encouraging an emotional, blind, knee-jerk reaction to events showing injustice, but rather he tacitly seemed to advocate a systematic yet iterative model of analysis, planning and action followed by more analysis to ensure we are not swayed away from the original target.

This approach is very humanitarian too, as the target was injustice rather than serving particular groups or individuals. If we are to contextualize it to today's business world, his mantra could be 'justice for real success'. So humans need to address what constitutes justice to all human beings and what constitutes genuine success to business, bearing in mind that for many business writers, the real purpose of business is to serve, first and foremost.

Hence such an approach is very compatible with the social marketing approach as advocated in this book. It combines values, process, outcomes and a constant concern for improvements.

Additionally the scheme reminds us that although SM has generally been applied primarily to focus on social ills, in principle it can apply to any situation (local or international) that may require attending to with a view to promoting a healthier local or global society. Accordingly, local or international politics should be legitimately targeted as they may be the source of many social ills.

If we take the political perspective, we may consider a newly independent country. In this context, what constitutes success is not just the departure of the colonizing forces from the country, allowing the country to have a government and a military force made up of the citizens of the country. Rather, true independence is also cultural and psychological. How can a nation be truly free if its conscious or unconscious judgements about values are dependent on the values left behind (in its citizens' psyche) by the so-called 'departing colonizer'? If the departure is only physical then the freedom has never been gained. There are too many arguments regarding the legacy of colonialism (e.g., Fanon, 1963; Said, 1979; Spivak, 1988; Loomba, 2005). These go beyond the physical violence inflicted on the colonized people, the plundering of their natural resources or the subsequent economic dependency on the ex-colonizer. Perhaps an insidious legacy that tends to go undetected by its victims, for obvious reasons, is that 'they start seeing themselves through the eyes of the coloniser and speak with the coloniser's voice' (McCowan and Unterhalter, 2015, p. 41). In psychological theory, once individuals adopt certain beliefs and make them part of their identity, it becomes very difficult to dislodge them, as any attempt at challenging such characteristics could provoke an aggressive reaction. It is ironic that one of the leading authors that diagnosed this condition,

Franz Fanon, developed many of his ideas influenced by his experiences in Algeria. This argument applies to anybody who mindlessly adopts the lifestyle and values of the previous colonizer. This argument equally applies to any simplistic solution that some people pick up, promising their people that it would solve all their problems. The first task for any nation to help itself is to learn to think for itself and be involved responsibly in finding a common solution. I believe social marketing can be a very effective tool that can help in such situations. What makes it particularly effective is its natural ability to make use of as many disciplines as possible to help produce constructive, future building solutions.

My second influence in deciding to write this book is my professional life trajectory, which started in educational sciences then developed to include counselling, psychotherapy and, finally, the discipline of marketing, as I was lucky enough to find myself looking after a national body that sets standards of marketing best practice for the whole of the UK and beyond. These three facets of my background made me aware that there are several social ills that would benefit from a more encompassing initiative. For example, as I worked in counselling and psychotherapy I became aware that the cost of one-to-one sessions over many months, if not more, is not very effective given the size of the population that suffers from psychological problems, as highlighted by several studies (e.g., Layard et al., 2007). The pervasiveness of psychological illness, however, should not be taken as a simplistic problem, as suggested by many writers, who regarded simplistic approaches as missing the wood for the trees (Marzillier and Hall, 2009; Bentall, 2003; Dowrick, 2004). In particular it was claimed that the medical model was too reductionist and argued for the need to adopt a broader perspective that helps assess more accurately both the mental conditions and what contributes to them. Such an approach helps clarify not only what constitutes a healthy versus unhealthy mental condition (e.g., intense pressure or sadness does not necessarily mean a diagnosis of depression that requires psychological support), as argued by Horwitz and Wakefield (2007), but also take into consideration the variety of factors that may be at play (including economic hardship) to provide a more accurate assessment of the situation. As we will see, SM offers just such an approach. We hope you will enjoy reading the book.

Note

1 Regarding Big Society issues, a good introductory paper is Morris and Gilchrist (2011).

1 From Commercial to Socially Responsible Marketing

Since the introduction of modern marketing as a promising business discipline, sometimes attributed to Theodore Levitt (1960), noises have been made that the concept seemed to be too concentrated on tangible/commercial products. Despite the potential relevance of the marketing paradigm to almost anything we can think of (i.e., 'being customer-centric'), arguments were being made about the restrictive nature of the application of the concept of marketing. Indeed even Kotler, generally credited as one of the key influences on this discipline, soon made the argument that marketing is not just about promoting toothpastes (see Kotler and Levy, 1969; Kotler and Zaltman, 1971). Other voices joined and started to argue for the inclusion of other topics such as non-profit marketing and religious marketing (e.g., see Evans and Moutinho, 1999).

So what is social marketing? Is this just another case of hyperbole?

The aim of the next section is to introduce the concept of SM and define it broadly. Subsequently its precursors will be reviewed in turn for the rest of this section of the book.

There are many great products, services and ideas about how to make the world a better place but, as many marketing gurus would advocate, bad marketing usually leads to failed business enterprises. The reverse is also true: 'how many "unnecessary" or, even destructive products affect huge sections of our societies as a result of clever marketing (fatty food, alcoholic drinks, cigarettes, etc.)?' (Fourali, 2010).

The Journey from Marketing to Social Marketing

As is regularly argued (e.g., Fourali, 2010), social marketing (SM) is a relatively recent concept derived in the 1970s as a result of the development of the marketing concept. Hence it would make sense to first look at the broader concept of marketing before venturing toward any definition associated with SM.

But trying to define a concept is no small feat. Perhaps the following anecdote may demonstrate the point: a few years ago I was asked by the director of research of the Chartered Institute of Marketing (CIM) to be involved in a project for reviewing its famous definition of marketing. After several meetings/discussions and sifting through many new 'definitions' suggested by the great and the good in marketing, it was decided to stick with the current (previously existing) definition as there was no agreement among the contributors about a new definition 'for the new millennium'.

Nevertheless, let's review some of the well-known marketing definitions before contrasting them with the social marketing perspective.

> Marketing is a social and managerial process by which individuals and groups obtain what they need and want through creating and exchanging products and value with others.
>
> (Kotler et al., 2001)

> Marketing is the management process responsible for identifying, anticipating and satisfying customer requirements profitably.
>
> (CIM, 2016)

> Marketing is the activity, set of institutions, and processes for creating, communicating, delivering, and exchanging offerings that have value for customers, clients, partners, and society at large.
>
> (AMA, 2016)

> Marketing is the process of achieving corporate goals through meeting and exceeding customer needs better than the competition.
>
> (Jobber, 2003)

As we can see above only one definition mentions the word 'social' as part of the definition of marketing. This was the one proposed by Kotler et al. (2001). This comes as no surprise as Kotler was one of the two authors generally credited with presenting the SM concept, as we will see later.

A more functional approach to defining the aims of marketing (responding to the question: 'what is the key purpose of marketing?') was produced by the now defunct UK-based Marketing and Sales Standards Setting Body (MSSSB), following extensive consultations with marketing professionals inside and outside the UK (as will be shown later in the section on World-Class Standards for SM), as follows:

> Marketing's key purpose is to advance the aims of organizations (whether private, public or voluntary) by providing direction, gaining commitment and achieving sustainable results and value through identifying, anticipating and satisfying stakeholder requirements.
>
> (Fourali, 2008)

This definition already took into account the fact that there are public and voluntary dimensions to marketing. However, is this enough to position the above definition as 'social marketing' especially when other concepts lay claim to the words 'social' and 'public'? For example, consider cause-related marketing, where an organization allocates a percentage of its funds/budget to a social cause; societal marketing, which reflects responsible business practices such as having policies regarding recycling, fair-trade or sustainability; and pro-social marketing reflected in building up a case for a social cause (NSMC, 2006).

It has been argued that SM as a new concept was first proposed as a separate discipline in the 1970s by Philip Kotler and Gerald Zaltman when they realized that the same marketing principles/techniques that were being used to sell traditional products/services (such as toothpaste or gyms) to consumers could be used to 'sell' socially beneficent ideas, attitudes and behaviours (Weinreich, 2013). However, 25 years after the publication of this article, Kotler stated that other people already used the principles of SM without calling it SM. He quoted Wiebe (1952) who asked 'why can't you sell brotherhood like you sell soap?' Nevertheless, the origin of social marketing is debatable since people have been thinking about and implementing ideas about bettering social conditions for centuries, if not millennia. A useful question to raise following this development is: is there an agreement among SM practitioners about what constitutes social marketing?

Perhaps to start with let's look at some well known SM definitions:

> The application of commercial marketing technologies to the analysis, planning, execution, and evaluation of programs designed to influence voluntary behavior of target audiences in order to improve their personal welfare and that of society.
>
> (Andreasen, 1995)

> [SM is the] systematic application of marketing, alongside other concepts and techniques, to achieve specific behavioural goals, for a social good.
>
> (French and Blair-Stevens, 2005)

> [SM is] a process that applies marketing principles and techniques to create, communicate, and deliver value in order to influence target audience behaviors that benefit society (public health, safety, the environment and communities) as well as the target audience.
>
> (Kotler et al., 2006, pers. comm. reported by Smith, 2008)

Although all these definitions cover both behavioural and social aims, it seems that the National Social Marketing Centre (French and Blair-Stevens, 2005) does not preclude the use of other concepts and techniques from the work of social marketers. In other words, they allow the creativity of the marketer to make use of non-traditional marketing concepts/techniques if this serves the purpose at hand.

Nevertheless Stephen Dann (2009) argued at the First World Social Marketing Conference that there was a need for a new definition of SM. He

made use of a concept analysis software tool, known as Leximancer, to analyse no less than 45 then-existing definitions of social marketing. His suggested new definition was as follows:

> [SM is] the adaptation and adoption of commercial marketing activities,
> institutions and process as a means to induce behavioral change on a
> temporary or permanent basis.
>
> (Dann, 2009)

In my view, this definition seems to miss a key component of what constitutes
an SM perspective and that is the 'social good' dimension, unless the definition was only meant to reflect the general trend of views rather than what
'should' be included.

The author of this book was lucky to have been given the opportunity
to manage a national project for developing the very first national occupational standards for SM. The project was undertaken under the aegis of
the MSSSB, headed by the author. The project allowed him to link up with
many gurus of SM including Philip Kotler, Alan Andreasen, Jeff French,
Gerard Hasting, Craig Lefebvre, Ed Maibach and many others too many
to list here (e.g., see details of First World Social Marketing Conference
held in Brighton, UK at WSMC, 2008). The kind advice received from all
those involved was decisive in getting some common agreement on the key
components of SM. Our perspective in this project was not to just define
the topic but rather to come up with some kind of functional description of
SM to serve as the guiding reference for determining best practice. Hence,
instead of trying to encourage practitioners to provide us with yet another
definition of SM, we simply sought their help to provide us with 'the purpose of SM'. After many discussions and conceptual iterations, we came up
with the following key purpose of SM (this procedure will be presented in
more details later):

> To [a]pply marketing alongside other concepts and techniques in order to
> influence individuals, organizations, policy makers, and decision makers
> to adopt and sustain behaviour which improves people's lives.
>
> (Fourali, 2008)

Note that this definition reflects a few components of the National Social
Marketing Centre (NSMC) approach. This reflected the general agreement
among the contributors to the project that the NSMC was somehow closer to
the general perception of the aims of SM.

More recently, a consensus definition was produced following consultation
involving 167 members of the International Social Marketing Association,
the European Social Marketing Association and the Australian Association
of Social Marketing (Lefebvre, 2013a). The definition was meant to reflect
both the nature and purpose of social marketing. The resulting definition

these organizations endorsed, which came to be known as the 'consensus definition' of social marketing, states:

> Social Marketing seeks to develop and integrate marketing concepts with other approaches to influence behaviours that benefit individuals and communities for the greater social good.
>   Social Marketing practice is guided by ethical principles. It seeks to integrate research, best practice, theory, audience and partnership insight, to inform the delivery of competition sensitive and segmented social change programmes that are effective, efficient, equitable and sustainable.
>
>   (Lefebvre, 2013a)

This definition is clearly a good basis to build consensus. It seems that other definitions may need producing as the field develops to account for new developments. Perhaps the strongest element of this definition is that it made explicit the ethical dimension of SM with even an example of an ethical principle in the form of 'equity'. On the other hand, one still feels that the multi-disciplinary nature of SM may need to be made more explicit. Perhaps the 'fixing a problem situation' (reflected in the 'social change' expression) may also be moderated, as SM could be preventative in the sense of 'immunizing' individuals and communities from the likely occurrence of unwanted situations (e.g., through acquiring attitudes and lifestyles) and encouraging a happier outlook on life (e.g., developing resilience). Perhaps this is another area that SM may need to outgrow. Changing behaviour is important but preparation for a variety of scenarios (through developing the right attitude) can be seen as a more effective approach. After all, one of the weakest areas of the behavioural approach is that not only can it be superficial (as in the simple stimulus-response that may overlook the proverbial 'black-box' represented by the conscious thinking mind) but it may also not be inclusive enough of the varieties of situations that a programme may be trying to address. In a way, the ethical dimension suggests that behaviour has to be underpinned by core beliefs; however, these beliefs currently seem to be primarily located in the mind of the project managers rather than the target population. Such core beliefs are at the heart of sustainable change as advocated by cognitive psychologists. Given these observations an alternative, functional, definition may therefore be:

> SM is a multidisciplinary programme of change guided by a marketing philosophy, and inspired by strong ethical standards, to prevent, induce and/or sustain behavioural changes underpinned by core healthy beliefs that maximise the greater social good.

When considering the above, perhaps one may agree with the view that SM can be conceptualized as a mindset that reflects strategic planning, including partnerships development, with a view to influencing the behaviour of individuals, influential persons or policymakers for beneficial social and environmental changes (CDC, 2013). Nevertheless it is important to identify the key elements of this mindset or 'codify' it in order to not only ensure there are common grounds for recognizing SM but also provide a reference template to guide the implementation of SM programmes. In this respect French and Russell-Bennett (2015), building on earlier attempts (Andreasen, 2002; French and Blair-Stevens, 2005; Robinson-Maynard et al., 2013), came up with a helpful framework for determining the key dimensions that make up a SM programme. We feel the framework could have benefitted from a practical illustration to demonstrate its utility. We also feel that the idea of iteration that is inherent in adopting an action research perspective (see Chapter 8) would help improve the model through integrating within it the idea of cycles of research, implementation and evaluation. This and other issues will be discussed later in the book.

The next question one might ask is 'how does SM differ in practice from marketing?' This is the focus of the next section.

Differentiating Social Marketing from Marketing

Initially SM was very strongly associated with marketing. Researchers saw marketing as a tool that can be applied to a variety of situations including commercial and humanitarian/social objectives. This view is very much reflected by Lefebvre and Flora (1988), who argue that the key aspects of the marketing plan need addressing in order to market health. These key aspects involve analysis, planning, implementation and control. More specifically, market research enables the clarification of population needs and preferences. This would help determine the goals of the programme and the most likely target audience, as well as finalize the expected behavioural change. As part of the marketing plan, a channel analysis would help identify the most cost-effective way of reaching the target audiences. Within such an approach, both the '4 Ps' and the constant monitoring of project results will help fine-tune the strategy. Lefebvre and Flora (1988) argued that such monitoring of the results would eventually come to represent the bottom-line test about the effectiveness of the programme.

Such approaches seemed to be the norm and at least seemed more effective than traditional educational or psychological methods (Fourali, 2010). Whenever such an approach was criticized (e.g., see Bloom and Novelli, 1981 who reviewed ten years of SM research), the answer tended to be that perhaps the marketing methods adopted were not rigorously applied (Kotler et al., 2002). In fact Peattie and Peattie (2003) suggested a closer concept to SM in the form of relationship marketing from which SM could learn more.

It may be argued that marketing forays into the social fields, initially in the 1950s and 1960s primarily through health promotion initiatives (such as the prevention of sexually transmitted diseases), was a result of linking two key factors (Cheng et al., 2011; Donovan and Henley, 2010):

1. the perceived success of marketing techniques in generating commercial profits; and
2. the recurrence of epidemiological research evidence linking 'lifestyle' and behavioural habits and some serious diseases and social problems.

Social programmes leaders saw a huge opportunity in making social changes if the power of marketing could be harnessed to help change/minimize self-destructive lifestyles.

This was seen as a capitalist way out of its responsibilities to society through blaming the victims. This argument would highlight the capitalist philosophy's tendency to put the full responsibility firmly on the shoulder of the individual rather than the systemic/broader macro-level factors. Clearly this criticism does not hold water, as social marketing is a tool, like other tools, that can be improved and used to help address social ills. Theoretically, SM should be encouraged to address all significant causes that help solve a particular problem (bottom-up or top-down). The fact that some initiatives may not go far enough may be the result of philosophical, budgetary or methodological restrictions rather than an SM inherent problem.

In a milestone article called 'Ready to fly solo? Reducing social marketing's dependence on commercial marketing theory' Sue and Ken Peattie (2003) put forward the argument that there may be enough reasons for SM to 'formally' separate itself from traditional/commercial marketing. So what justifications did they offer? They start by arguing that:

> an over-emphasis on the direct translation of mainstream marketing principles and practices into social contexts may create practical problems and also confusion regarding the theoretical basis of social marketing.
>
> (Peattie and Peattie, 2003, p. 365)

They identify a number of areas that make social marketing different. For instance, they differentiate social marketing from cause-related marketing (e.g., involving promotional campaigns that build brand values through social contributions) or corporate social responsibility (e.g., involving community investment). The difference is that such initiatives, although seeming in appearance to tick the SM boxes, in reality are very different as their end aim is enlightened self-interest as they aim to harness social values to meet corporate and marketing aims. Fourali (2009a) argued that in genuine SM humanitarian interests override commercial ones. He stated that the bottom line or even the existence of a company, although very important, is subservient to the wider goal of achieving a social good.

Peattie and Peattie (2003) listed a number of concepts that needed revisiting as they could not be taken in the same sense as traditional marketing. This involved broadly the following twin concepts:

1. The concept of exchange: Although this is a key concept in SM as well as marketing (and economics generally), however, its meaning tends to be different. While marketing tends to focus on the twin goals of customer satisfaction and profit, a social marketer focuses on inducing behavioural change as a result of various incentives (e.g., information and tangible products). This is a different type of exchange. It is clear that changing behaviour may have to pass by emotions and cognitive dimensions, however, the ultimate goal is to induce sustained change in behaviour.
2. The social marketing mix: this is the famous 4 Ps (product, promotion, price, place). If we take these in turn, we will note that,
    a) instead of talking about products social marketers talk about social propositions;
    b) instead of talking about price, they talk about cost of involvement (including psychological cost);
    c) instead of talking about place, they talk about accessibility;
    d) instead of talking about promotion, they talk about social communication;
    e) instead of talking about competition between products or companies or brands, they focus on competing ideas, and the need to win the battle for attention and acceptance to secure sustained behaviour change.

However, the concepts listed by Peattie and Peattie omitted the remaining elements that make up the 7 Ps (people, physical evidence, processes), maybe because these concepts apply equally to marketing or SM with perhaps some slight improvement such as the people involved in 'selling' the new behaviour are a good example and a model to follow, the physical evidence may be more than just a good layout of merchandise, but also reflecting sensitivity linked up to historical contexts. The processes/procedures (systemic or otherwise) should also reflect integrity, fairness and a sense of responsibility.

More recently a NESTA study (2008) analysed 81 case studies and 21 literature reviews in order to identify the most effective characteristics of SM. The study argued that the areas that mostly benefitted from SM projects tended to be in public health. They argued that SM is an ideal tool for encouraging sustainable behaviour. They identified an external and internal/psychological source of influence. Externally, their list included using multiple/interlinked mechanisms (finding synergies), involvement of leaders and champions, financial incentives, raising awareness and regulation. At the psychological level, factors included framing the problem (e.g., climate change) as a common enemy to unite people, focusing on what can be done and not overwhelming the people, and avoiding guilt/blame as motivator as these may encourage people to use escape/counter-blame strategies (NESTA, 2008).

Indeed, given the nature of this subject, is there an argument for finding another label/name for this discipline? Such an argument is easy to understand in the light of the multidisciplinary nature of this approach, the association of 'social' with 'social media' as well as the 'unhealthy' association with the word 'marketing' in SM. This later point was highlighted at a recent international conference on SM by perhaps the biggest advocate of SM, Kotler, who suggested another alternative name in the form of 'social causal marketing'. Other contenders could include 'social healing and emancipation strategies' or 'communities healing theory and practice'. After all, what is more important is the focus rather than the discipline and for this purpose a multitude of disciplines/sources are called upon. Answers on a postcard, please!

The above suggests that there are similarities between marketing and SM. However, there are also plenty of differences, reflecting separate rules and aims. Accordingly Bloom and Novelli (1981) argued that SM has a bigger challenge on their hands than commercial marketers. Hence they require greater 'ingenuity and imagination'.

Why is Social Marketing Important?

Having reviewed what SM stands for and how it differs from marketing, one might wonder what is the need for yet another 'marketing discipline'.

For starters, SM is not just a marketing discipline although it is closely aligned to the marketing philosophy (focusing on the need of the target 'customer'). Nevertheless, in order for a discipline to find a champion, at least in the early stages, perhaps it is not bad that it is being currently linked mainly (at least in perception) to marketing.

The development of the first world-class standards faced several challenges from various 'marketing profession representatives' who claimed that the marketing concept is already wide enough to encompass any dimension within marketing and therefore there was no need for further development of best practice professional standards for this 'sub-discipline'. Despite the many challenges faced by the UK Marketing and Sales Standards Setting Body, reason eventually prevailed and the community of professionals, together with the funders, agreed to proceed with developing world-class advice for the marketing professional.

Accordingly there has been a number of arguments raised by several social marketers to argue the case for a separate study of SM. Chapman (2015) identified three lines of enquiries in marketing (commercial, public and social); however, for simplicity, we may adopt the commercial versus the social dimensions since the public dimension has been identified by many as equivalent to SM (Lannon, 2008).

The focus of traditional marketing has been seen as too commercial, with the primary aim to derive profits from various business ventures.

There has been enough criticism of marketing as one of the main causes of human ills for anybody to query (e.g., see Stearns, 1999): 'What? You mean you want to help resolve our social problems invoking the help of the very cause that brought it about in the first place?' The answer is 'well ... yes and no'. If something works very effectively for destructive purposes then maybe it can work equally effectively for constructive purposes. And this is where SM comes into its own.

As argued in the introductory quotation, the best business ideas may go unheeded if unsupported by good marketing. Consequently, the advice is to use marketing to help make our ideas more effective.

The importance of SM can be easily gleaned from the amount of projects done in many social areas. Fourali (2009a) listed the following areas that ben-efitted from SM work (Table 1.1).

Despite the long list of social areas that have benefitted from SM, such a list can be much longer. The issue of citizenship, for example. How can commu-nities be encouraged to assume responsibilities for their own neighbourhood? For example, the author visits regularly an idyllic seaside resort called Belge near Tipaza, an Algerian city famous for architectural antiquities, recognized by World Heritage. Whenever summer comes, the streets of this little village seem to become a rubbish-dumping ground for visitors. With a modicum of citizenship, the place could maintain its beauty. Clearly the local council also has a role to play.

Another ongoing issue that seems to have escaped the radar of most social marketers (Fourali, 2009a) is that of wars (civil, military, economic, religious or otherwise). The argument is that if SM has something to say to reduce violence at home or to help fight abuse and inequality then clearly the same principles (although perhaps in a much more complex environment) may be invoked.

Several studies have highlighted the superficiality, not to mention, missed opportunities to develop strategies that make peace sustainable. As argued by

Table 1.1 Issues addressed by social marketing

blinding trachoma	physical activity
community involvement	racism
diabetes	reducing prison numbers
doping in sport	safe driving
energy and water conservation	smoking cessation (or drug
environmental protection	abuse)
fighting abuse and inequality	smoking in pregnancy
HIV/AIDS prevention	social enterprise
injury prevention	social exclusion
junk-food advertising	sugar-free medicine
mental health	suicide and domestic violence
obesity	transportation
oral and bowel cancer prevention	waste prevention and recycling

Cochrane (2008), wars are not inevitable but are instigated or terminated by a mixture of structural and human factors. Cochrane (2008) reminds us that 'unfair peace' is not sustainable as it simply postpones the claims of the 'losers'. Peter Wallensteen (2007) supported this argument by his finding that 20 per cent of 'peace' achieved through 'victory' led to a recurrence of violence within ten years. Cochrane states:

> the 2003 Iraq war, supposedly won by the US coalition force in May 2003, 'yet by the end of 2005 2180 American troops had been killed in a war that had seemingly been "won" two and a half years earlier'.
>
> (Cochrane, 2008, p. 71)

The above statement in fact seems to disregard the hugely disproportionate loss of lives among the Iraqis (and, by extension, the whole of the North Africa and the Middle Eastern area) who were caught up in the conflict and are still paying as a result of, to put it mildly, rushed errors of judgements.

More recently Antony Adolf (2009), inspired by Maslow's hierarchy of needs, derived a 'Pyramid of Peace' that reflected a number of principles that would ultimately help develop a more sustainable world peace. This 'Pyramid of Peace', ranged from corporeal peace, corresponding to Maslow's basic survival/physiological needs, to the highest level, more encompassing peace, or world peace, as shown in Table 1.2.

What the pyramid provides is an argument that true lasting peace can only be brought about by ensuring that the five levels of provision have been achieved. Clearly a peace achieved by force through military victory does not end a conflict, since it just forces resistance underground.

How many times have we been told that a peaceful initiative did not lead anywhere because there was one group that was against peace, when what actually happened was that a group – because of economic or military power – forced a peace on a poor, heavily disadvantaged social group that made it very hard for them to survive in the imposed conditions of peace? Such imposed peace is, to say the least, a recipe for disaster, even if we do not consider the ethical dimensions. Arguments have been given that such imposed arrangements were cynically put into place for that very purpose, with the view to progressively further political, economic or geographical hegemony.

Given the importance of human agency in acts of war, it is important to address the issue of socially destructive attitudes (underpinned by, among others, religious, racial or economic factors) and the factors that contribute to social tensions. As human agency is very much an area of focus for SM, we believe this discipline can offer a way forward to ease and remove the causes of tensions, thereby helping to minimize the 'causes' of wars. It is interesting that recently Kotler (2013), arguably the best-known living marketer, was willing to work with people involved in conflicts to help build up a peace movement. For instance, he stated that he met with the younger bin Laden brother (of the notorious Osama bin Laden) to help develop the movement (Kotler, 2013).

Table 1.2 Levels of peace and associated supporting measures (adapted from Adolf, 2009)

Level	Type of Peace	Supportive measures
Fifth (highest) level	World	1. Legitimacy and law 2. Incentives and deterrents 3. Continuous investigation and critical dialogue
Fourth level	Inner	1. Quietude and plenitude 2. Recognition and respect 3. Spiritual and intellectual attainment
Third level	Socio-economic	1. Access to employment 2. Removing discrimination 3. Reducing wealth disparities
Second level	Sanctuarial	1. Minimal interpersonal harm 2. Minimal structural harm 3. Minimal state (induced) harm 4. Minimal harm against nature
First level	Corporeal	1. Nutrition 2. Shelter and sanitation 3. Health care 4. Education

Some similar movements aim to link the three Abrahamic faiths to support conflict resolution. These are important initiatives that make sense whenever there are disaffected communities. They help find common ground. For instance, there are several initiatives around the world that have sidestepped the easy labelling and vilifying of certain groups, with legitimate grievances, for the sake of political expediency. Such initiatives include recognizing the importance of religion and spirituality in people's lives and developing programmes that combine religious and secular values to develop understanding and congruence between the two perspectives for constructive and integrative purposes (see Sajoo, 2015). Extremism is a very risky approach whatever form it may take: ranging from a radical exclusive approach that claims a monopoly over truth (be that a religion or ideology) to a complete denigration of anyone who prefers to lead a spiritually grounded life as done by some 'new-born' scientists (see Dawkins, 2006; Flew, 2007; Prayson, 2012; Fourali, 1994).

It is important to realize that SM will depend on the 'local' values that a society espouses. This aspect is partly addressed in the section on 'Philosophical considerations associated with SM' in Chapter 3 of this book. What may constitute a worthwhile activity in one country may not be considered worthwhile elsewhere. Accordingly, an 'SM project' may be welcome in one country but not in another. In fact, it may not be welcome by some members of a society who, if powerful, may prevent certain changes from taking place. It is clear that some societies may identify more with certain cultures and values and less with others. Hence, when given a chance, such a culture would take every opportunity to work towards achieving the sought-after culture and aims. An example to quote perhaps is how in Poland, where Russian used to be a second language, after the unravelling of the communist bloc, it was decided to move towards a more Westernized culture with a strong focus on English as second language. One may also contemplate a situation where there is a lack of agreement about the future cultural direction of a country (in practice rather than in theory) thereby reflecting an 'unresolved situation' where there is a status quo showing a 'balance' of contradictory forces. Perhaps a good example of this situation is that of Algeria, where despite the soundbites that Algerian authorities proclaim, in line with the aims of the glorious war of independence, total freedom from French hegemony at economic, military and social levels, the reality is still very different. The social dimension includes linguistic and cultural influences. Despite these aims, and after more than 50 years of 'independence' a good part of the Algerian society, perhaps mostly from the upper echelons of society, still appears to position itself in relation to French society. Even politicians seem to find it hard to detach themselves from the French language.[1] Indeed, at the time of writing, I listened to two presentations from Algerian government representatives given in French and both took place in London, where all attendees are expected to be fluent in English and would probably favour a presentation in English. In this scenario, an SM project about cultural unity would be tokenistic and perfunctory if not backed up by a strong sense of direction supported by leaders who talk the talk. Of course this is no value judgement of the two politicians. Rather this situation is an indictment of our Algerian society and the lack of leadership in furthering the cultural independence agenda. Perhaps it is also important to highlight at this level that the above arguments are not directed against France or the French, among whom I have been lucky to make many friends. Rather these are arguments about the adverse effects of colonialism and the need to address all vestiges of such colonialism so that Algeria, as a nation, and its people can regain full independence (including psychological and cultural) to enable them to move forward with greater confidence.[2]

At times it may be difficult to differentiate SM from other initiatives. For instance Kotler at the World Social Marketing Conference held at Toronto in 2013 (Kotler, 2013) argued that SM includes activism and social movements (such as collective bargaining, minority rights, fighting pollution, etc.). Perhaps a more recent and significant social movement over the past few years is the so-called Arab Spring (with terrible consequences for people involved and, arguably, serious consequences for any hesitancy from the international community). The approach was associated with Ralph Nader (Justin, 2002) and Saul Alinsky (Horwitt, 1989). SM has also been associated with advocacy and lobbying and consumer movements associated with economic or financial discontent (Kotler, 2013). SM makes use of all directions of communications: top-down, as when a government intends to influence an individual's behaviour; horizontal, when the aim is to encourage peer influence;

and bottom-up, when individuals work together to influence companies or governmental institutions. Clearly, given the global interconnectedness of our current world, it seems that now people and organizations need to work together across boundaries to help get results at the international level.

A reader may wonder at the evidence about effectiveness of SM. SM effectiveness has been endorsed by the 700 or so participants (many of them SM practitioners with many years under their belt) that took place at the first international conference of SM held in Brighton, UK, in 2008. Nevertheless, the reader who may like to refer to recent work supporting this view can consult work such as Lannon (2008), Stead et al. (2006) or Hastings and Domegan (2014). In particular Stead et al. (2006) carried out a systematic analysis of 54 interventions associated with health issues (e.g., smoking, drug avoidance and obesity). They evaluated the findings through the level of compatibility with the effectiveness 'benchmark criteria' produced by the National Centre for Social Marketing. Their results support the view that there is clear evidence that social marketing principles can be very effective across a range of behaviours for various target groups and in different settings. However NESTA (2008) warns that the studies may still need to demonstrate SM effectiveness in other areas. This argument was also raised by Hastings and Domegan (2014), who listed a number of effective SM projects in the form of case studies but also highlighted significant areas for improvement. They cite the lack of evidence to support effectiveness of SM in environmental issues such as climate change.

Perhaps the most recent comprehensive review of evidence on the effectiveness of social marketing campaigns is the one provided by the Centre for Disease Control and Prevention (see Community Guide, 2015; Robinson et al., 2014). The research covered 22 studies focusing on 25 different groups. It focused on the following health-related products: child safety seats, condoms, pedometers, recreational safety helmets, nicotine replacement therapy and sun-protection products. The results demonstrated effectiveness of all campaigns in achieving the intended behaviour change, irrespective of the number of channels of communications used, when supported with freely available or reduced price products. Hence, in line with this outcome, it is fair to suggest that the more comprehensive the social marketing approach is (acting at several levels including facilitating access to products), the more effective the result will be.

What is Different about SM?

Fourali (2009a) identified four dimensions of SM that represent its selling point. Perhaps the most important level of what may be termed the SM enterprise is its humanitarian perspective, which overrides all other concerns. Accordingly, its success or failure is measured not in terms of how much profit it derives but how much benefits that humans, in all their variety, may derive in the long term. This means that, in the first instance, reducing human ills and misery would assume priority. However, what is meant by focusing on the 'human good' by social marketers is both reducing human misery and increasing human happiness. Clearly between these two options one may argue that reducing misery may be seen as more important than increasing the happiness of those whose condition may be considered as meeting the 'minimum for normal function'.

Another dimension that Fourali (2009a) identified is that SM offers a more effective tool for change than other alternatives. He compared the nearest other approach, counselling, and found that, although effective, it is not efficient. Education may be put in the same category. Although these two approaches may apply to groups (such as group counselling or classroom education) and, in the light of technological developments have achieved more reach (e.g., online counselling or education), these approaches are not addressed as part of a strategic plan that integrates all disciplines and associated techniques. They are merely, and generally passively, adopting new 'channels' of access without aiming to be integrative in perspective and proactively capitalise on the new tools and opportunities offered by adjacent disciplines. Should they do so, and adopt a public interest focus, the difference from an SM approach would significantly reduce. By comparison, SM, by definition, is a multidisciplinary area that combines not only techniques borrowed from marketing, but also all the other sciences that support its healthier aims, thereby combining the strengths of both marketing and social practice.

A third dimension is SM's 'preventative effects'. As well as the above-stated advantage of 'reach', SM does not need to wait for a problem to arise before helping address it; preventative measures (rather than curative) may be adopted. In some cases this is the only effective option. As an example, the problem of violence (domestic or otherwise) has led many policymakers to identify social marketing as one of the best available instruments to address the problem since they found out that the origins of the violent mentality are in an individual's early stages of development when he or she picks up wrong models from the surroundings (Donovan and Vlais, 2005).

Another element of the SM's potent mix is what Fourali (2008) termed its 'collateral positive effects on other practices'. This characteristic reflects the advantages of having a mutually supportive and beneficial effect among the various fields of studies from which social marketing borrows. Fourali (2009a) argues that the testing of some social science theories are no longer the preserve of the disciplines in which they arose. Rather SM provides the opportunity to test those theories in a wider, real and multidisciplinary context.

Clearly the aim of this book is not to take sides or encourage 'destructive revolutions' (given some of the recent extreme actions for change that have been occurring around the world), including the 'Arab Spring'. However, it may be an important (and pacifist) way forward for authorities (with genuine intentions) to consider adopting the 'wisdom' that an SM perspective would bring to the table. At the time of writing, it is still unclear as to whether the long-awaited 'Spring' has produced (will ever produce?) a blooming, life-affirming, community-geared harvest.

Notes

1 Some Francophiles argue that French is a treasure to value or, as they put it, borrowing a famous statement, 'le Francais est un butin de guerre' (French is the spoils of war) a sentence linked to the famous Algerian writer Kateb Yacine (Maina, 2013). However, even this writer also stated in 1966: 'The use of the French language is to serve a neocolonial political machine, which only perpetuates our alienation. Yet the usage of the French language does not mean that we are the lackeys of a foreign power and I write in French to tell the French that I am not one of them' (Turkovich, 2014). Clearly this suggests that the writer would have felt more authentic if he could avoid using French (as French is a constant conscious or subconscious 'reminder' of his subjugation). Given the several options Algerian society has in terms of alternative languages (English, Spanish, Chinese, not to mention Arabic), one would feel surprised why many Algerians (some of whom at the highest level of government) still relentlessly show deference to anything that's French, reflecting perhaps an inadvertent belief that the salvation of Algerians resides with France. Many Algerians would feel betrayed by this nonchalance towards the long-sought aims consecrated by the founders and the many martyrs of the Algerian revolution.

  In the light of the above, one might argue that the spontaneously improvised football chanting by Algerian crowds of 'one, two, three, viva l'Algerie' at international football games and demonstrated at the Brazil 2014 football world cup, conveys the message that Algerians aspire to a much more varied and internationally inclusive perspective than being circumscribed by a French culture that still triggers some very familiar emotions: feelings of pain, frustrations and an eerie outlook (recognized or not) of secondary human value.

  At this juncture it is important to perhaps restate the obvious in saying that the above arguments are not just a groundless rant against a past colonizer. Indeed, I know many French friends and influences (including teachers) that stood against injustice irrespective of its origins. This is about the insidious effects of colonialism and a refusal to normalize a state of subservience in any form. It is about encouraging ex-colonized nations left reeling from many years of covert and overt destructive influences to remove the shackles of dependence in all their forms and discover their unique capabilities to move confidently, yet constructively, forward while removing any vestiges of subservience.

2 A particularly insidious way of 'legitimately' countering any claim of unfairness by powerful groups is by referring to scientific 'facts' such as argued by the Eugenic 'scientific' movement. Many groups realised that a scientific garb provided a compelling legitimacy (not to mention other advantages) in the form of 'expert leadership'. Some groups who suffered as a result of this scientific categorising decided to take on the discrimination by 'reputable' academics and 'scientists' by working hard to join this category of powerful people and eventually arguing their case, using their 'authoritative' scientific arguments, to achieve more rights and honours (see for example Efron (2013) who offered some useful arguments to explain the shifts in the makeup of the list of Nobel prize winners). Indeed one might call such 'scientifically' discriminative arguments as 'Paradigmatic bullying' given that they make use of an established paradigm that confers legitimacy for bullying or abusive purposes. Note that suffering such bullying does not make a group of people immune from bullying others as demonstrated by history.

2 Precursors and the Development of Social Marketing

From Early Pioneers to the First World-Class Standards

SM, it may be argued, was a by-product of the development of marketing. In fact its widely considered inception, through an article that signalled the first announcement of SM, had as its title 'Broadening the concept of marketing' (Kotler and Levy, 1969) although the actual title was not formally formulated until later (Kotler and Zaltman, 1971; MacFadyen, et al., 1999). Indeed the jump was relatively simple from a remarkably successful commercial marketing to a marketing whose aim is to enhance people's healthier behaviours and, consequently, lifestyles. This was especially reinforced by the general finding that many social ills originate from unhealthy behaviour (such as smoking and obesity). Nevertheless, the principle had already been in existence well before the publication of these articles as shown through the publication of Wiebe's paper (1952) where he enquired whether it was possible to 'sell brotherhood like soap'.

A few marketers looking at the evolution of the SM concept tried to first disentangle this idea from other similar concepts. In particular, Kotler argued that SM should be differentiated from a host of concepts and tools (Kotler, 2013). In terms of concepts, he argued that SM should be differentiated from 'persuasion', 'social innovation' or movements associated with libertarian values. These are briefly presented as follows:

- **Libertarian/Laissez-faire philosophy:** according to this view, people should be free to lead their life the way they want. For instance, if people want to be obese then they have the right to do so, especially if they are not hurting others. Clearly this argument may not stand up to scrutiny as the next natural question would be 'how far this concept of freedom can be "tolerated" by society since people could eat, smoke or drink themselves to death?' Additionally, even the idea of freedom has to be 'qualified', as psychology tells us that some self-destructive tendencies are based on certain backgrounds rather than being part of our biological make-up; and if they are this does not make them right (some of these issues will be discussed in the next chapter on key values).
- **Persuasion:** as Kotler rightly pointed out, this is primarily focusing on the promotional side of the 4 Ps and, obviously focuses on the psychology of

persuasion which will be touched upon when we address the psychology dimension later in this book.

- **Social innovation:** this concept focuses on new technological developments that help improve human welfare. Examples may include a drug that discourages drug users from using drugs or technological developments such as having a facility in a car whereby a belt is put for you.

Although the above approaches may not be equated with SM, they nonetheless may be part of an SM strategy. For instance 'freedom of choice' is paramount to commitment to a programme. However, this freedom of choice should be based on clear and reliable information that takes into account information from short- and long-term perspectives. It is also a freedom that takes into account psychological as well as contextual elements that, in turn, may influence this very 'free choice' (for instance, a person who freely made a choice to drink may reconsider after realizing the long-term effects on significant people in his/her life as well as the available help). This aspect also links up to the point on 'persuasion' given the strong relevance of psychological and contextual contexts to cognitive conviction. Finally, it is easy to see how social innovation can support an SM programme. For instance consider the use of nicotine patches to support a 'no smoking' campaign.

Recognizing the potential of the various tools that SM can make use of, Kotler (2013) also mentioned the following elements that SM can capitalize on:

- **Activism:** Kotler referred to upstream movements such as those led by Saul Alinsky, who helped organize and gave voice to poor communities in north USA, or Ralph Nader who, among others, campaigned for a safer record of American cars, an issue that was previously generally not deemed serious enough to pursue among politicians, given the strong lobby of the American Automobile Association.
- **Advocacy and lobbying:** These activities, which may be carried out by 'activists', aim to harness the power of people through organized awareness and collective bargaining for the benefit of a just cause (e.g., environmental protection).

Both activists and lobbyists aim to start a social/consumer movement that enlist the help of 'ready' groups in society with various issues of concern (e.g., ecological, economic or financial discontent), which would eventually influence, in a horizontal peer-to-peer manner, larger sections of society. Such movements, after reaching a tipping point, may work through collective bargaining to eventually lead to an irreversible change with the view to achieve significant improvements associated with the issue addressed (within a company or society in general). Note that although these techniques may be used cynically by powerful groups (consider 'plants' in open forums whose aim is to influence discussions while claiming to be without invested interests), they are nonetheless a very important process for improving the quality of life of society. Although they may be abused by powerful institutions, including governments, the value of their adequacy can generally be estimated through a sober and non-partisan evaluation of the pros and cons of the movement in the short and long term and in terms of size of beneficiaries (religious, non-religious, ethnic, gender and other social groups).

Finally social engineering (SE) was also mentioned as another concept that may be linked to SM. SE is associated with using education to induce long-term changes in society, usually through targeting children with specific programmes (e.g., changing attitudes such as racist views) that make use of cognitive and behavioural techniques. Arguably such programmes may also use other tools such as TV and cinema programmes. When the purpose is laudable, SE is a good way forward. Unfortunately totalitarian regimes have also made use of it with disastrous effects. Hence there is a need to question the ethical basis of such initiatives and those associated with SM. This is taken up in the next section of this book.

Perhaps another concept associated with SE is macro-social marketing (MSM). This seems to have derived from the concept of macro-marketing, which, according to Hunt (1981), refers to the impact of marketing systems on society and vice versa. In particular, Kennedy and Parsons (2012) demonstrated how MSM/social engineering was used successfully by the Canadian government to curb the spread of smoking habits. They argued for a MSM approach that focuses on structural/environmental factors that contribute to a social ill (e.g., smoking) and give primary importance to implementers and controllers of society-wide strategic interventions (which mostly means government-level action). French and Gordon (2015) remind us that despite the effectiveness of such approaches, it is arguably more effective to adopt the more inclusive social ecological perspective. Perhaps a well-known such model is that of Bronfenbrenner (1979; Tudge et al., 2011) that advocates for the need to be more inclusive of all the systems of influences that affect an individual (e.g., adolescent smoker) in their environment. This ecological scheme focuses on individual characteristics (sex, health, age, etc.), a first level of influence known as a microsystem (family, school, peers, etc.), a second level known as a mesosystem (connection between two or more systems such as interaction between teacher and parents or place of worship and neighbourhood, etc.), a third level known as an exosystem (media, social services, industry, etc.) and the largest level known as a macrosystem (cultural values, social customs and laws). All these dimensions are in turn heavily influenced by the timing of the changes and interaction between the systems. Figure 2.1 presents a different version of Bronfenbrenner ecological framework (1979, Tudge et al., 2011) as it looks heuristically clearer in that it separates the actual topographic systems (individual, micro, exo, macro) from the more pervasively functional systems reflected in the mesosystem (interaction between systems) and chronosystem (timing of events within or between systems). Some SM researchers prefer to simply talk about upstream (national policy level), midstream (support programme run by institutions

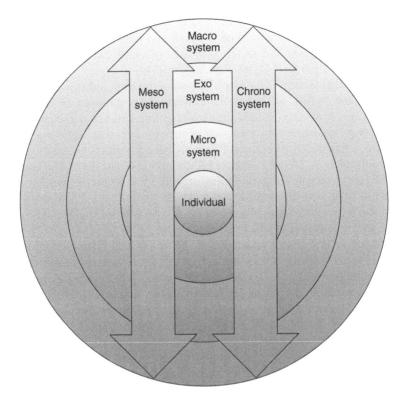

Figure 2.1 Ecological model systems (adapted from Bronfenbrenner, 1979)

Note: In this illustration we may include any dimension that may help explain the lower levels. For example, at the macro-level, we may include the traditional PESTLE dimensions.

such as payment to pupils to stay at school) and downstream (tactical support such as campaigns and counselling clinic support) levels, although such representation sacrifices the interaction and timing aspects. We feel that such ecological approach is more encompassing, although we feel it could be more inclusive as shown in Figure 2.1. For instance, we feel that the macro-level should reflect all dimensions and not mainly the socio-cultural and legal dimensions. Hence our suggestion is to adopt the PESTLE (political, economic, social, technological, legal and environmental) dimensions.

SM and Social Movements

Only in the face of [...] opposition has significant social change been achieved. If institutions had a capacity for constant evolution, there would never have been a crisis demanding transformation ... Resistance helps change happen.

(Palmer, 1997, pp. 164–165)

A number of studies have been carried out about what triggers social movements and the successful ingredients that are needed to maximize their success (Bate et al., 2004). This is quite a relevant issue in the light of the recent events popping up around the world with, in some cases, disastrous outcomes. One of the most challenging aspects about social movements is that once they 'take off', their direction is difficult to predict. Hence it is most important for the influential elements to not only understand them but also encourage a degree of (responsible) management to prevent them from getting out of hand and, in some cases, ending up with a situation worse than before they started.

Perhaps a most enlightening definition about social movements is the one offered by Blumer:

> Social Movements can be viewed as collective enterprises seeking to establish a new order of life. They have their inception in a condition of unrest, and derive their motive power on one hand from dissatisfaction with the current form of life, and on the other, from the wishes and hopes for a new system of living. The career of a social movement depicts the emergence of a new order of life.

(Blumer, 1969, p. 99)

In a way, one may see social movements, especially the fact that there is dissatisfaction with a current form of life (such as an irresponsible environment degradation, an unjust government or international tensions that may lead to mutually destructive wars) as a prelude to adopting an SM approach to help address the situation in an inclusive and evolutionary manner. However, slow evolution or 'incremental changes' (perhaps linked to demagogic/false promises) may also lead to a more radical social movement. Perhaps an extreme metaphor that could be invoked to link social movements to SM is that of a human body showing some symptoms of malaise or sickness. Such situation could either be addressed systematically (authentically, inclusively and voluntarily) at an early stage using SM or, if not addressed early, this may lead to more radical movements, the outcome of which may be hard to predict. Following the body metaphor, it could lead to drastic surgery or even the death of the person (in SM terms, the destruction of society, its systems and material facilities).

Given the similarity of aims between SM and social movements, any understanding of one of them would help enlighten the other. For example, reasons for enlisting the support of people to a movement is of interest to both. A number of factors are at work (e.g., see Bate et al., 2004; Klandermans, 2004):

- Values/purpose of movement. These may be the key reasons why an individual is inspired not only to join a movement but to also endure hardships in the face of difficulties. Others may simply be in search of meaning and a movement may provide such meaning (an existential perspective).
- Cultural resonance/similarities. A common 'cultural' understanding and background may be decisive in bringing people together and move them to help achieve a vision they identify with.
- Expected level of success of a movement (e.g., achieving social and political outcomes).
- Group identification may also be an important crowd-puller.

The above factors may be evaluated at a number of levels to attract or maintain the individual support.

- **Rational:** Whether this is a logical action to take given the individual interest.
- **Emotional:** People may be induced by feelings (e.g., injustice and anger) to either join a movement or leave it.
- **Social:** To be successful, the aims of the movement need to be supported by all or most of society.
- **Behavioural:** Taking part in the movement should live up to expectations (e.g., confirming injustice or relation with other members).
- **Organizational:** The organization and the structure of the movement in terms of management, resources and allocation of roles and responsibilities may also have a key effect on its success. This factor is akin to that of running a sound business.
- **Leadership:** This is decisive both in terms of the individual leader and the process of leadership. Leaders who frame (present) events and movements in a language that aligns with key individual values would tend to attract more supporters. If such framing provides a unifying vision that galvanizes groups for action using both emotional and rational arguments then this would increase the odds of success of the movement.

Table 2.1 summarizes the dual dimensions referred to above. This summary may be the basis of a test reflecting the levels of attraction of a movement.

This table suggests that each of the identified four influential factors may be subject to evaluation in terms of six criteria. For example, the values, purposes and benefits may be evaluated rationally (e.g., objective assessment of their importance), emotionally (based on instinctive feelings), socially (based on social attraction), behaviourally (positive or negative experience of previous engagement), organizationally (the perception of adequacy of management and resources) or on the basis of leadership (compelling vision/story). Perhaps further studies could work at determining the comparative weighting/influence of each of these factors.

Table 2.1 Key factors and their levels of evaluation that determine the level of attraction of a social movement and, by extension, a social marketing programme (adapted from Bate et al., 2004; Klandermans, 2004)

	Influential factors			
	Values/ purpose/ benefits	*Cultural resonance*	*Expected level of success*	*Group identification*
Levels of evaluations	Rational Emotional Social Behavioural Organizational Leadership			

As with all marketing 'products', the reason behind the attraction may be tangible or intangible. According to the above scheme, both tangible (e.g., material benefits) and intangible dimensions are reflected.

Given the overlapping nature between social movements and SM, social movements should be studied by all SM workers to help identify factors that enthuse and gain support for a movement with a view to try to extrapolate the learning to inform an SM programme.

'Can Brotherhood Be Sold Like Soap?': The Birth of Social Marketing

The sections above looked at a number of initiatives that have been associated with SM. Now if we focus on the specific evolution of the concept of SM there may be a two-level approach. First, the development of the concept of SM as another stage of development of the marketing concept (which may be termed the marketing phylogenetic development) and, second, the actual evolution of the concept of SM after it came into being (or ontogenetic development).

At the phylogenetic level, there has been several versions about the stages of business philosophies before reaching the current stage of marketing. For instance, the following stages have been suggested (Brassington and Pettitt, 2006):

- **Production stage:** At this stage, there is so much scarcity of a product that producers are confident that the product will sell once it is made available in the market. So at this stage, the issue is primarily about 'how much can we produce?'
- **Product (quality) stage:** Companies aim to focus on improving the quality of their products to differentiate them from those of the competition.
- **Selling stage:** With available, high-quality products and a well-trained sales team, business can only thrive.

- **Marketing concept stage:** People buy what they need. So the role of the marketer is to understand the needs of their customers and provide them with the solutions.
- **Social marketing:** Although we identify social marketing as a key stage here, since it is the focus of this book, other authors identify other elements such as societal marketing or sustainability stage, as shown in Table 2.2. Here the idea and philosophy of marketing becomes more encompassing and long-term, hence responsible to social and environmental aspects.

Although there are broad agreements about the history of social marketing, there are, nevertheless, a number of disagreements regarding timing and key concepts associated with each stage of development. There appears to be two ways of classifying marketing development: one according to the development of what constituted marketing at different periods of history; the other associates with this history a number of key conceptual developments that helped redefine marketing. Table 2.2 attempts to integrate these two perspectives based on several views on the history of marketing (e.g., Baines et al., 2008; Brassington and Pettitt, 2006; Dibb et al., 2006; Jain, 2009). Table 2.2 presents a view on each of the stages and how they were supported by new insights represented by key concepts.

The representation suggests that there was no equivalent of SM until after the appearance of the concept of marketing. This is seen as an incorrect assessment of the human history. Kotler and Roberto (1989) argued that SM has roots in public education and that there has been initiatives that may be considered SM in nature since ancient Greek and Roman times, such as campaigns to free slaves and public health initiatives (although these were primarily media campaigns rather than comprehensive SM). French (personal communication) argued that this perspective is rather Eurocentric, as strategies for influencing people's views and behaviour have also existed in Chinese, Middle Eastern/Persian and Indian cultures.

Nevertheless, the above representation is shown only for heuristic reasons rather than reflect definitive clear-cut historical stages of development. Actually, in order to reflect the flexibility in the stages, the representation did not put a time limit for each stage for a number of reasons: the first one is that the stages would tend to be cumulative as each earlier stage would inform the next stage (concerns regarding quality or selling techniques do not disappear in the later stages but tend to be integrated to the later stages) and the other reason is because there are overlaps between the various stages. Another reason, perhaps, is that just because there is an awareness or traditions about certain marketing developments in one country does not mean that this will be reflected in other regions or countries (hence the idea of brand appeal based on 'country of origin' of goods). According to the above scheme, one is tempted to venture an adaptation of Haeckel's recapitulation theory (Gould, 1977) that 'the "ontogeny" of marketing in a developing country recapitulates

Table 2.2 Evolution of the concept of marketing and relevant key issues addressed at each stage

		Evolution of the concept of marketing				
		Production stage (1890s onwards)	Product stage (1920s onwards)	Selling stage (1930s onwards)	Marketing stage (1950s onwards)	Social/societal/ relationship/ethical/ sustainable marketing stage (1970s onwards)
Selected concepts associated with different stages of marketing evolution	Exchange	↑				
	Transaction	↑				
	Quality of product		↑			
	Communication skills			↑		
	Customer focus/value				↑	
	Stakeholders				↑	
	Branding				↑	
	Market space/ CRM, digital marketing				↑	
	Relationship development				↑	
	CSR				↑	
	Publics services/ social/ environmental goals					↑
	Service dominant logic					↑
	Co-creation of value					↑

its "phylogeny" (whole history) elsewhere', especially since the concepts are complementary. To make matters more complex (and somewhat contradictory), work by Manoff (1985) and Rice and Atkin (1989) suggested that the earlier, more comprehensive SM applications only started being applied since the 1960s/70s, first with developing countries, tackling areas such as sanitation and family planning, and then, in the 1980s, in developed countries, starting especially in Canada and Australia where issues such as disease and injury prevention, drink-driving, smoking and immunization were among the most common to be tackled. This statement only serves to stress that the history of marketing (or SM) may not be as tidy as some of the books would have us believe. Additionally, it is possible that a useful idea may not be first largely adopted in the country where it appears but more taken up by a developing country with a more acute need that is looking for effective and efficient approaches. This is nothing new since it is well-argued that, for example, the idea of Total Quality Management (TQM) was first largely adopted in Japan before the USA even though many of the key quality gurus were from the USA. The idea of integration of each previous concept into the new stage does not necessarily mean that the concept's meaning may stay stagnant. For example, although the idea of 'barter' (exchange) has probably existed since the appearance of the first two people, its importance remains key in SM.

Donovan and Henley (2010) argued that while initially the onus was on influencing the individual to help him/her change behaviour and unhealthy lifestyles, this approach was later moderated after overwhelming evidence regarding the influence of social, economic and environmental factors. Hence SM adopts a multiple perspective approach and is arguably a more complex project to manage. As mentioned by Kotler in a recent international conference on SM held in Canada (Kotler, 2013) and by Andreasen (2006), to be effective SM's influence needs to be directed at several levels: obviously, downstream, focusing on influencing the targeted individuals (target audiences); the horizontal or midstream, through the use of peer influence (family members, co-workers, etc.); and upstream, aiming to influence companies and government institutions (e.g., activists fighting pollution). Andreasen (2006) also talks about vertical and horizontal considerations. The earlier focuses on the sources and modality of addressing social problems, while the latter focuses on the 'stakeholders' (players that need involving) associated with the social issue.

In terms of 'ontogenesis', the SM concept seems to have evolved in parallel with the concept of marketing. In particular, it shares with marketing the concept of exchange of costs and benefits as well as the need to adopt a rational planning process that proceeds from market research to objectives, targeting and tactics of implementing the plan. However, as stated above, SM is different from commercial marketing in both its purpose (social welfare and not commercial benefits) and process, as it requires more in-depth analysis requiring a variety of approaches that borrows from several disciplines and a particular focus on action research. The above recurrent question

'Can brotherhood be sold like soap?' from Wiebe (1952) both reflected and announced for the twentieth century, very well the concern of social marketing as a new discipline.

The idea of applying the principles of marketing to social concerns was not welcomed by everybody on the basis that either the concepts of marketing, such as that of 'exchange', a key marketing concept (Bagozzi, 1975), are being diluted (Luck, 1974) or 'misused' for cynical aims (Laczniak et al., 1979) such as in social control. Such misgivings were no obstacles to the development of the marketing concepts that quickly moved from the marketing of products and services to the marketing of events, experiences, events, places/countries and even ideas. Arguably, at the heart of all marketing resides the marketing of ideas. This is part of the reason marketers prefer to talk about brands rather than products, as products are never perceived as separate elements from the multitudes of associations that are triggered by them and influence their perception/value. Accordingly, it was no surprise to also extend the marketing concept to social welfare in the form of social marketing. As in most developments, the SM concept was a culmination of efforts of a group of activists, in this case SM workers who were trying to find effective ways of addressing social problems. It is always difficult to allocate names to the SM pantheon, as there are always risks of overlooking the work of some very significant workers. If one must list a few key names one may perhaps agree to some extent with the list of MacFayden et al. (1999) and try to improve on it. Although Phil Kotler is the most obvious name, there are nonetheless other significant names whose work was also decisive in developing or disseminating SM. Among these names, one may mention Paul Bloom and Bill Novelli who helped establish the theory and practice of SM on a firm footing (e.g., Bloom and Novelli, 1981); Karen Fox who helped evolve social advertising as part of SM promotion (e.g., Fox and Kotler, 1980); Dick Manoff who helped test some SM concepts in developing countries (e.g., Manoff, 1985). Other significant names include Jeff French (e.g., French and Blair-Stevens, 2005) and Gerard Hastings (e.g., Hastings, 2007) who influenced the development of SM in the UK; R. Craig Lefebvre and J.A. Flora (1988) who helped disseminate SM in the public health field; and Alan Andreasen whose work on SM spans several decades (e.g., 1972, 1995).

Despite SM's firm establishment as a discipline, there still appears to be confusions with other 'types of marketing'. Donovan and Henley (2010) identified several marketing activities, some already listed earlier, that need to be differentiated from SM. They listed the following:

- **Not-for-profit marketing:** The use of marketing to advance non-profit organizational goals.
- **Cause-related marketing:** This applies when an organization representing a social cause partners with a commercial one as when a percentage of profit made from selling a commercial product goes to the partner organization with a social cause.

- **Pro-social marketing:** This applies when a commercial organization takes on a responsibility for promoting and sponsoring activities associated with a social cause (e.g., anti-bullying, domestic violence prevention, etc.).
- **Societal marketing:** This is to be differentiated from SM, as it usually refers to the work of organizations who, while focusing on making profit, still ensure their activities are socially responsible. For instance, they make use of biodegradable material, encourage recycling and minimize energy resources intensive activities (Kotler et al., 1998).
- **Corporate philanthropy:** This usually refers to philanthropic activities in the form of secondment of staff to carry out charity works or the use of company funds to help the needy (e.g., building wells or houses in needy areas of developing countries).

In fact the above concepts are only a select few from an ever-growing list of marketing related sub-disciplines. One might throw in for example:

- arts marketing, or the integration of a marketing perspective into the artistic planning process (Hill et al., 2003);
- health care marketing, or the use of marketing techniques to develop, promote and sell health care 'products' (R.K. Thomas, 2008); and
- political marketing, or using marketing tools to study public opinion to develop, assess the impact and improve campaign communications (Kavanagh, 1995).

It is clear that despite arguments from many companies that are involved in 'charitable' and 'responsible' initiatives, these companies are also aware of both direct and indirect benefits that accrue to them from various stakeholders who not only view the 'charitable' company more positively but would also be more willing to do business with them. However, the above list may still need clarifying. For example, when we talk about organizations, we may find it useful to specify commercial, non-profit/charity or government organizations as some have as part of their *raison d'être* the mission to carry out SM initiatives to support the populations they deal with. The above also highlights the need to be specific, with a clear title about what social marketing is about, as this variety of titles can be very confusing for a reader not acquainted with the concept. In the light of the above and the common confusion with social (media) marketing, there may be an argument for opting for a clearer title such as 'social cause marketing'. This issue, together with other suggested options, is taken up further later on in this book.

Despite concerns from some practitioners (e.g., Glenane-Antoniadis et al., 2003), SM has moved on significantly since its early days when it was practically equated to marketing in general (the 'traditionalist' view) and has become acquainted with a more interdisciplinary and eclectic view. This later view is more ready to capitalize on any new theoretical or procedural advances that may help produce more effective results.

The Legal Perspective

Clearly one may be considered naïve (at least) to believe that the law exists to ensure the welfare of society. Consider the following statement provided by Hastings.

> If, for example, an unelected government were to kill millions of people, there would be an outcry, UN resolutions and serious talk of military intervention; yet the world's five big tobacco companies have been doing this for half a century and no one talks of invading Philip Morris International or arraigning the CEO of British American Tobacco in The Hague.
>
> (Hastings, 2013, p. xvi)

Clearly different people understand different things when faced with the words 'welfare' or 'rights'; and our later section on ethical dimensions associated with SM will help develop these ideas further. Nevertheless because of the prominence of the value of law in any social enterprise, it is worth addressing this dimension in this section.

All marketing practitioners (whether working in commercial or social marketing contexts) ought to consider what the law of the land that affects their activities may have to say so as to avoid breaching them. Ideally, the law is only the first step being considered by organizations. This is because there are several areas where the law may be wrong, unclear or even socially destructive, as argued by Hastings in the quotation above, inspired by the movie *The Matrix* with the difference is that this quotation is 'real' and based on facts not fiction. Indeed among the pseudo arguments identified later in this book, where ethical issues will be discussed, is the Friedman Doctrine, which argued that as long as an organization stays within the law then this is good enough. However, we all know that the law may allow behaviour such as child labour and other unethical practices depending on which country's law we happen to be dealing with.

Kolah (2013) argues that the law has three possible functions:

1. It may act as a barrier to market entry (e.g., use of intellectual property rights to protect a marketing position).
2. It may be a prerequisite for sales and marketing activities (e.g., abiding by an advertising regulatory body such as the Advertising Standards Authority, that all marketing communications should be legal, decent, honest and truthful).
3. It may be used as a tool to induce a competitive advantage (e.g., comparative advertising or product placement on TV or cinema).

Among the key texts in the UK being referred to by marketers (including social marketers) are (Chaffey et al., 2009):

- Privacy and Electronic Communications Regulations 2003 (EU Directive).
- Trade Descriptions Act 1968.
- Sale of Goods Act 1979.
- Health and Safety Act (e.g., children).
- Food Safety Act 1990.
- Data Protection Act 1998.
- Consumer Protection Act 1987.
- Office of Fair Trading (OFT) Control of Misleading Advertisements Regulations.
- Office of Telecommunications (Ofcom) Clearance of Broadcast Advertising.
- Financial Promotions Monitoring Team of the Financial Services Authority (FSA) – Financial Services and Markets Act 2000.

The digital world itself attracts several laws such as:

- Data protection and privacy law.
- Disability and discrimination law.
- Brand and trademark protection.
- Intellectual property rights.
- Contract law.
- Online advertising law.

Clearly the above is just one country's perspective on the law dimension, and different nations may adopt different approaches based on social, cultural and historical perspectives. Perhaps a more encompassing source of regulation is that presented by the International Chamber of Commerce (ICC) Consolidated Code revised in 2011 (Kolah, 2013). The ICC is in a unique position, as it reflects the marketing communications practice regulations of many countries. According to this model, all communications should be legal, decent (not offensive), honest, socially responsible (respect human dignity) and truthful.

When taking into consideration the idea of going beyond the law, one needs to remember that all work should ultimately aim for maximizing, in the short and long term, human health and happiness. Wells et al. (2000) argued that marketers should use objective and accurate persuasion and not encourage acquisitiveness, even when allowed by the law, which reflects a philosophy of happiness based on materialistic ownership. Hence the arguments produced by the British psychologist Oliver James (2007, 2008) called 'affluenza', a term reminiscent of a medical condition, which combines affluence and influence and is frequently used by critics of consumerism.

The laws should address most issues associated with irresponsible marketing. However, it is clear that not all businesspeople are too concerned about the law. Svend Hollensen (2011) argued that there is a ladder of attitudes towards responsibilities. This ranges from 'not applying the law', to 'applying the law and nothing else' to moving beyond the law and applying 'the spirit of morality' that may be, or may not be, behind the existing law. Clearly, although the last stage may be the most effective in developing a responsible society, in practice it could mean different things to different people. However, this challenge should be seen as an opportunity for continuously reviewing the law rather than applying it blindly.

In terms of the current approach of sensitive areas for marketers in general and social marketers in particular, Wells et al.'s (2000) categorization seem to offer a good framework for aiming to systematically avoid areas of risk. They identified six issues in marketing communications that law-makers have to be particularly sensitive to.

- Puffery/exaggeration.
- Taste (sex, vulgarity and violence).
- Stereotyping (women, ethnic groups).
- Advertising to children.
- Advertising controversial products (e.g., cigarettes, alcohol, irresponsible holidays).
- Subliminal advertising – research has shown that ads using covert sexual priming linked to products such as alcohol may affect interest and behaviour of consumers. This is clearly a breach of ethical standards.

The above general law requirements should apply to all marketers, including social marketers, and therefore should be heeded whenever producing any SM programme.

Fourali (2006) put marketing in the spotlight by addressing the general negative views against this discipline. He demonstrated that despite the general perception that marketers are seen as useless at best and irresponsible at worst, marketing has much to offer based on its core philosophy of focusing on the needs of the customer. If this is done properly (i.e., focusing primarily on the current and future needs of customers), then the marketer should be able to better serve society.

It is clear that the law is not a sufficient factor to help develop a better society, although it may help (e.g., judging from the new laws preventing smoking in public buildings in some nations). In fact, given that laws evolve as society evolves, it is important that social marketers are at the forefront of helping develop a healthier and happier society rather than rely on private corporations whose benefit is primarily in arguing that a person cannot do without their product and service, thereby promoting a materialist philosophy that works against the much sought-after health and happiness. As demonstrated by James (2008) and Wilkinson and Pickett (2009), the more materialistic a society is, the more unequal it is, and the greater is the resulting unhappiness of its citizens. Part of the promise of SM is to help develop active citizens who see it as part of their responsibility to help create a more responsible and caring society. If such an attitude is adopted by most members of our society, the effects of their involvements will, eventually, be seen in the change of our laws. Indeed it has been argued that one of the key aspects that helped steer our world from an imminent nuclear war catastrophe was exactly such social activists who refused to adopt a mutually destructive 'them and us' perspective as advocated by their leaders. In this respect the OECD (2001) identified three levels of involvement of citizens in government policymaking, ranging from a simple unidirectional communication providing information, to consultation with a view to getting feedback from selected groups, to active inclusive participation encouraging all citizen engagement with proposed policies and seeking improvements or alternative options (French and Gordon, 2015). Nevertheless there seems to be an increasing demand for the third level of involvement (i.e., inclusive active encouragement of citizen engagement). This is due to the fact that policymakers are coming to realize that in order to ensure a long-term success of public policies they need to consult with and mobilize as many citizens as possible. The two main reasons for this is that, first, such involvement is increasingly being *demanded* by citizens (consider placards such as 'not in my name' at anti-war rallies) and, second, the latest research and advice that are being offered on how to design successful policies argue for such involvement (French and Gordon, 2015; Shafir, 2013; Oliver, 2013). In order to implement an effective citizen participation, the OECD (2001; French and Gordon, 2015) advises that the process should have the following criteria:

1. All participants should be involved in the agenda-setting.
2. Allow adequate time for decision-making.
3. Focus on common values rather than debate.
4. Communication should be based on inclusion, courtesy and mutual respect.

Perhaps the reader may feel surprised that the above advice for full involvement of citizens in policymaking was not adopted earlier. Indeed received advice – including criteria such as the need to be inclusive/non-discriminatory, need for in-depth research to determine complexity of issues, being clear about the aims of a policy and, finally, coordinating efforts – have always been seen as decisive in business or corporate decisions. Accordingly it should come as no surprise that such criteria should be part and parcel of a social policy design (Cornelissen, 2014) if it is to succeed.

In the light of the above arguments on the need for more advice on SM and the realization of the benefits of encouraging the uptake of SM as a promising discipline, many SM professionals started producing books on the new discipline and sharing their ideas about what a quality SM programme should include. With a view to further this aim, a number of marketing professional bodies, from around the world and including those based in the UK, started working together to develop the very first world-class standards of marketing best practice. This is the subject of the next section.

The Birth of the First World-Class Standards for SM: A Promising Tool for Best Practice

One of the most significant events associated with the development of SM as a mature discipline was the development of the first world-class standards of SM. These standards help determine what constitutes best practice among social marketers. Such clarification would be very welcome by the many thousands of SM practitioners across the world who want not only an agreed view on what SM is but also a detailed practical description of the steps that SM practitioners undertake in order to fulfil their projects' objectives.

The following is based on the work of the Marketing and Sales Standards Setting Body (MSSSB) and more particularly on the work of Fourali (2009a) who oversaw the design and delivery of the projects assumed by this UK national body during the years of its existence. Nevertheless, the success of all major projects relies on the contributions of many organizations and individuals. In this respect, I would like to particularly acknowledge the decisive support of the National Social Marketing Centre (NSMC) under the leadership of Professor Jeff French that helped initiate the work and provided professional and material support until its successful completion. This, of course, is in no way meant to underplay the very good support received from all those who contributed to the project, some of whom have already been mentioned in the list of acknowledgements in the Preface.

In the UK and in Europe more broadly there was a systematic attempt at defining the vocational dimensions of various professional areas. Such clarification would then lead to determining the best practice standards of professional working. UK industries saw this clarification as decisive to enable various necessary functions associated with each industry. Such functions include (Mansfield and Mitchell, 1997):

- **Performance management:** The standards would determine the level of satisfaction with current performance and help improve it.
- **Assurance of product and service delivery**: The standards would help compare the delivered outcome with the expected delivery.
- **Recruitment and selection:** The standards would represent an ideal reference for identifying the skills of potential recruits.
- **Job design and evaluation:** The standards represent a good basis for designing and evaluating job specifications for SM practitioners.
- **Identifying learning needs:** The standards help identify any gaps in the skills of staff with responsibilities for SM.
- **Delivering and evaluating learning programmes:** The standards represent a good basis for designing an SM learning programme.

- **Public recognition certification of competence:** The standards represent a good basis for recognizing competence of social marketers if they gain the necessary SM skills to become recognized practitioners.
- **Regulating professional and occupational qualifications and institutions:** Based on the above, it would be possible to regulate the field of SM practice as there will be a basis to establish national requirements that, if met, would lead to licence to practice. Such regulations would provide a credible certificate for organizations looking for professionally qualified practitioners.

The MSSSB already had valuable previous experience of developing national occupational standards for marketing, sales and cross-sectoral workers in these professional areas.

Following an early 'state of play' review about how best to develop social marketing in the UK, the stakeholders, primarily marketing practitioners, advised that there was a need to develop credible competence standards that can back up any professional development initiative. Accordingly the researchers consulted on the most helpful way forward for developing the 'standards of best practice' and the general view was to adopt a method called 'functional analysis' based on the UK experience (Mansfield and Mitchell, 1997) in developing other standards in adjacent occupational areas (e.g., marketing, management, customer services).

The functional analysis consisted of starting with an agreed key functional purpose of social marketing and then proceeding to develop the elements that help achieve the identified key purpose. Accordingly, the consultation process (using a combination of secondary information, questionnaires, focus groups and interviews involving contributors from both inside and outside the country) led to the following key purpose of SM to:

> Apply marketing alongside other concepts and techniques in order to influence individuals, organizations, policy makers, and decision makers to adopt and sustain behaviour which improves people's lives
>
> (Fourali, 2008)

This definition led to a 'downward arrow' question in the form of: 'what do we need to do in order to achieve this?' This question was asked repeatedly and further specifications prescribed until the participants were satisfied that the information provided was clear enough for any user of the future standards. Accordingly the outcome was at four levels as follows (see Figure 2.2 showing the structure of the national occupational standards (NOS), and Figure 2.3 showing the key functions and associated areas of competence below):

Level 1: The identification of five key functions of SM (see A–E in Figure 2.3).
Level 2: The unpacking of these key functions into areas of competencies.

Level 3: Each of these areas of competencies was made up of one or more self-contained units of activities.

Level 4: Each of these units of activities were described in terms of:
- the title of the activity being described;
- outcomes of performance (what is the expected outcome of a successful performance);
- behaviour that underpins successful performance;
- knowledge and understanding (and attitude) that underpin successful performance.

Hence, according to the received advice, the sum of the key functions, areas of competencies, with their associated units of activities represent the field of activities undertaken by social marketers. This does not mean that SM workers had to cover and be competent in all the units (a total of 61). The NOS simply mapped and specified the dimensions of competencies that made up the field of SM. Indeed it is possible that a 'social marketer' may cover only a few units, associated with one area of competence, in their whole career as the other activities may be contributed to by other members of the team or even external agencies (such as a research agency). Note that although the list of functions and associated competences are very unlikely to be assumed by all SM workers, the functions are meant to be comprehensive and reflect a strategic picture that covers (1) researching, (2) identifying and evaluating strategies, (3) managing and (4) delivering SM interventions, and (5) promoting SM best practice. Such larger picture should be obvious to an overall manager of an SM project.

A more recent review of the SM standards (UKCES, 2013) focused only on three of the original five functions, perhaps to simplify the design of training

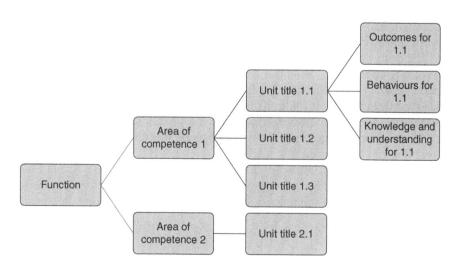

Figure 2.2 Structure of the National Occupational Standards (NOS)

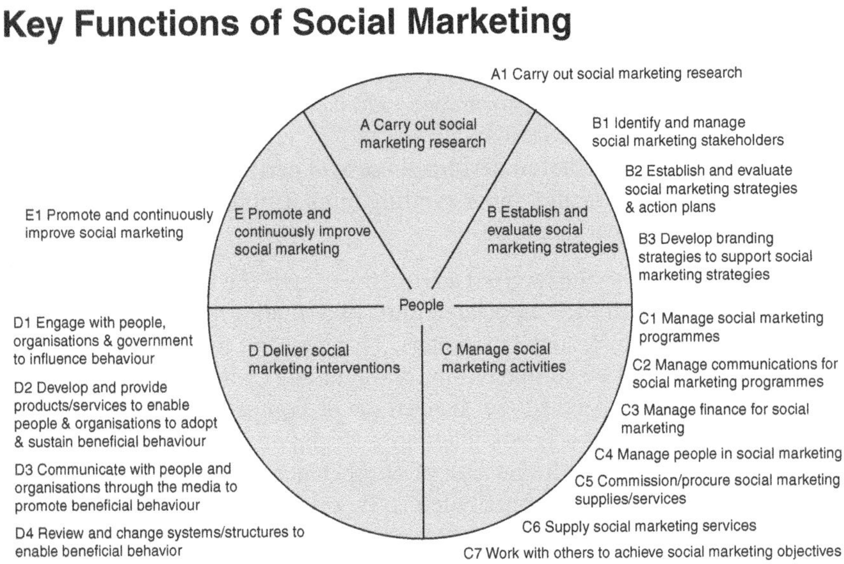

Key Functions of Social Marketing

A1 Carry out social marketing research

A Carry out social marketing research

B1 Identify and manage social marketing stakeholders

B2 Establish and evaluate social marketing strategies & action plans

E1 Promote and continuously improve social marketing

E Promote and continuously improve social marketing

B Establish and evaluate social marketing strategies

B3 Develop branding strategies to support social marketing strategies

People

D1 Engage with people, organisations & government to influence behaviour

D Deliver social marketing interventions

C Manage social marketing activities

C1 Manage social marketing programmes

C2 Manage communications for social marketing programmes

D2 Develop and provide products/services to enable people & organisations to adopt & sustain beneficial behaviour

C3 Manage finance for social marketing

C4 Manage people in social marketing

D3 Communicate with people and organisations through the media to promote beneficial behaviour

C5 Commission/procure social marketing supplies/services

D4 Review and change systems/structures to enable beneficial behavior

C6 Supply social marketing services

C7 Work with others to achieve social marketing objectives

Figure 2.3 Functions and areas of competence for NOS SM

programmes (see Table 2.3). These functions in turn represented only nine of the original 61 units. These functions reflect primarily three steps: research-ing/planning (A1 units); developing/providing products and services (D2); and supporting best practice (E1).

The description of the NOS was to introduce a significant milestone in the development of SM: the development of the first internationally supported occupational standards that provided a strong basis for defining both the scope, purpose and competence skills associated with the work of SM.

The draft standards were presented at the first international social market-ing conference held in Brighton, UK, which attracted 700 participants. The subsequently received feedback was very encouraging including the following received from Professor Philip Kotler, regarded as one of the foremost living social marketers: 'I am impressed with the clarity and the comprehensiveness of this work on setting standards for social marketing definition and certifica-tion' (Fourali, 2009a, p. 23).

Since their design, the above standards have become the basis for all UK nationally recognized SM professional qualifications as well as being consid-ered a strong frame of reference by many SM organizations around the world.

Table 2.3 Latest UKCES SM NOS

A1.1	Plan, manage and evaluate social marketing research programmes
A1.2	Collect data on the knowledge, attitudes and behaviours of target groups
A1.3	Analyse, interpret and synthesise data and research findings to inform social marketing strategy
A1.4	Develop understanding of theories and evidence about what might influence the behaviour of target groups
A1.6	Develop social marketing propositions and test their potential to influence the behaviour of target groups
D2.1	Develop and provide products to enable people and organisations to adopt and sustain beneficial behaviour
D2.2	Develop and provide services to enable people and organisations to adopt and sustain beneficial behaviour
E1.4	Provide learning products and tools to develop effective practice in social marketing
E1.5	Provide education, training and support for effective practice in social marketing

3 Philosophical Considerations Associated with Social Marketing

This section looks at the philosophical views associated with the ethical dimension of SM. Indeed it is very hard to address SM without referring to the values and principles that underpin the work of the social marketer. Although this is an area that affects all marketers, it particularly affects social marketers, especially since they generally claim that their work is primarily motivated by social welfare; an argument that perhaps many commercial marketers may reject outright as they have no qualms about stating that their primary aim is to make a profit and as long as this is allowed by the law, they are OK with any business practice.

However, the reader may still wonder why is there a need for a chapter on 'philosophy' when marketers, whoever they are, are only there to do what they are expected to do. Well, even such a statement may be subject to philosophical arguments (especially when such statements have been used in perhaps other more gruesome situations such as 'my actions may have been barbarous but I was only obeying orders'). Philips (2010) identified several purposes in seeking the help of philosophy. These purposes are presented below:

- To be reflective about our practice.
- To avoid inconsistencies in our beliefs.
- To be aware of what we are committed to as a consequence of holding the principles we claim to hold.
- To expand our horizon of possibilities by considering alternative goals that might never have occurred to us if it was not for the work of some philosophers.

One might also add:

- To challenge our positions as well as established views and avoid knee-jerk reactions.
- To consultatively develop robust arguments having considered the pros and cons of various positions.
- To address tacit beliefs and assumptions and transparently subject them to our and others' power of analysis.
- To clarify what we stand for and be more authentic.

For those who may argue that philosophy is primarily a navel-gazing activity, it may be useful to remind them that a big contingent of philosophers, known as pragmatists and neo-pragmatists, argued that as well as developing ideas and arguments, philosophy should also aim to test them in the real world through research and practice, while at the same time exposing and evaluating 'the taken-for-granted presuppositions implicit in their practice' (Oancea, 2012, p. 71). Philosophers also support the construction of knowledge through the creation of new language and developing new questions to help deeper analysis of the problems at hand. Philosophers help question narratives and power relations that may help the development of new research, practice and policies. A reverse argument about the tacit philosophical pervasiveness of human endeavours is that policies, politics and law are public incarnations of chiefly ethical aims. Gaining clarity of the latter helps develop sound and principled policies of the former (Levenstein, 2013).

One of the aims of philosophers is to determine value-based arguments that may guide professional practice. There are several well-known professional (including ethical) standards adopted by marketing organizations (see AMA, 2013; CIM, 2016; MRS, 2013) and they generally tend to agree on key ethical principles such as 'do not harm', be transparent and be responsible. However, it may be useful to try and identify how such values are derived by ethical philosophers as, depending on the choice of arguments, the approach to SM practice may be affected.

Hollensen (2011) argued that the level of ethicality can range from a person's lack of consideration for either law or ethics, to being mindful of the law, to going beyond the law and focusing on the spirit of the law. However, Andreasen (2006) reminds us that a safe bet in trying to motivate human beings (including legislators and politicians) is to remember that people generally focus on fulfilling their individual interests. This was argued long before by Adam Smith and the free market economists. This view may assume that people's 'interest' is necessarily selfish. Despite such assumptions, perhaps peddled by some evolutionary theorists with a restricted perspective, recent studies argue that there is enough evidence to show that there are universal values that are found throughout all human beings (Sober and Wilson, 1998; Brown, 1991; Kinnier et al., 2000; Peterson and Seligman, 2004) and such values tend to be rather pro-social. These include wisdom, courage, humanity, justice, temperance and transcendence (Peterson and Seligman, 2004). These appear to be part of our biological make-up. The general view is that these have been developed to support human survival, above and beyond the individual or even group survival (Sober and Wilson, 1998). Subsequently these basic survival values became the basis of 'moral intelligence', which arguably has been seen to be at least as important as IQ and/or emotional intelligence by some authors (Lennick and Kiel, 2007). The survival idea has also recently been extended to business survival (Lennick and Kiel, 2007, Barratt, 2006; Kotler et al., 2010).

Despite the variety of 'needs' that motivate humans, it is still useful to look at the ethical principles that may justify not only whether it is reasonable to undertake a project but also on what basis can we make a decision when faced with several options within each project. Hence the aim of the next section is to look at the various 'competing' ethical arguments that individuals may use to argue their respective cases.

Basis for Ethical Reasoning

There is a tradition among SM writers to refer to selected ethical principles that may be associated with SM practice (e.g., Donovan and Henley, 2010; Hastings, 2007). Indeed there are many ethical views and theories that have been argued by philosophers (e.g., Frey and Wellman, 2005; LaFollette, 2007). The purpose of this section is to present a brief summary of some of the most influential arguments that may be provided by social marketers to build a basis for justifying their practice. Table 3.1 provides a summary of alternative ethical arguments that have been derived primarily from Hill (2011).

The table shows that it is never straightforward to argue an ethical case. Additionally there are different ways of organizing the arguments. For instance Gerard Hastings (2007) refers to three broad ethical arguments:

1. The deontological argument, which focuses on motives for a behaviour rather than outcomes. This reflects, at least partly, a psychological perspective as it focuses more on the motivation behind action rather than the ethical principle behind it.
2. The teleological argument which is reflected in the utilitarian view in Table 3.1.
3. The theory of rights, also covered in Table 3.1.

Levenstein (2013) recently argued that broadly speaking there are two main discernible schools of thinking: deontology (focusing on rights and duties) and consequentialism (utilitarianism). While the first one considers as paramount the 'inner' rights of individuals, even if there is only one person concerned, the latter starts from the rights of the majority, bearing in mind that humans compete for scarce resources and have to share them. Levenstein suggested that these schools are not inherently incompatible and can be combined to provide a more effective practical way forward. He argues that while rights are not absolute reality (a noble fiction?), they may be used to develop a system of interpersonal respect. These derived rights may be the starting point for a utilitarian policy. For example, once a set of rights has been derived, the violation of such rights must not exceed the minimum required to protect the greater interest (Levenstein, 2013). As we will see later, todays 'division' of resources flies in the face of both ethical schools.

Perhaps another view to consider is that advanced by Fourali (2000) who, focusing on educational opportunities, summarized three broad perspectives based on the predominating three theories of social justice as suggested by Howe in 1999 (see Table 3.2). Clearly such views may apply to other contexts and not just educational opportunities.

Table 3.1 Key ethical positions and their justifications (based on Hill, 2011)

Types of reasoning	Name of argument	'Justification'	Criticism
Pseudo-arguments	Friedman Doctrine	The only social responsibility of business is to engage in activities designed to maximize profits as long as they stay within the law.	The law may allow unethical behaviour (e.g., sweatshops, child labour or land pollution).
	Cultural relativism	All ethics are culturally determined.	Is it OK if a culture supports extremely unethical behaviour such as slavery?
	Righteous moralist	The same rules should be applied everywhere.	Is it reasonable to expect that people in different countries are paid the same if it means businesses will go elsewhere?
	Naïve immoralist	If all visitors/business people from other nations are adopting the local customs then it is acceptable to do the same.	Is it ethical if the 'local custom' is to pay protection money or promote child exploitation?
Genuine arguments	Utilitarian	The best decisions are those that maximize the greatest good for the majority of people.	Two problems: (1) lack of accuracy in risk-reward estimates (e.g., promising genetically modified crops may lead to worse consequences in the long term); 2) may cause injustice to minorities.
	Kantian view	People, as conscious moral beings with dignity, should be seen as ends in themselves and not as means to the ends of others.	The system appears oblivious to the importance of moral emotions such as sympathy or caring.
	Rights theories	Human beings have fundamental rights and privileges that apply everywhere (e.g., UN Universal Declaration of Human Rights).	Rights go hand-in-hand with obligations and the responsibilities of all moral agents (i.e., people or institutions capable of moral action).
	Justice theories	There should be a just distribution of economic goods and services. Most famous is Rawls theory. Liberty and goods and services to be distributed equally except when an unequal distribution would work to everyone's advantage. Variations in income may be considered acceptable if the inequality benefits the least-advantaged members of the (global) society.	As Sen (2009) argued, there may be a sense of injustice at many levels. It is therefore important to be aware of the danger of imposing a 'justice' when there is no agreed dominant reason for the diagnosis of injustice.

It was argued that despite criticism against liberal egalitarians they seem to be least prone to injustice since (Fourali, 2000; Elliot et al., 2010):

- liberty is hollow unless supported by equality (or in the case of some SM projects, social responsibility);
- flexibility in terms of having to balance principles, while criticized as a negative aspect, can be seen as a strength since it does not hold itself hostage to a rigid principle.

Fourali supported the view that Rawls (1972), one of the strongest proponents of liberal egalitarianism, has come up with a very strong procedural argument for justice. Rawls did this by introducing the idea of an 'original position' to prevent bias towards our own current condition/interests. This original position is demonstrated by encouraging thinkers about justice to reason from behind a veil of ignorance about their wealth, beliefs, abilities, social position or any other information that may give them a stake in the issue at hand. If a 'disinterested' position is assumed then we remove the possibility of favouring anybody, which is at the heart of so much injustices. Govier (2002) used this approach following the blind persecutions that followed the events of 9/11 (anybody whose looks or name reflected a Middle

Table 3.2 Three perspectives on justice (adapted from Fourali, 2000)

	Libertarianism	*Utilitarianism*	*Liberal egalitarianism*
Position	States should refrain from exercising power.	An action is right if it maximizes the total good.	The principle of equality is paramount and any inequality must be justified.
Consequence	Hence should not intervene and redistribute resources to achieve equality among its citizens.	Interventions to support disadvantaged groups are welcome.	Interventions are primarily for removing disadvantages and prior to maximizing the good.
Negative impact	Educational achievement may be largely dependent on the lottery of conditions that the learner has access (or no access) to.	If programmes prove to be less effective in helping disadvantaged groups these may be replaced by programmes that may benefit less disadvantaged groups.	May affect liberty and also criticized for not having an overarching principle and having to balance competing principles.

Eastern link was 'fair game' to target within Western countries) and to criticize knee-jerk reactions either from people, institutions or governments. The argument of 'probability of occurrence' based on assumptions made about the ethnicity or race of 'potential sources of danger' may have several angles ranging from the reason of 'imbalance' between sources of crime to its effects in maintaining the cycles that created the imbalance in the first place. For instance we may ask: why are certain groups more likely to commit a crime? Have they been particularly discriminated against? If so, targeting them may help maintain the sources of the 'crime'. For example, who is the real criminal when a government abuses a group of people (e.g., taking their land, taunting them, restricting their movements, preventing them from accessing basic provisions so that their survival is limited) then screaming 'crime!' (not to mention 'terrorists!') when elements of such group lose all hope for change and act in desperation? SM aims to address the heart of a problem to genuinely encourage people to change. Any government with tokenistic 'faffing about' can never be seen as a genuine partner in helping get to the heart of a problem and resolving it. By ignoring problems, the responsible (or irresponsible in this case) actors are only transferring them to the future, when they may come back with even more force than when they appeared the first time.

An interesting consequence of identifying moral principles is to determine ways to measure our level of moral standing that may reflect our bias. A famous measure of moral judgement is the one proposed by Kohlberg. His method consisted in presenting subjects with scenarios reflecting moral dilemmas (e.g., stealing medicine or food when in dire need) and gathering their views and position vis-à-vis the situation. As a result of his research, he derived a Piagetian linear stage model involving six stages that can be more generally grouped into three levels of two stages each (see Table 3.3): pre-conventional, conventional and post-conventional stages (Kohlberg, 1971, 1986; Kohlberg and Lickona, 1976; Colby and Kohlberg, 1987):

> Each of the earlier stages provides a new and more comprehensive perspective that integrates the preceding ones. According to Kohlberg, fewer than 20% of American adults ever reach Stage 5, and almost no one reaches Stage 6.
>
> (Johnson, 2012)

Kohlberg wasn't without his critics, as it was reported that there was an unconscious degree of bias reflected in the way interviews were interpreted – for example, a feminist would tend to perceive a feminist perspective, while others either reported the views of philosophers such as Rawls or simply stated that their subjects were not aware of any deliberation process as their views were arrived at 'spontaneously' (Rest et al., 1999). Rest and colleagues argue that the latter view is not unusual, as people do not need to be aware of how

Table 3.3 Kohlberg stages of moral development/position

Level 1 (pre-conventional/personal interest stage)
1. Obedience and punishment orientation (how can I avoid punishment?)
2. Self-interest orientation (what's in it for me? Paying for a benefit)

Level 2 (conventional/maintaining norms stage)
3. Interpersonal accord and conformity (social norms; the good boy/girl attitude)
4. Authority and social-order maintaining orientation (law and order morality)

Level 3 (post-conventional/broader principles)
5. Social contract orientation
6. Universal ethical principles (principled conscience)

---

their immune or digestive systems function to be able to benefit from them. They also refer to work that highlights the regularity of unconscious-based decision-making processes in our day-to-day activities as demonstrated more than two decades ago (Uleman and Bargh, 1989).

Other criticism included assuming Foundational Principles, as deductivistic rather than inductivistic, adopting an individualistic rather than community-based orientation, making an unwarranted assumption that there is a consensus for deontic/moral principles reflecting universal values and, finally, offering a partial theory that used a limited pool of population, focuses primarily on rationality and does not include the emotional dimension (see Rest et al., 2000). Kohlberg (1986) himself recognizes the limits of his approach. Nevertheless, he produced a useful framework, that could be improved upon, that enables some rational way of identifying moral positions.

What the reader should perhaps take from the above views is that we need to be careful about what we may consider an 'ethical argument', which may only be another term for self-serving expediency. Indeed Hill (2011) identifies no less than four false (or straw-man) common arguments (see Table 3.1): For instance, the argument of a cultural relativist who feels that morality depends on the time and place, and therefore that it is pointless to aim for universal rules. This argument may also be implied by some post-modernists who argue that morality is relativistic and 'socially constructed'. This argument may be further supported by the view that we have gone beyond the three 'post traditions' (post-colonial, post-structural and post-modernist) (e.g., see Andreotti, 2011), backed up in turn by Sen, who states:

> we have a strong sense of injustice on many different grounds, and yet not agree on any particular ground as being the dominant reason for the diagnosis of injustice.
>
> (Sen, 2009, p. 2)

Although there is some truth regarding changes in moral perspectives reflecting geographical and historical changes (among others), it would be hard to reject all broadly agreed standards of morality on this basis as this may do a disservice to the work of social cause workers who are looking for some mutually agreeable principles that could be used as a basis for peace between warring factions (note also the OECD view mentioned in the previous chapter that encourages engaging citizens by focusing on common grounds!). Now, despite the relativity argument, many current decisions made anywhere in the world may affect a number of groups situated in a faraway corner from the place where the decision was made. This is the effect of our present-day global societies, where the life of a person living in a remote village in Africa may be influenced by a decision from a CEO located in New York or Beijing. Hence it is clear why Hill (2011) also provides four valid arguments based on well-debated issues on what constitutes a moral argument.

Integrating the Ethical Perspective

Although there have been several views on ethical behaviour, ranging from the philosophical and the procedural to the practical aspects, Rest (1986; Johnson, 2012) provided a framework that can be used to help integrate the various sources of focus and, consequently, of concern (see Table 3.4). He argued that as a prerequisite to any ethical decision and action, a person should demonstrate the following:

1   Moral sensitivity, or the ability to recognize a moral dilemma (or polylemma).
2   Moral judgement, or the ability (and maturity) to exercise a balanced and inclusive moral judgement (this topic will be reviewed below).
3   Moral focus, or the ability (motivation and commitment) to follow through with their judgement and making matching choices.
4   Moral character, or the ability to overcome challenges or obstacles that a moral agent comes across (physical, social, emotional) and follow through with the implementation of their choices in accordance with a planned approach. The challenges that moral agents meet at this level may prevent the majority from following through with their moral decision. This argument is backed up by findings showing a low correlation between moral judgement and moral behaviour (Johnson, 2012).

This approach seems to offer a good organizing framework for the various perspectives adopted by workers on ethics with a view to help increase the soundness of the process of making sense of and determining choices systematically. Such approaches include (Johnson, 2012):

1   Kidder's (1995) nine steps for clarifying, testing, making and reviewing ethical decisions.
2   Day's (2006) SAD template which stands for situation, analysis and decision. Accordingly, this author advises workers struggling with ethical problems to first define clearly the *situation*, where they occur. Then

analyse and interpret the competing ethical principles associated with the situation and then, finally, make a moral *decision* that is backed up by moral theoretical reasoning.

3   Nash's (1989) 12 requirements (in the form of questions) that seem to be particularly suited for guiding organizations (including a government) in making and evaluating moral decisions in the short and long term.

Table 3.4 demonstrates how Rest's framework can integrate the various perspectives but also gives an idea about where each of the discussed authors can be located within the Rest's four areas of focus.

John Elkington provided an argument about the need for all businesses to go beyond the simple profit making perspective (Elkington, 1998). His approach became known as the triple-bottom-line argument. This argument holds that the purpose of businesses is threefold, covering commercial profit but also reflecting care towards society and the physical environment. It is possible to argue, therefore, that this model reflects internationally agreed moral aims. It is worth noting that Elkington's approach could easily be added to Table 3.4 above after determining the equivalence to Rest's (1986) four dimensions. Nevertheless, we feel that Elkington's model misses a very important dimension, individual aims, that most people (organization leaders or general staff) directly or indirectly go for. Indeed while the triple-bottom-line aims are very worthwhile, perhaps the main source of motivation supporting the maintenance of these aims lies in the individual's personal reasons and values on what constitutes a worthwhile aim. Hence, and as shown above via Andreasen and Adam Smith views, any list of business aims that neglects the personal dimension may not help sustain the other identified aims (see Figure 3.1). Arguably personal aims are much broader than the economic aims (making a profit). This also links to the 'perceived value' concept that is crucial to the exchange principle routinely referred to by social marketers (Bagozzi, 1975, 1978).

If we just focus on the triple-bottom-line aims, there may be a debate about prioritizing which of the three values is more important than the rest and in which context, but the pervasiveness of the triple-bottom-line among responsible business circles reflects a consensus on moral aims. Throwing the fourth, individual, dimension into the mix sets the cat among the pigeons as it reminds us that the so-called rational debate may be fraught with hidden personal reasons.

Given the variety of arguments that moral agents may provide, it may be useful to remind practitioners about the need to be transparent and inclusive in trying to reach a multilateral consensus. In turn, this consensus should be open to scrutiny whenever there are any concerns raised so that a review of the principles as well as process and outcomes are undertaken.

It is clear that some of the best thinkers may reveal their weaknesses in some situations. As an example, Fourali (2014b) referred to Martha Nussbaum (e.g., see Nussbaum, 2000), who is generally perceived as a highly

Table 3.4 Using the Rest model as an integrative framework for the various ethical studies

Example of studies	Rest's four ethical dimensions (1986)			
	Moral sensitivity	Moral judgement	Moral focus (commitment)	Moral character
Kidder's nine steps (1995)	1) Problem recognition 2) Allocating responsibility 3) Fact finding	4) Determining the validity and acceptability of issue 5) Determining the ethical/value dilemmas 6) Selecting the relevant ethical principle (e.g., utilitarianism? Human rights? Community etc.) 7) Consider a third way/creative solution to reconcile differences	8) Moral courage to decide	9) Review and reflect on the decision
Day's SAD (2006)	1) Defining the situation	2) Analysing competing ethical principles	3) Ensure the moral decision is backed up by theoretical reasoning?	
Nash's 12 requirements/ questions (1989)	1) Problem definition 2) Seeing the problem from the other side of the fence 3) Origin of the problem (contributing factors)	4) Clarifying effect of loyalties (e.g., to self, group, family, organization) on values 5) Determine the intention behind a decision? 6) How likely is the intention to be reflected in the results? 7) Determining harmful consequences to all affected 8) Can you consult with the stakeholders before taking a decision	9) Can your choice stand the test of time? 10) Are you ready to disclose your decision to all affected?	11) Can you handle the variety of interpretations that the public derives (rightly or wrongly) from your action? 12) Are there any exceptions to your stance (are there exceptions to your rule)?
Kohlberg (1984, 1986)	Kohlberg's 1–6 stages can all be located in this column as they refer to how people determine their moral judgement			

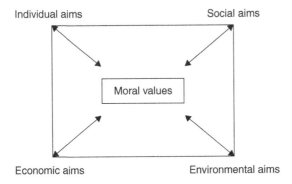

Individual aims   Social aims

Moral values

Economic aims   Environmental aims

Figure 3.1 Moral values and the aims of the quadruple-bottom-line

influential philosopher of justice but has been heavily criticized by human rights campaigners, such as Noam Chomsky and world-renowned scientist Stephen Hawking (*Guardian*, 2013) for her stance against the academic boycott of Israel despite the appalling, inhuman behaviour of Israel towards the Palestinians, which for many amounts to apartheid.

Perhaps one way to help us test our integrity is through the approach suggested by Gardner et al. (2001). This test suggests that professionals should ask three questions associated with what they call the '3 Ms' (mission, model to follow and mirror):

1. **Mission:** What is the defining feature for my job (e.g., 'healing for medicine' and 'justice for a lawyer')?
2. **Best model to follow:** What defines best practice for my profession (e.g., the Hippocratic oath or any other professional standards as defined by professional bodies)? Such a question should be linked to 'who best represents a good model to follow for my profession?'.
3. **Mirror:** What the world would be like if everyone was to behave in the way I have? This question, which is really a reformulation of the Golden Rule (treat others how you would like to be treated), could be linked to whether the person would be proud to look him/herself in a mirror after taking an action. However, the overt reaction to this last point is by no mean a measure of the person's level of ethical responsibility.

Clearly the model or, ultimately, the Golden Rule may be adapted for any situation and not just professions. When I introduce the Golden Rule to my business students, I tend to reformulate it in the following words: 'Treat others how you would like others to treat you or your most valued/loved people'. This is because there is always the cynical reaction of 'as we live in the jungle of survival of the fittest, then I am happy to take on the risk'. However, many tend to be more cautious if the rule is presented in terms of the 'significant other'. Nevertheless, the model may be criticized for being reductionist, since each one of us may represent more than one 'profession' (or responsibility). However the combination of the 3 Ms should help us determine what may be considered an acceptable (to say the least) way forward.

SM may also have another tacit agenda and that is to remove inequalities, especially when studies tend to argue that the more materialistic a society is, the more unequal it is, and the greater the resulting unhappiness of its citizens (see James, 2008; Wilkinson and Pickett, 2009). Such lack of justice or fulfilment, which may not be reflected in an ever-increasing hoarding of material wealth, may be the cause behind the malaise that may lead to destructive behaviour. Understanding a problem does not mean condoning it. But being indifferent to its consequences (i.e., looking the other way) may be, in ethical terms, almost as bad as committing it.

The Post-Modern Perspective

It is difficult to avoid mentioning the post-modern perspective when addressing issues of standards or purpose. As argued by Fourali (1997), in an article where he demonstrated the concept of fuzziness and the associated fuzzy logic methodology, the last few decades of development of literary theory have led to the demolition of many assumptions that used to prevail in relation to texts. In line with several post-modernists, he argued that it is no longer assumed that literary work contains universally acceptable truths and values, that texts have precise and definite meanings that all readers can derive and that there are agreed 'objective' values that determine what is good and bad writing. Indeed the reasoning goes beyond language to encompass any 'cultural artefact' since 'meaning is neither inherent in language, nor in the world of things, but is "constructed" by conventional frameworks of thought and language' (Gray, 1992; Lyotard, 1985). Many post-modern texts are therefore organized to reveal how meanings and values are temporary and self-generated constructions (Buci-Glucksmann, 1985). By extension, it may be argued that the meanings and values of not only artistic work (e.g., music, painting etc.) but, potentially, any social work, may be affected by temporary and self-generated constructions. This view is very similar to recent psychological views that stress the relativity of meaning constructed by different individuals (Gardner, 2004; Beck, 2001) or even the relativity of what constitutes acceptable standards of best practice. The later point can easily be demonstrated by referring to significant differences between various versions of the *Diagnostic and Statistical Manual of Mental Disorders* generally known to the mental health community as the DSM. It is not unusual to see that some differences are not simply the result of new findings but rather the result of socio-cultural factors (e.g., see Widiger and Sankis, 2000). This was reflected in ancient Greece by Epictetus, who suggested that people are not affected by 'events' but rather by their perceptions of them. There seems to be a convergence towards this view of the world or, as the epistemologists call it, 'paradigm' or rather 'paradigms'. One of its foremost promoters, Kuhn (1962), initially argued that we cannot rely heavily on the much-praised 'here and now' empiricism for discovering reality only to be rebutted by Feyerabend (1975) who attacked Kuhn's monism by arguing that at any one time there are several competing theories about the 'observed' reality. Feyerabend clarifies his position further (Stokes, 2004) by arguing that there are no facts since all factual statements are theory-laden. Clearly this may be seen as a step too far. However, as long as we remain cautious about how theory (and personal views/ideologies) may affect our portrayal of the reality and realize that it may be a matter of degrees rather than 'throwing out the baby with the bath-water' then such warnings may come in very handy.

The post-modernists (and post-structuralists) recommended the use of methods such as 'deconstruction' (Derrida, 1988) that challenged ideas of objectivity by highlighting the need to unravel grand narratives (or generally unquestioned 'universal truths') to discover how knowledge is legitimized (Lyotard, 1979). Other developments also challenged the so-called objective dichotomy between researcher–researched as demonstrated by post-colonial criticism (e.g., Said, 1979) and critical theory including neo-Marxist, race and feminist ideas (e.g., Habermas, 1987).

While the above challenges provided a breath of fresh air in the sense that we no longer have to accept a 'reality' as absolute truth, by the same token it also let out the proverbial Pandora's box evils of 'anything goes' (a favourite expression by Feyerabend!) even if it helped challenge any comfortable truth that we may have been acquainted with.

'Propaganda' or SM?

Although propaganda may be more accurately linked to 'social advertising', the reader may rightfully raise this question. Can one lie with SM? Can self-centred totalitarian regimes cynically make use of the developments of SM to 'sleep-walk' their populations to outcomes that match their every whim? History seems to suggest that the answer is 'yes' and there are plenty of examples of leaders who because they were convinced about what constituted the good for the people, lead their societies to utter destruction.

Kotler saw a link between SM and 'social engineering' (Kotler, 2013), a less negative word than 'propaganda', perhaps with good reasons. One way to help develop society is to educate children from an early age to provide them with the attitudes and skills to become healthy human beings. However, Kotler was also aware of the dangers, as history shows that such an approach, if abused and based on totalitarianism, may lead to 'propaganda', which in turn may lead to extremist movements such as national socialism.

In fact Popper in *The Open Society and Its Enemies* (1945) already suggested that any result or approach be continuously revised and improved using the concept of 'falsifiability'. Such an approach, if adopted by a society, should be able to circumvent the crystallization of some policies into 'finished truths' that do not need improvements (or new interpretation) according to changes in society and environment.

Propaganda may be defined as the act by an individual (especially with powerful means), group, institution or state that proactively promotes a value judgement that favours one version of reality over another, with a view to filtering out key aspects of the opposite view and making the chosen perspective the basis of decisions reflecting absolute and exclusive right and wrong that, eventually, advantages one or more groups over others.

Accordingly, one might argue that communications that promote certain cultures or countries (e.g., 'country marketing' for touristic purposes) may be seen as a form of propaganda. The answer is that would be so if the communication meet the following four conditions:

1. Favour one view over another.
2. Filter out key information/facts about competing views.
3. Urge the target group to make a decision about absolute and exclusive right and wrong (we are right and they are wrong). Note that this may be overtly or covertly encouraged.
4. Direct or indirect consequences (individual, institutional, etc.) that leads to advantages achieved by the 'chosen' group or loss incurred by non-chosen groups.

It may be argued that only if all criteria are met can we talk about propaganda, while bearing in mind that propaganda, like many other concepts, may be located in a continuum ranging from least harmful to extremely harmful. For instance, with a view to reducing self-harm, an initiative might encourage certain views about drug taking, warning users about health consequences and even filtering out information (e.g., that cigarettes may be as bad a drug as 'pot', if not more destructive). Clearly this is not as big a propaganda initiative compared to one that proactively designs and broadcasts messages that encourage ethnic cleansing.

There are many governments that have been accused of engaging in propaganda initiatives. These are not just the so-called usual suspects emanating from well-known totalitarian regimes. Recent developments showed that so-called 'civilized' countries also presented and supported one view/ideology of the world to win support for it. However, in the long term, the effectiveness of such an approach is counterproductive as eventually the facts will become known and will not only reduce the potency of the message but will also lead to a loss of trust of the sources of 'propaganda' messages. Consider, for example, the public relations blow to the US government (and other governments) after the WikiLeaks revelations. Perhaps the biggest challenge nowadays to propaganda is the availability of alternative information easily accessible on the internet.

It is suggested that to avoid a propagandist perspective and adopt a responsible 'social engineering' position, decision-makers need to take into account three key dimensions according to the following questions:

1. **Is the policy based on verified truth?** To illustrate this question in the tobacco industry context, we may ask whether smoking is actually destroying individual and social lives and whether it is being actively (directly and indirectly) encouraged by corporate bodies.
2. **Is the policy being considered for adoption relevant to the context at hand?** This would address questions such as: has the policy been subjected to rigorous research? Will its application adversely impact some minority groups?
3. **Is the knowledge/wisdom behind the policy being applied adequately?** This question is more about monitoring implementation and ensuring that the application reflects the earlier agreed aims. For example, it asks whether the application is still reflecting the principles of fairness, harm reduction and respect for individual freedom in the light of the feedback that is being received.

Depending on how rigorously these questions are addressed there are eight possible scenarios that may result as shown in Table 3.5.

However, as argued by Fourali (1997), the reality is mostly fuzzy (i.e., with shades of grey rather than 'black or white'). The optimal resolution should reflect the most appropriate balance of truth, relevance and rigorous application as shown through a list of continuums reflecting each of these concepts (Fourali, 1997).

Propaganda tends to reflect only perhaps cells 3, 4, 7 and 8, which are predicated with 'not true'. This is because irrespective of whether knowledge was relevant or applied well or not, propaganda usually reflects the non-democratic application of the truth that a select few see and tend to impose on the rest of society. This state of affairs does not only apply to Nazi Germany as traditionally argued but applies to current world realities as

Table 3.5 Possible scenarios that may result from the implementation of 'social engineering' policies. Note that responsible social engineers should aim for an outcome that reflects cell 1

		Knowledge (Truth by relevance)			
		True and relevant	*True but not relevant*	*Not true but Relevant*	*Not true and not relevant*
Application	Well applied	Cell 1 True Relevant Well applied	Cell 2 True Not relevant Well applied	Cell 3 Not true Relevant Well applied	Cell 4 Not true Irrelevant Well applied
	Not well applied	Cell 5 True Relevant Not well applied	Cell 6 True Not relevant Not well applied	Cell 7 Not true Relevant Not well applied	Cell 8 Not true Irrelevant Not well applied

has been demonstrated by several SM workers and critical theorists (Fox and Prilleltensky, 1997; Derrida, 1988; Said, 1979, 2001). Hence the importance of 'digging deeper' to go beyond the 'presented facts' is particularly important advice. As an example, one may mention the work of the late Edward Said (1979, 2001). Said highlights the bias that some social researchers have brought into their studies of Middle Eastern societies because they did not weigh up how their conclusions were mediated by their cultural perceptions, generally designed by the West to justify imperialist and colonial policies. In terms of systemic aspects being brought to bear on the problem, one may mention the work of Fox and Prilleltensky (1997) on critical psychology, who take a broader view about psychological practice influenced by a raft of factors including economic and social dimensions. Fox (2008) in particular illustrated the importance of the broader political/social factors through the Palestinian/Israeli conflict and showed how the resulting dominant discourse 'dismisses Palestinian suffering as self-induced and politically justified'.

If anything, the above arguments raise awareness of the need to encourage more active and responsible citizens within our societies. Accordingly, one can envisage a meta social marketing initiative where the aim is to raise awareness to the insidious effects of initiatives (corporate or otherwise) that may claim social causes but when considering the bigger and long-term picture, one may find that the destructive consequences may outweigh their social benefits. Such meta social marketing initiatives would aim to educate society to be more alert to threatening initiatives through a broader critical ability and more investigations and open discussions of any initiative. Such initiatives would therefore help encourage a more preventative approach that aims to protect societies from destructive threats.

Criticism of SM

Fourali (2010) stated that, like most initiatives, there are reservations about marketing in general, and social marketing in particular. Such reservations include accusations about dishonest means of inducing changes, focusing too much on profit issues at the expense of the bigger issues such as environment and social ills, and using means that are either too slow to take effect or are inadequate (Crompton, 2008). In this respect David Norman from WWF UK stated: 'Environmental challenges will not be met while maintaining a narrow focus on the happy coincidence of economic self-interest and environmental prudence' (Crompton, 2008, p. 2).

Lefebvre and Flora (1988) level another criticism as they see SM as a form of 'blaming the victim' since it identifies the problem at the individual level and aims to change him/her.

As argued by Lefebvre and Flora (1988), most of the above criticisms may be seen as a very narrow way of conceptualizing SM. As argued in this book, one of the strengths of SM is that it provides priority to social concerns (including environmental). The SM approach allows for creative thinking that uses top-down, midstream or bottom-up strategies and, as long as the outcome is effective, there are no limits to what may be undertaken. The sphere of focus (e.g., socio-political and economic) as well as the disciplines referred to, are only limited by the social marketer's imagination.

Additionally, most of SM's detractors have not managed to suggest alternative strategies. The irony of such an argument is that, if new effective ways of inducing changes are found, SM would be very keen to adopt them because, as argued above, SM is not restricted (or wedded) to a particular approach or a specific target group. Many of its initiatives include persuading policymakers who can influence laws that override any economic benefits that may adversely impact society.

Nevertheless, and notwithstanding the above criticisms and responses, one should still consider situations where SM is yet another tool in the hand of people with self-serving intentions rather than genuine attempts at serving society. A case in point is when SM is accused of language assumptions leading to human rights abuse. Such assumptions may conjure ideas of you are 'with us/in' or 'against us/out'. Such a situation may include tangible (e.g., obesity/fatness) or intangible ('I am/am not Charlie') examples, each of which reflects judgemental assumptions whose main aim is 'classification of members of society with a view to bestow value judgements on a particular topic'. If somebody states 'I am not Charlie' this may trigger the following assumptions:

- People can either be with us or against us – there is no middle or other alternative ways.
- Those who state 'I am Charlie' are good and those who state 'I am not Charlie' are evil (i.e., 'all bad').
- You are against us/society.
- You are against our way of life (implying there is one way of life).

Cleary the result of such conscious or subconscious analysis may lead to a witch-hunt against those who do not fit the 'standards' or toe the line.

Indeed the reverse can also be true, as there may be members of society who invoke SM or any other concepts of discrimination in order to encourage 'guilt trips' for anybody who may promote an initiative to improve society and minimize 'abuse of the system'.

These ideas suggest that SM, like all sciences and especially social sciences, are subject to vulnerabilities. So it is important that part of any SM study should differentiate the factual from the subjective (or abusive) and even if an initiative for addressing a 'social problem' is warranted, this should not be necessarily taken as a green light for adopting a number of unwarranted assumptions.

It is true that SM and its protagonists have their weaknesses. This does not mean that the concept is wrong; it just provides us with the opportunity to improve the methodology. Nevertheless, and despite any reservation, SM is a proven tool that is too effective to overlook, particularly when the issues at hand affect a large proportion of the population.

How Does the Above Relate to SM Practitioners?

It is clear that SM practitioners have to be even more careful in trying to assess the so-called 'reality' and understand how to challenge it and adopt a flexible attitude to truth. Such a perspective would require a continuous review of the perceived 'reality' in the light of agreed principles such as 'inclusion' and 'common good', while realizing the dangers of adopting any 'unified view'. The contribution of philosophical thinking is key in helping SM practitioners deliberate about the relevance of concepts, values and suggested courses of action. Hence philosophical awareness and tools are very much part and parcel of the bread and butter of SM practitioners, especially given the vulnerabilities the SM profession may present due to its cross-disciplinary nature. Perhaps the biggest benefit of such a perspective is the erosion of any false sense of self-confidence that should encourage the adoption of a more humane and humble perspective. To facilitate the development of SM initiatives underpinned by thought-through philosophical and ethical dimensions, perhaps the following lessons may be derived:

- SM researchers should allow debate of underpinning moral values to differentiate between 'straw-man' or short-termist arguments and genuine ones. Part of winning supporters for SM projects is to be able to develop sharp arguments to be able to challenge such short-term or straw-man justifications.
- The consultation with all stakeholders associated with an issue is key in helping identify robust solutions. Part of the debate should address the relativity of values as argued, for example, by post-modernists with a view to reaching convergence towards common grounds.
- In line with this last point, social marketers may also need to encourage a debate around individual responsibility in contributing (or not) to a social ill. The three-step questioning technique highlighted by Gardner and colleagues (2001) offers a good scheme for encouraging authenticity in engagement. Having said that, it is clear that some individuals may have much more options than others (e.g., given their wealth, intellectual or social capital). It is important to be sensitive to such differences. Such an issue was raised during international discussions on global warming, when it was argued that different demands on different regions or country should be made taking into account different circumstances.
- Sometimes solutions result from thinking creatively at micro-, meso- or macro-levels. For example, a government keen on cutting down pollution may provide tax or funding incentives that would encourage more creative thinking at the micro-level.

- There are many varieties of human societies (underpinned by cultural, social and individual differences). Hence a savvy social marketer should aim to understand local values before devising a programme of action. Nevertheless, given the multicultural communities many of us live in and the global consequences of many projects (e.g., moving toxic material from one country to another), there is an argument to also look at common ground values to ensure support from all communities. Consequently, a number of suggestions have been made regarding determining universally shared values. Such debate should be pursued and the results refined.
- Solutions do not have to be located exclusively within one or two factors of the quadruple-bottom-line. Perhaps the best solutions may relate to all four (think of Unilever's water purifiers). However, it is important to remember that psychology is a key determinant in helping sustain social or environmental solutions. Understanding what constitutes satisfaction is a prerequisite to attempting to raising interest in a target population and providing an attractive exchange offer (at either the individual or business level) (Bagozzi, 1978).
- Like most credible decisions, ethical decisions also require systematic critique and application of relevant models with a view to substantiate decisions and actions based on several sources of evidence and arguments (triangulation). This chapter highlighted several models that could be consulted for guidance to maximize comprehensiveness of approach, thereby ensuring that the adopted decisions and actions are more robust and, hopefully, fairer.

Finally there is an argument that ethics is an unavoidable issue. The fact that we are making decisions throughout our daily lives does not make it less of a serious issue to address especially if the consequences can be disastrous to many (in some cases to millions). How many Governments waged wars on the pretext of flimsy or, in some cases, non-existent 'proofs', as demonstrated by damning evidence such as the collusion between British and USA Governments to go to war in Iraq based on what amount to blatant lies (e.g. See Murray, 2016)? The result, and pain inflicted to many by such disastrous decisions, can be (and in most cases are) felt by millions in many years to come.

4 Mapping the Field of Social Marketing

The Complexity of the Sources of Behavioural Influence

As the primary aim of SM is to prevent or change destructive behaviour and maintain constructive behaviour, it is paramount to have a closer look at the factors that current research identifies as decisive in directing human behaviour. Clearly behavioural change is a very complex area recognized by many. Take Tim Jackson's telling statement:

> In summary, my behaviour in any particular situation is a function partly of my attitudes and intentions, partly of my habitual responses, and partly of the situational constraints and conditions under which I operate. My intentions in their turn are influenced by social, normative and affective factors as well as by rational deliberations. I am neither fully deliberative nor fully automatic in this view. I am neither fully autonomous nor entirely social. My behaviours are influenced by my moral beliefs, but the impact of these is moderated both by my emotional drives and my cognitive limitations.
>
> (Jackson, 2005, p. 6)

The above opinion has been reflected by many social marketers too. SM literature reflects many potential influences on our behaviour combining both theory and practice. In this chapter we will briefly remind ourselves about the complexity involved in addressing SM projects and then, in the following chapters, proceed to focus in turn on each of the key identified areas.

Understanding the Complexity of Individuals: A Necessary Prerequisite to Helping Them

Fourali (2014a) presented a paper at Oxford where he demonstrated the complexity of humans and their interactions. Two diagrams were made use of. The first diagram produced the social influences and the second one showed the other influences beyond the social influences (see Figures 4.1 and 4.2 below).

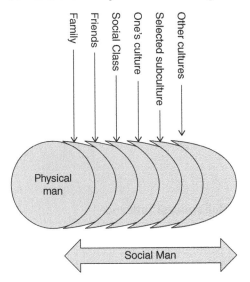

Figure 4.1 Social influences on individuals since birth

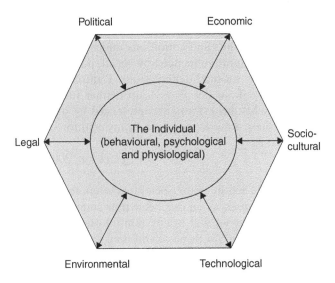

Figure 4.2 Variety of influences on an individual

In Figure 4.1, it is important to note that the relative influence is not necessarily linear and the weight of influence of each of the social dimensions will depend on the specific circumstances of each individual and the interaction of all the dimensions. So for one individual, a teacher may have more influence than even family members if, for instance, the family members were not that present or did not represent a 'good' model.

Now if we consider Figure 4.2 we will notice that the previous diagram reflected only one dimension among several dimensions that may influence an individual. Again the decisive influence of any of the above may depend on each individual case and the combined iterative interaction of all effects as demonstrated by Fourali (2009b) in a paper focusing on the dynamic benefits of adopting a fuzzy logic perspective to understanding human behaviour. Note that whilst the primary interest among social marketers is behavioural influence, the influence may also be psychological and/or physiological.

Social Marketing: A Semantic Perspective

The social sciences are key to SM. So much so that the word 'social' is one of the two words that make up the name of this discipline. One may see two reasons for this importance: the first one is that this discipline has at its primary interest to serve society as a whole and ultimately the global social community. Arguably this aim may be the source of controversies as shown in the section in Chapter 3 called 'Philosophical considerations associated with SM', which ought to be (re)visited for more details. Although the main priority of social marketers is human welfare, it does not mean that the other factors are to be excluded from the equation. For instance, other considerations may boost this primary aim even if in the short term it may be seen as contravening the primary aims. Consider the issue of profit-making. Although 'profit' is seen as secondary to SM, since we are not dealing with commercial marketing, nevertheless profit is needed for 'sustainability' of SM initiatives as ideally one of the criteria of effectiveness of an SM initiative is its ability to maintain itself. The last point is particularly relevant when we consider that many initiatives that depended on a one-off support ended being dropped once the funding 'dried up'. It is worth noting that many SM initiatives are carried out by governments who are happy to fully sponsor certain projects using taxpayer's money and, at least in the initial stages, may not worry about sustainability. However, relying on government initiatives may be very risky as the decision to support projects may be dropped as a result of other (political?) priorities taking over.

Nevertheless the word 'social' would, ultimately, refer to the global social community, although generally the focus tends to be at local level given the prevalence of certain problems in certain geographical areas.

The second reason for the importance of the word 'social' in SM is to reflect the multidisciplinary nature of this field as it needs to refer to the advice/wisdom of the various sciences that make up its discipline depending on the topic or problem at hand. Clearly given that the word 'marketing' makes up the second part of the name of this discipline, its importance is therefore undeniable. As stated earlier and in the light of the negative associations with the word 'marketing' in the general population psyche, one possible argument would be to determine perhaps a more appropriate name for such a noble discipline. The jury is still out on this.

Given the nature of SM to aim to influence social behaviour to a more constructive and healthier one to replace the existing one, in the next chapters we will focus on the second meaning of the word 'social' and will look at the most recurrent disciplines that reflect the main sources of influences on human behaviour. We will then try to identify some key aspects of theory and practice that relate to or have been used by SM.

An Integrative Picture of Behavioural Change?

Marketers have for a long time focused on what affects consumer behaviour. Clearly there is no surprise here as businesses not only need to understand what causes the buying behaviour so as to produce relevant products and services that serve the behaviour, but they also intend to attract consumers to try and adopt new products that may not have any precedent in the market. Marketers came up with several frameworks to broadly identify the influential factors on consumer behaviour as well as how they interact between each other. Perhaps two among the most influential and useful frameworks were those provided by Schiffman et al. (2012) and Brassington and Pettitt (2006). The author felt that both frameworks had useful dimensions that perhaps the other one did not reflect adequately. Additionally, both perspectives seem to primarily focus on the buying behaviour as they both refer to purchasing rather than 'behavioural change'. Consequently, the author decided to produce a version that combines the advantages of both perspectives while making the outcome broader for use as it refers to behavioural adoption rather than 'purchasing' (see Figure 4.3).

Figure 4.3 seems to have a clearer relevance to social marketing than those referred to earlier. Hence the reference in the title to behavioural change or influence rather than 'consumer behaviour'.

The diagram identifies both context and chronology of behavioural influences. The context could be external, internal and the result of the influence. The chronology shows the steps that a 'customer' may undertake before adopting or repeating a behaviour such as purchasing or changing a lifestyle behaviour.

	Input	Process	Output
External influence ↑ ↕ ↓	• Marketing effort (4 Ps) • Socio-cultural environment • Other situational factors (PESTLE)		
Internal influence ↑ ↕		• Decision-making steps • Psychological precedents • Past experience	
↓ ↕ **Consumer behaviour**			• Behavioural adoption (trial) • Post-behavioural adoption (evaluation/ decision)

Figure 4.3 Factors of behavioural change/influence (adapted from Schiffman et al., 2012, and Brassington and Pettitt, 2006)

Table 4.1 Competition for SM initiatives (based on Peattie and Peattie, 2003)

Behavioural adoption and maintenance	
Acting for (battle for attention and acceptance)	*Acting against (battle for attention and acceptance)*
Social marketing proposition	Commercial counter-marketing
Social encouragement (from significant others)	Social discouragement (from significant others)
	Apathy
	Involuntary disinclination

There have been other frameworks specifying some of the factors involved in behavioural change but in our view, Figure 4.3 is much more comprehensive. Nevertheless, the more specific diagrams are also useful as the more specific we are about a particular case, the greater the need for clarifying the differences and relevant factors about the case.

The issue of differentiating consumer behaviour from behavioural influences is taken up by Peattie and Peattie (2003) in a landmark article called 'Ready to fly solo? Reducing social marketing's dependence on commercial marketing theory' where they argued that SM needed to adopt its own specific concepts and tools of research. They present a diagram that balances the factors that may contribute to a new behaviour and those acting against it. This is very much akin to adopting the 'T approach' in selling (Futrell, 2010) or the pros and cons method in cognitive psychology. Hence to demonstrate their view we will adopt the T approach (see Table 4.1).

The Relevance of the Social Sciences

As demonstrated above, SM needs to make use of a number of disciplines from the social sciences. As argued by Jackson (2005) it is actually difficult to find any 'pure' influence on behaviour. Accordingly and for the sake of simplicity we will aim to identify some key composite areas to help locate the sources of the influences.

A NESTA (2008) paper focusing on environmental/climate issues argued that the main theoretical aspects that can inform social marketing may be located in the fields of the sociology of consumption and psychology. This is not surprising as some of the key models referred to in SM work borrowed from psychology and sociology. Nevertheless, there is an argument that economics are also very important in mediating our behaviour and therefore should be considered as part of this section (e.g., see R.K. Thomas, 2008).

One can envisage a diagram mediating the psychological and economic dimensions via the sociological dimension as shown in Figure 4.4.

Although one would expect a three-way presentation covering, in turn, psycho-socio, socio-economic and psycho-economic factors, for simplicity's sake we will aim to cover all three dimensions within the psycho-socio and

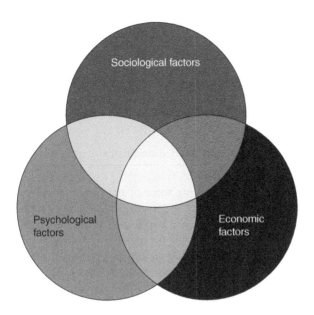

Figure 4.4 Interplay between psychological, sociological and economic factors

socio-economic dimensions. Additionally, and given the importance of the marketing dimension to SM, we will also address the effect of this discipline on SM in a separate chapter. Accordingly we have organized our treatment of the various SM factors as follows:

* psycho-social dimension;
* socio-economic dimension;
* marketing.

Clearly such delineation between subjects may sacrifice the integrative nature of the combined forces that influence behaviour. In particular, a number of views may be located at the conjunction of these three categories of influences. Consider, for example, the position of behavioural economics (Simon, 1979; Kahneman, 2003). Although this approach may be considered at the junction of psychology and economics, we feel it may be presented within the psycho-social perspective and have done so accordingly (see Chapter 5).

Hence the three categories of theories will be addressed in turn in the next three chapters.

What about Education?

A reader may feel uneasy about 'leaving out' education from the list of the key facets influencing behaviour. In fact the relevance of education is reflected in the common grounds between education and SM. Fourali (2010, 2013) argued that there is a clear link between education and SM both at the systemic level, as when considering what is valued in educational establishments, but also in terms of the value that marketing could bring to disseminating progressive and inclusive educational practices. Education, like psychology/counselling and SM, is about changing behaviour (hopefully underpinned by inner insights) using as many disciplines that may help this process as possible. Arguably there is a lot of overlap between the aims of education and those of SM and both can learn from each other. As an example, if we consider the psychological overlap, recent educational studies tend to highlight common grounds in the form of the importance of reflection, relationships and transformation (e.g., Schon, 1987; Mezirow, 1995; Land et al., 2008). Such common grounds are addressed in Chapter 5.

Apart from these overlaps there is a developing view that education should be put back on track to serve rather than become a tick-box discipline that is more interested in meeting administrative rituals for funding and career promotion (some of these issues are also taken up in Chapter 8).

There have been several criticisms about the aims of education during the past few decades reflecting views covering philosophical and political as well as educational positions (e.g., Elliot, 2009). In particular, one of the claims levelled against 'conventional approaches to education' has been that it is removed from the real social issues that it should target (e.g., Levin and Greenwood, 2013). In turn, this situation has been blamed for leading to the destructive types of leadership that were one of the main contributors to the 2008 financial crash, which could have been avoided if not for the so-called expert popularity of 'positive leadership'. According to critics of this type of leadership, it leads to a blind allegiance to organizational aims that 'lies at the heart of many of the financial miscalculations that drove the Great Recession' (Collinson, 2012).

SM can offer a lot at this level in terms of changing attitudes and moving from 'frozen' rituals to influencing changes if the academic community joins forces and decides to work together to help prevent their field from falling in the tracks of irrelevance and supporting political expediency.

Another area debated in educational studies over many years that SM could perhaps benefit from is the value-added studies that highlight the importance of moving target populations along a continuum of improvement rather than necessarily aiming for a simple 'black or white/good or bad' type of argument. Unfortunately the black and white approach tends to promote unfairness if the system for assessing the value of 'education' or effectiveness of an SM programme is a simple two-box option (e.g., 'pass or fail'). Education and SM should aim to be inclusive and sensitive to any improvement, be that a small skill improvement (although still short of a 'pass') or a little change of attitude or health improvement. How many schools or universities have lost out to so-called better-performing educational institutions when the starting point and environmental conditions have not been taken into account? This is a well-known issue in educational circles that reflects an indictment of the so-called 'league-table approach to assessing quality of education', where the main concern is simply the level of achievement at the end of the programme (not how much improvement has been made since the starting point). Educationalists are quite aware that value-added (or improvement) between the starting point and the current results, taking into account availability of resources, should be part of any credible analysis before claiming fairness of comparison. One of the criticisms for such added-value/'multilevel' considerations is their complexity. However, how many social issues can be explained in terms of one or two factors? Even if such complexity is confirmed, does this mean that for simplicity's sake we should sacrifice such principles of validity and reliability of findings, not to mention fairness? Surely this is not what was meant by the law of parsimony. Nevertheless, Fourali (2009b) argued that there are opportunities for simplifications given the recent uptake of new methods such as fuzzy logic.

5 The Psycho-Social Dimension of Behaviour

It may be argued that human needs may explain most if not all enterprises. If so, understanding those needs and motivations is key to understanding the psychology behind unhealthy behaviour that social marketing is so keen to help with.

The following will aim to provide a broad view of the key theories that have been advanced to explain behaviour and then provide more details to some of the ones that have been of particular help to social marketers. In particular, we will look at the following models/theories that are considered to be highly relevant to the work of a social marketer:

- Addiction theories.
- Theories of change.
- Behavioural economics (linked to concept of nudging).
- Cognitive behavioural theory/therapy (CBT).

The above approaches to understanding and changing behaviour present a number of perspectives that may provide the social marketer with useful insights about the problem being addressed with a view to suggesting possible solutions. They are critically addressed in turn while providing suggestions about some future considerations. As will be discussed later, there are links and overlaps between the above perspectives, although each one of them provides specific insights that may help the social marketer.

The Insights Provided by Addiction Theories

In order to attempt to present a bird's-eye view of the various explanatory models for different behaviour, we will refer to the classification presented by West and Brown (2013), with some adjustments, with a view to simplifying the picture for the reader.

West and Brown (2013) were particularly interested in addiction, a self-destructive behaviour, when proposing their classification of the main theories advanced to explain it. We feel that the theories used to explain addiction fit our purpose very well, as they help shed the light on factors that impel an individual to carry out behaviours that are self-destructive or, at best, maladaptive. Indeed, conversely, the theories can also be used to account for the development of healthy behaviour too. Hence, in the following presentation we will refer to these various suggested theories simply as potential explanatory models for individual behaviour. Such a perspective highlights the social scientist dual role as a provider of explanatory models but also, at least potentially, as the provider of resolutions of social problems based on what constitutes a healthy society. Accordingly, the theories presented would constitute initial prompts for potential explanations regarding the sources of unhealthy behaviour. This strategy should not be surprising, as one of the key aims of marketing is to serve the 'needs' of the targeted populations (i.e., the customers). So understanding the characteristics of such needs would help the marketer better serve the 'customer'. Clearly this also helps remind us that what a customer perceives as a 'need' may be simply 'psychological' and not a need in the usual sense to help biological survival. There are plenty of studies demonstrating such needs; for instance, through the concept of brand loyalty where customers would buy a product primarily because of values associated with such products that a person would identify with (e.g., Keller, 2012). This point brings us back to our earlier discussions on ethics, as profit-based marketers may like to present any of their products, tangible or otherwise, as 'necessary' for survival. Such arguments unfortunately tend to be pretty successful when supported (albeit cynically) by research recommendations from social science and particularly persuasion or motivational studies. This latter point should remind us about the huge difference between the purpose of commercial marketing and that of SM.

In the light of the above, and given the multiplicity of theories invoked for explaining human behaviour, we believe addiction theories, because of their complexity and their tendency to be self-destructive, may offer very useful pointers to social marketers to guide them as to the reasons a situation may occur. This does not mean that other theories should not be considered. Indeed, the social marketer is primarily led by the phenomenon (or social problem) s/he may be focusing on to decide what theory may be relevant. For example, a social marketer interested in domestic or communal violence may consider several converging factors (backed up by theoretical models) that can offer insights and solutions to the problem. Nevertheless, because of the substantial overlap between the issues associated with addiction (perhaps very simply defined as 'a broadly maladaptive overpowering behavioural tendency') and those tackled by SM researchers, there is an argument that SM workers should study theories of addiction for a number of reasons including:

- At their heart, these theories aim to explain what attracts, induces or maintain an individual behaviour.
- Most theories apply to many psychological conditions (anger, anxiety, depression, etc.). So social marketers who feel that addiction may not be

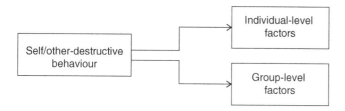

Figure 5.1 Two main groups of theories for explaining maladaptive behaviour

the primary factor they are dealing with may readjust the explanatory models for their own purposes.

- Addiction theories are closely aligned to motivation theories making them very relevant to the task of behavioural change.
- Social marketers have already started making use of addiction theories as demonstrated, for example, through the adoption of the trans-theoretical model by Andreasen (2006) and Hastings and Haywood (1991) as shown below.

West and Brown (2013) classify the addiction theories for explaining behaviour under two labels: individual- or group-level explanations as shown in Figure 5.1. We will take each level in turn and present it briefly. The reader who needs more details may like to refer to the references provided for each perspective, as there is little space for in-depth presentation. Note that the list of factors/influences presented below is compatible with those presented earlier, based on Schiffman et al. (2012) and Brassington and Pettitt (2006) with the difference being that there are several options presented to account for the psychological perspective.

Individual-Level Theories

The following is a brief introduction to each of the main individual-level theories. As stated earlier, the reader interested in a more detailed presentation can refer to the authors listed in each introduction. Table 5.1 reflects well-known theories associated with explanations of unhealthy behaviour located within the individual. We will review each of these theories and associated key arguments.

Automatic Response Theories

Four groups of theories could be linked to automatic response theories. These are learning, drive, inhibition dysfunction and imitation theories. The first one, in the tradition of behaviourism, stresses the importance of linking stimuli to responses and associated positive or negative reinforcement

Table 5.1 Individual-level explanatory models of self/other-destructive behaviour (author's classification)

Automatic response theories
Decision process theories
Level of reward theories
Needs-related theories
Lack-of-control theories
Disease theories

in developing or maintaining behaviours (Berridge et al., 2011; Nevin and Grace, 2000). The second group of theories, the drive theories, sees behaviour as induced by developed drives as a result of changes in neuro-physiological homeostatic mechanisms (see Jellinek, 1960; Riley et al., 2011). The third group of theories, the inhibition (of impulses) dysfunction theories, reflect a lack of mechanisms for controlling impulses located within the brain circuitry (Lubman et al., 2004; Goldstein et al., 2001). Finally, the fourth group of theories identifies imitation as a key factor in developing new behaviour. This involves (consciously or automatically) copying behaviour patterns and adopting ideas and identities. This approach was initially associated with the work of Bandura to account for social learning, but other researchers followed suit (see Bandura, 1977; Heyes, 2011).

Decision Process Theories

Two theories may be classified under this label depending on whether a decision process for undertaking a behaviour is carried out rationally or reflects some bias. In the first instance, decisions are carried out following a rational cost–benefit analysis and opting for a behaviour that attracts higher advantages (Edwards, 1961; Keeney and Raiffa, 1976; Kahneman and Tversky, 1979; Ajzen, 1991). In contrast, biased decisions may be the result of errors underpinned by cognitive or emotional causes (Skog, 2003; Ainslie and Monterosso, 2003; Field and Cox, 2008; Slovic et al., 2002; Kandel et al., 1992; Janis and Mann, 1977).

Level of Reward Theories

A behaviour may be determined by the level of satisfaction/pleasure an individual derives from undertaking it. The higher the pleasure, the greater the risk of indulging in the behaviour and subsequent addiction to it (Koob and Le Moal, 2008; Kanayama et al., 2009; Cawley et al., 2004).

Needs-Related Theories

As their names indicate, these theories focus on the type of needs a person may be addressing when carrying out a behaviour. Three main thrusts can be identified: acquired, pre-existing and identity needs theories. The acquired needs theories argue that destructive behaviour, such as addiction, reinforces itself through the steady development of physiological and psychological needs (through 'force of habit') (e.g., Koob et al., 1992; West, 2013). The pre-existing needs theory proposes that destructive behaviour may involve engaging in activities that help eliminate or moderate the effects of pre-existing (unresolved) needs (Khantzian, 1997; Flores, 2004; Cooper et al., 1995). The identity needs theories argue that destructive behaviour may be induced or maintained through an individual's perception of one's identity ('that's who I am!') (Kearney and O'Sullivan, 2003; Gibbons et al., 2003; Harris et al., 2007).

Lack-of-Control Theories

These types of theories tend to be broader with a multilevel perspective. Three groups of such theories have been identified in the form of self-regulation, broader integrative and trans-theoretical or change models. The self-regulation theories argue that a destructive behaviour may reflect a person's inability (through lack of strategies, skills or capacity) for self-control to adequately address the impulses/desires that lead to the destructive behaviour. One possible weakness reflecting this incapacity is a lack of mental energy (i.e., ego-depletion) (Miller and Cohen, 2001; Fernandez-Serrano et al., 2010; Madoz-Gurpide et al., 2011; Hustad et al., 2009; Ryan and Deci, 2000; Gollwitzer, 1999).

The second group, the broader integrative theories, argue that destructive behaviour may be the result of complex processes combining influences and interactions involving, among other things, pre-existing conditions, behaviours, social and environmental determinants that may lead to the initiation and, subsequently, the maintenance of such behaviours (Blaszczynski and Nower, 2002; Hussong et al., 2011; Orford, 2001).

The third group, the process-of-change theories, focuses on the importance of matching helping strategies to the level of readiness of a person to address a behavioural problem. Accordingly, a number of stages of readiness for recovery are identified that help with diagnosing the problem and the level of commitment for addressing it. For instance the trans-theoretical stages include recognition of a problem, initiation of change, recovery or relapse (Festinger, 1957; Blume and Schmaling, 1996; Petty et al., 1991; Prochaska et al., 1992; Hayes et al., 1999, Hendershot et al., 2011; Marlatt and George, 1984).

Disease Theories

This group of theories have a biological basis and more specifically reflect a neurological 'anomaly', or disease, which translates into executive malfunction. Such malfunction will affect both the individual's behaviour and their ability to resist against the occurrence of the destructive behaviour (Brewer

Table 5.2 Group-level explanatory models of self/other-destructing behaviour (author's classification)

Social support theories
Economic theories
Marketing communications theories
Systems of management models

and Potenza, 2008; Everitt et al., 2008; Baker et al., 2011). Note that in the section above on automatic response theories, we listed a third group of theories called the inhibition (of impulses) dysfunction theories, that reflect a lack of mechanisms for controlling impulses located within the brain circuitry. Although this is a slightly different type of theory, because of their focus on a neurological basis, the reader may feel that this type of theory should also feature here (see Lubman et al., 2004; Goldstein and Volkow, 2011).

Group-Level Theories

Having presented above the individual-level theories, we will now review some key theories that consider social, economic and other environmental dynamics. The selected theories are listed in Table 5.2.

Social Support Theories

As their name indicates, this type of theory stresses the importance of individual social connections in trying to account for destructive behaviours. This was demonstrated by the observation that one key element in peoples' changing unhealthy habits is reflected in the degree of social support they attract or lack of it (Ferrence, (2001; Rende et al., 2005; Young et al., 2011).

Economic Models Theories

As has been highlighted by many of social scientists, the economic model reflects the view that poverty has a strong relation with destructive behaviour, whether it is low educational attainment, health, crime or addiction (Piketty, 2013; Kotler, 2015). This approach considers that people weigh up the cost of indulging in a behaviour against the cost of alternative options/choices before deciding on what is the most attractive option (French et al., 2006; Mytton et al., 2012).

Marketing Communications Theories

Marketing communication theories as applied to behaviour (e.g., see West, 2013) tend to focus on models of persuasion rather than on a full-blown marketing approach. Even persuasion may be seen by some marketers as a too restrictive a goal for a marketing communication that, for example, may just want to act as a reminder for an already established (persuaded) customer. We therefore differentiate this approach from general marketing and most certainly from social marketing theories. The marketing dimension of SM has a full chapter devoted to it in this book (Chapter 7). The reader may also refer Chapter 4, which also describes a number of elements associated with marketing including understanding the determinants of the consumer behaviour that, incidentally, also reflects the views expressed in the above framework for understanding behaviour.

Management System Models

According to these theories, behaviours may be the result of interacting components of the social system. For example, if we take alcohol addiction as an example, the interplay between the competing agencies – such as alcohol industries, government, communities within which people live – would affect the degree of occurrence of alcoholic behaviour in a society. The outcome is a balancing effect of the various influences that the agencies exert on social life (Borland et al., 2010; de Savigny and Adam, 2009).

General Considerations

The above representation reflects the categories identified by West and Brown (2013), although it is a more simplified version with some adjustments where needed. For example, we tended to select only one or two references/representatives for each model/theory. We also made adjustments to the categories with a view to simplify and make them more meaningful for the reader.

It is clear that there are several links between the above models/theories. In some cases, two or more theories may be covered by a broader theory. For instance rational emotive behaviour therapy (REBT) theory and cognitive theory (CT) could cover rational choice, 'biased' choice' and learning theories (e.g., see Ellis, 1962, 1994; Beck et al., 1979; Fourali, 2000). It seems that neither REBT nor CT were mentioned by West and Brown's presentation. Perhaps these theories were perceived as too general, given their eclectic nature, and therefore not helpful to identify key specific determinants of behaviour. Also, as those theories may apply to a variety of behaviours, this may have been seen as beyond the specialist focus on addictions that was the area of interest of these authors.

It is also clear that there are significant overlaps between the various theories. For example positive reward and acquired need theories reflect, at least partly, the learning theories. Additionally the inhibition dysfunction theories also strongly relate to the biological theories presented separately above. A weakness perhaps of the above schema is that the listed theories may not seem to highlight clearly the cultural influence, recognized in many works (e.g., Hofstede, 1984; Schiffman et al., 2012; Hill, 2011) despite references to organizational systems and social network theories. Although there is an overlap with these ideas, it is clear that even without social networking influence, the pressure of a local culture (e.g., local values) may still have a significant effect on both groups and individuals. In fact, more recently there is a growing interest in linking mental resilience (or toughness) to culture as argued by Sheard (2013) and Terracciano and colleagues (2005). These authors quoted the example of the Japanese reaction to the terrible destruction caused by the earthquakes of 11 March 2011 in Japan:

> There was no looting or panic in the aftermath of the earthquake. Nobody barged the queues as the emergency supplies arrived; rather, there was self-control and orderliness – an extraordinary stoic mentality the Japanese call *gaman*.
>
> (Sheard, 2013, p. 115)

Clearly theories are as such just representations of what may be happening when trying to understand what factor/s may be compelling an individual or group to behave one way rather than another. One does not have to show loyalty to one theory over another but rather should refer to them as potential frameworks for understanding and acting to improve a particular situation. Such a position is particularly advised in the light of the huge debate on the primacy of economic, social or psychological health, which will be reviewed later. Clearly the arguments also reflect ideological loyalties (e.g., 'socially responsible government' versus 'nanny state') that only reinforce the need to adopt a more eclectic approach. The theories highlight the importance of avoiding simplistic answers to what is usually a very complex area. Indeed, politicians would like us to believe that there are simple ways of dealing with issues such as obesity or even terrorism ('responsible versus irresponsible', 'them versus us', etc.). However, the above has demonstrated that a genuine attempt at addressing these issues will need to diagnose all the potential influences and proceed to systematically address all relevant ones.

Despite the reservations, the above categorization is a good attempt at a tidy organization of the various key ideas to help SM researchers weed through them with a view to locating potential key determinants of a particular social problem.

Despite the variety of the theories, judging from their respective popularity, it seems that not all theories have been considered of equal relevance. We therefore discuss below some theories that have been and/or should be of particular use to social marketing professionals.

Theories of Change as Social Marketing Tools

Although a number of conceptual tools have been listed above in association with the process of change theories as another tool to help understand the stage of readiness of an individual, these theories are by no means all similar. As argued by Stevens (2013) 'establishing change readiness may be one of the key factors in determining whether a given change intervention will ultimately be successful or not' (p. 333). At the same time, Stevens (2013) highlights the fact that there are many theories purporting to clarify such change. He identified conceptualizations promoting changes as follows:

1. Cognitive facilitation of change through determining dimensions of discrepancy, appropriateness, efficacy, principal support, personal valence (e.g., Armenakis and Harris, 2009).
2. Stages of changes that reflect the progress/readiness of an individual towards a healthier outcome. This will be looked at more closely as it has been of particular interest to SM workers (e.g., Andreasen, 2006).
3. Factors enhancing commitment to change such as affective, continuance, and normative commitment (e.g., Herscovitch and Meyer, 2002).
4. Factors influencing receptivity to change. This approach identifies multidimensional attitudes toward change as well as broad evaluation of change as positive or negative (e.g., Devos et al., 2007).
5. Factors reflecting capacity for change (e.g., Campbell and Campbell, 2009; Soumyaja et al., 2011). These may apply to organizational-level (e.g., culture or climate for change, trust in management, resources, structure of organization) or individual-level attitudes (e.g., ability to cope with change, practical intelligence, self-efficacy or low dispositional resistance to change).
6. Multidimensional situation inducing either an individual or group of individuals to accept (cognitively and emotionally) a particular course of action. The situation may be defined in terms of content, process, context as well as people involved (e.g., see Holt et al., 2007).

However, perhaps the most popular model associated with understanding and encouraging behavioural change, first in addiction/health psychology and, later, in social marketing, is the one proposed by Carlo DiClemente and James Prochaska as the trans-theoretical model of change (DiClemente and Prochaska, 1998; Andreasen, 2006; Hastings and Haywood, 1991; Cirksena and Flora, 1995).

The model was primarily developed to help address the needs of addiction problems and more specifically smoking addiction with a view to motivating change according to the specific needs of the various groups of smokers. Accordingly its key advantage is reflected in the model's ability to identify different groups of people according to their readiness for change and recovery. The model built upon and transcended a number of then-popular models such as the social learning theory, the Health Belief Model and the theory of reasoned action (Whitelaw et al. 2000). Figure 5.2 summarizes the key elements of the model (DiClemente and Prochaska, 1998; Whitelaw et al. 2000).

Stages of change	Types of problems encountered at any level	Examples of processes promoting change
→ Stage 1: Pre-contemplation	• Symptoms-related difficulties • Situational challenges • Unhealthy thinking • Family/systemic difficulties • Interpersonal conflicts	• Awareness/consciousness raising (learning and understanding the problem behaviour) • 'Counter-conditioning' (fighting conditioning through substituting new alternative behaviours for problem behaviour) and • 'Stimulus control' (preparing for and reacting constructively to established prompts)
→ Stage 2: Contemplation		
→ Stage 3: Preparation		
→ Stage 4: Action		
→ Stage 5: Maintenance		

Figure 5.2 Trans-theoretical model of change and associated characteristics

The model is cyclical in that the various groups may slip back to an earlier stage given any challenge. This is reflected by the number of arrows between the various stages. For example, a smoker who is in the stage of 'maintenance' may 'relapse' and give in to an urge. This could take him/her back to either the 'preparation' or 'action' stage.

The above framework is naturally attractive to social marketers as it helps easily apply a marketing strategy that aims to focus on identifying needs and matching services to those needs. Thus an SM strategy would select the various groups at the various stages and target a group either because of its size or criticality. For instance, it may aim to move a very large population, who may not be aware of the destructive effects of smoking or alcohol (i.e., at the pre-contemplation stage), by encouraging more awareness of the problem and hoping to induce a large proportion of this target group to become 'contemplators' who start considering the option of giving up the destructive.

A variation to the above trans-theoretical model is the one proposed by Fourali (2009b). Figure 5.3 illustrates the steps of this model. This model reflects the stages of readiness as a movement spanning the following stages:

Stage 1:   (similar to pre-contemplation stage of the trans-theoretical model): At this stage there is a complete denial of any responsibility in helping create or maintain the problem at hand (e.g., addiction).

Stage 2:   At this stage there is a slight improvement in that the person with the addiction is now primarily focusing on environmental (past or present) explanatory factors.

Stage 3:   At this stage the explanations are more inclusive and consider a variety of options but tend to be presented in terms of either/or scenarios rather than a combination of factors.

Stage 4:   At this stage the subject recognizes the grey areas associated with many situations and accept the need to live with uncertainties.

Stage 1	Stage 2	Stage 3	Stage 4	Stage 5
'There is nothing that one can do'	Problems addressed in terms of changing the environment/ situation	Issues presented as either/or scenarios	Issues evaluated flexibly through levels of greyness	Issues (and greyness) subsumed within higher level issues/values
No responsibility to be assumed	Some responsibility depending on resources available	Help/responsibility sought associated with all dimensions/modalities including own attitude/ perceptions		

Figure 5.3 Stages of changes according to the beyond opposites approach (Fourali, 2009b)

Stage 5: In this final stage, the challenges, reflecting various degrees of greyness and uncertainties, are subsumed within higher more encompassing principles/values that provide the subject with a stronger basis for change and maintenance of change (e.g., a higher purpose to live for).

The Contribution of Behavioural Economics

Behavioural economics (BE) has been proposed by two main authors, Herbert Simon (1979) and Daniel Kahneman (2003). BE theory came to challenge the view that men are rational in undertaking decisions based primarily on costs versus benefits and personal preferences. BE researchers argued, with evidence, that many decisions are based on erroneous thinking supported by many psychological experiments demonstrating lack of rationality. They used the concept of 'bounded rationality' to demonstrate interferences with human information processing, reflecting lack of information and/or computational capacities (Simon, 1979; Kahneman, 2003). As an example of lack of information (or feedback) Samson (2014) offers the case of smokers who are not aware of the effect of smoking until a significant period has elapsed and even then they are still none the wiser about the exact effect on cells and internal organs. Moreover, through the prospect theory, it was demonstrated that what appears to be rationally derived decisions regarding risk-taking (or avoidance) were in fact affected by the way in which choices are framed or presented (Kahneman and Tversky, 1979). Such arguments have been the subject of several studies, including the idea of schemas, which links up to the idea of 'framing'. In fact, several researchers seem to have made a career with the framing principle – for example, branding, schemas, cognitive structure, core beliefs, etc. – as they all revolve around the idea of understanding or creating a meaningful perspective that can serve a particular purpose (as in advertising). Nevertheless, BE managed to derive a number of rules (cognitive shortcuts, similar to computing rules), known as heuristics, that can be made use of to encourage socially sanctioned decisions based on the philosophy of liberal paternalism. The word 'sanctioned' has been purposefully selected here as there is a tendency by BE workers to talk about social benefits that may not be necessarily just but simply socially sanctioned, as suggested later. The heuristics support an intuitive system, called system 1, which contrasts with a more deliberative and analytical system 2 (Tversky and Kahneman, 1974). Samson (2014) listed 13 heuristics and Shah and Oppenheimer (2008) listed no less than 42 heuristics. Among the most commonly listed are the following:

- Availability, or ease with which an idea can come to mind, which will affect the judgement of an individual. For those who still cannot understand why companies still keep spending millions in advertising, the concept of availability can be decisive.
- Affect/emotions triggered with an object or event tends to affect the decision positively (if linked to warm feelings) or negatively.
- Salience, or information that stands out may affect positive or negative evaluation (e.g., brand name cues may suggest quality).
- Social norms such as reciprocity and fairness would affect judgement of an object or event. For example, if somebody has been nice to you in some ways it would be easier to reciprocate.
- Projection, as when people assume that tastes will not change (think of the statement 'I will love you forever').
- Representativeness, as in the case of a prototype-based evaluation (think of a brand packaging that resembles a well-established brand).
- Anchoring, or a base numerical value that would affect the judgement of a result, such as when a first given price of a product may become the reference for a decision about whether other products are cheap or expensive.
- Cognitive ease, or adoption of techniques that help reduce efforts in decision-making. Consider how many more people will make more efforts to calculate their taxes if provided with an easy software to do so.

The above and other heuristics in a way seem to summarize several insights that appeared under different theoretical labels. For example, the priming effect

(Chartrand and Bargh, 1999) or cognitive dissonance heuristics (Festinger, 1957) reflected in consistency heuristics, have long existed as separate lines of enquiries in their own right and not necessarily under the BE label. So in a way the BE heuristics argument reflected a mixed bag of rules demonstrated empirically under various theoretical labels. Such an idea has already been aired by Tim Harford who argued that BE has become a catch-all term for any type of psychological view (Harford, 2014). Hence it may be debatable about whose credit a social marketer should acknowledge when making use of a 'BE heuristic'. Is it BE or the actual specific theory that postulated a concept or model? If we follow the latter approach (ironically, compatible with the 'fairness' dimension, a listed heuristic), the best that a BE could become is an organizer of 'heuristics' to help SM make sense and choose relevant concepts/techniques, but only as a first port of call that should be followed by a closer study of the relevant theories associated with the selected 'heuristics'. Nevertheless, given that SM purpose is to make use of any advice that helps affect behaviour for the good of society, it is perfectly acceptable for social marketers not to worry too much about requiring a 'theoretically consistent eclecticism'.

Behavioural Economics and the Concept of Nudging

Clearly social marketers should learn from the advice of BE at both procedural and philosophical/value levels. This was made easier when a number of authors took up the ideas of BE and started promoting the ideas of liberal paternalism (overtly or covertly) and making use of the ever-growing list of heuristics to 'encourage' or prompt target groups to adopt behaviours that otherwise would be difficult to adopt. 'Nudging' became the favourite word to reflect such situations where a target person or group is 'enticed' to select a particular series of actions that serve a particular, socially sanctioned purpose via prompts in the form of well-positioned heuristics. Consequently, the new concept of nudging became popularized as it represented the liberal paternalistic philosophy (Thaler and Sunstein, 2008).

French and Gordon (2015) highlighted a number of weaknesses associated with BE. They argued that there is a lack of available research about the possible interactions between the various principles and heuristics. They also criticized the so-called neo-liberal paternalistic BE philosophy as it does not seem to seek full involvement of an individual in decision-making or community empowerment. Such an approach is akin to manipulation, even if done for benign purposes. Indeed, such a philosophy seems to suggest the Machiavellian idea that the aims justify the means (and we are not even considering whose aims are being debated). It's interesting to note at this juncture that Kahneman started as a psychologist for the Israeli army while trying to find ways of minimizing errors for the selection of soldiers, arguably helping to develop a more lethal army. This is an ideal example of how a scientist's skills can be misused for destructive means encouraged by a brutal government.

Kahneman and other BE promoters talk about adopting socially beneficial behaviours but not necessarily humanely beneficial behaviours, as we know that there may be a social group where it is highly encouraged to adopt certain behaviours because such behaviours are particularly beneficial to that specific group irrespective of whether other groups or the broader human society will benefit or not.

French and Gordon (2015) also highlighted that 'nudging' can be only one of a number of possible approaches to influencing behaviours. They derived a value/cost exchange matrix that contrasts two dimensions; first, whether the intervention seeks the conscious involvement of the target group in the decision to adopt a new behaviour or not, or, second, whether the intervention uses incentives/rewards or disincentives/punishments. They accordingly identified the following possible scenarios where a relevant behavioural change strategy may be adopted:

- An *active/conscious* involvement with provision of *rewards*, suggests a 'hugging' strategy.
- An *active/conscious* involvement with provision of *punishment*, suggests a 'smacking' strategy.
- An *automatic/passive* involvement with provision of *rewards*, suggests a 'nudging' strategy.
- An *automatic/passive* involvement with provision of *punishment*, suggests a 'shoving' strategy.

The above options reflected in the value/cost exchange matrix help remind a SM project manager that there are four options that may be adopted depending on context and philosophical position. We feel that there may be much more than the four above options if we consider that each dimension is a continuum rather than an either/or choice. For example, there may be middle-ground options between any two clear 'extreme' positions. Hence there may be both rewards and punishment provided to support a particular aim. Nevertheless, in line with the above options, French and Gordon (2015) identified a number of possible interventions that SM projects may make use of:

- **Design:** Through the planning and creation of optimal environments that support individual and community initiatives.
- **Informing and persuading:** Through appropriate, evidence supported communications.
- **Control:** As when making use of the law.
- **Education:** Through empowering people to take decisions and teaching them relevant change support skills.
- **Support:** Such as government or charity based resources to support SM initiatives.

As a mnemonic, one may suggest the word DICES to help the SM manager systematically consider all these five options.

We feel that this section on the psychological approaches that may be relevant to SM would also be incomplete without mentioning, at least briefly, the studies on persuasion. The social marketer's armamentarium would certainly be incomplete without reading through literature on techniques of persuasion. Arguably some of the key writing on persuasion may have been influenced by the above-mentioned heuristics. As an example we may cite Robert Cialdini's *Influence: The Psychology of Persuasion*, published in 1984. This book identified some six key principles, very similar to the above-discussed 'heuristics', that research seems to support, regarding their influence on people's behaviours as follows: reciprocity (returning a favour), commitment and consistency (e.g., finishing a job), social proof (social examples to follow), authority (respecting authority), liking (can be persuaded easily by people we like) and scarcity (try harder to obtain scarce commodities). Since then other principles have been identified (Goldstein et al., 2008).

Cognitive Behavioural Theory/Therapy (CBT): A Rational Tool for Social Marketers

CBT is more of an approach that encompasses a number of theories. CBT has benefitted from many reviews and is considered one of the most effective models of therapy (Butler et al., 2006; Hofmann et al., 2012). Arguably the trans-theoretical model presented above is a CBT tool as it focuses on the link between cognitive, environmental, emotional and behavioural dimensions. Perhaps the basic idea of this approach is reflected in the stoic view of Epictetus that people are not upset by events but by the meanings they assign to them. The origins of CBT are not new as they reflect Buddhist, Greek and Islamic work (Fourali, 2009b). For instance, Gautama the Buddha advocated awareness and equanimity to liberate oneself from suffering (Hart, 1987). Centuries later, the prophet of Islam encouraged his followers to have a positive perception/expectation of Allah as this perception will have a direct effect on their reality.

The current general model for understanding the aetiology and maintenance of a current situation can be illustrated by Figure 5.4 (Freeman et al., 2005).

Figure 5.4 shows the origin and effect of mental and emotional states. Given the interaction of the various elements of the model any improvement at any level would reflect improvements at other levels (Fourali, 2009b).

Clearly CBT is a good model (backed up with research evidence about its effectiveness) that can be added to the social marketer's armamentarium as it can get to the deep beliefs of the self-destructive behaviour and act on it by offering alternative beliefs and behaviours that can help halt the destructive behaviour and replace it with healthier alternatives.

As far as we know, it seems that most existing approaches addressed by SM appear to be geared towards identifying a problem and trying to resolve it. There are two aspects that make this approach not completely satisfactory

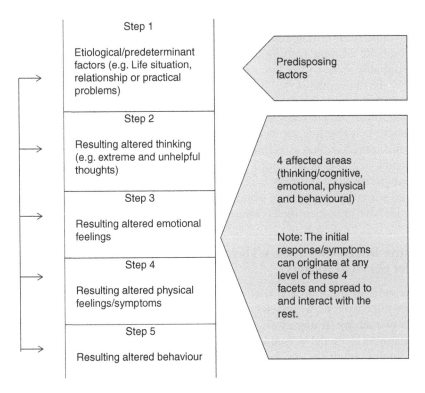

Figure 5.4 Five basic CBT steps to assessing mental health (Freeman et al., 2005)

(see Figure 5.5): first, in many cases problems could be prevented rather than faced after they occur. For both logical and practical benefits, prevention is better than cure. Second, it seems that this perspective is more about removing problems rather than finding ways of enhancing the life of citizens. For instance, instead of just addressing the destructive effects of alcoholism (which is a very worthwhile purpose) we could talk about helping produce a more worthwhile and happier society. This, in a way, could also be considered a preventative approach and therefore also economically valid (Kotler, 2015).

This second potential target can perhaps best be reflected by the views of positive psychology (Peterson, 2006; Seligman, 2002; Seligman and Pawelski, 2003; Positive Psychology Centre, 2014; Gardner et al., 2001). Positive psychology aims to foster positive emotions, positive individual traits and positive institutions through focusing on characteristics that research shows promote a healthier and happier outlook on life. Such characteristics include: courage, ability/capacity for love and work, creativity, compassion, resilience, curiosity, integrity, self-knowledge, moderation, self-control and 'wisdom' (Peterson, 2006). This approach is far from what may be seen as positive thinking, as the later may focus on blind commitment to positive thinking while disregarding

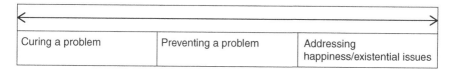

| Curing a problem | Preventing a problem | Addressing happiness/existential issues |

Figure 5.5 Potential areas of focus of SM

the 'reality'. Positive psychology tends to work with evidence to advance its triple study objectives of positive emotion, positive character and positive institutions (Seligman and Csikszentmihalyi, 2000).

Another dimension that may be considered a fully legitimate SM target that may be crucial to personal and social happiness is the issue of bringing communities together. This aim, in a way, focuses on the prerequisite of a society 'at ease with itself' that could represent the best antidote for war and conflicts, especially if such an aim becomes a key target for national and international organizations.

The author believes that the challenging aspects to positive psychology is how to produce happy yet responsible citizens of the world. We know that established science has a powerful influence on society's culture and what constitutes acceptable or unacceptable behaviour. It is this influence that we need to remain aware of when psychologists (and SM workers) are producing plans of actions. Clearly one of the easy objections is 'we are here to try and help individuals who may be vulnerable and could do without "extra responsibilities"'. It is felt that this goes against the long-term aims of positive psychology, which are to help deal with vulnerable people as well as perfectly functioning people who are unfulfilled or have not adapted to the demands and responsibilities of our modern and global world. Positive psychology should aim to address the increasingly global environment we live in and assume responsibility to prepare individuals to be healthy as well as being a force for good in our future society. This approach is not new and is already supported by psychologists both in the field of critical psychology (e.g., Fox and Prilleltensky, 1997) and positive psychology (e.g., Gardner et al., 2001).

Before completing this section, it is worth noting that given the recent evidence of studies highlighting the unconscious basis of many of our decisions (tacit within our above discussion about BE), it is important for SM to also make use of the techniques for understanding this effect and capitalizing on this understanding (e.g., see Uleman and Bargh, 1989; Zaltman and Zaltman, 2008). As suggested above when discussing the liberal paternalist philosophy of BE, there may be an argument from liberal proponents that we are restricting the freedom and even deceiving the people. This is not deniable and, as alluded to above, it is an ethical issue to be resolved by, on the one hand, contrasting the destructive causes on our societies and the best possible strategies available to us to counter them and, on the other, our respect for individual freedoms. Incidentally this debate is not new and the result of its outcomes may be seen among the many societies who restrict, by law, the freedom of self-harming people (e.g., people with proven suicidal tendencies). If this is acceptable, why should we condone the destruction, albeit slow and subtle in many cases, of our societies?

So Where Do We Stand in Relation to All the Above Views?

The above suggests that the world of a social marketer is a messy one with a multitude of variables to take into account. As ethics and values are at the heart of purpose and actions, they are perhaps the first dimension to consider. Indeed, as shown earlier with respect to BE, having a workable solution for changing or maintaining behaviour efficiently and effectively may not be the 'best' solution if the ethical dimension is wanting. Accordingly, maximizing transparency and inclusion should maximize the chance of having a more ethically robust decision.

Given the multiplicity of theories available to guide some of the behavioural change work, it was argued that 'motivation' theories (change and addiction theories, BE and CBT to mention a few) are perhaps the closest to the interest of a social marketer. Such theories help identify the precedents and prerequisites for triggering, maintaining or changing behaviour. With such advice, a social marketer may develop strategies to encourage healthy behaviour and discourage non-healthy actions.

It is also clear from the above that while searching for the most relevant models and theories, a social marketer should be careful to investigate the evidence basis for each of the theories reviewed. For instance, there has been a wide debate about the lack of evidence for some of the most well-known theories (e.g., psychoanalysis) and the subsequent search for more evidence-based theories such as CBT. This is another case where the standards of acceptability should not be dictated by Hollywood, among other media organizations.

The SM researcher needs to understand the broader perspective to get the context of the problem s/he is trying to understand. For example, it may be advisable to consider the PESTLE (macro-level) as well as dimensions of influence on individual (micro-level) behaviours (e.g., as suggested by Schiffman et al., 2012) before zooming into relevant psycho-social theories that help identify possible reasons for behaviour. This point, regarding attending to the various levels of a particular problem behaviour, will be taken up in the following chapters.

Part of understanding the issues to be addressed is the need to adopt a global perspective that is sensitive to social and environmental consequences. Many of today's metropolises are socially multicultural, thereby presenting an even more complex environment. Such understanding needs to systematically identify the most significant contributing factors to a problem (or solution). Unfortunately, most evaluations tend to adopt a rigid approach when trying to understand a particular context (i.e., select some variables and infer their relative contributions). A more adequate approach should be to adopt more dynamic evaluation procedures that take into account live updates of situations backed up by weighted iterations. Such an approach is very much available to researchers, given the development of IT capabilities. For example, and as argued elsewhere (Fourali, 1997, 2009b) it is felt that fuzzy logic offers some promises regarding more dynamic evaluation procedures. Almost 20 years ago, Fourali (1997) argued that the engineering field is much more advanced when considering evaluating and making adequate decisions in response to environmental demands. This situation still seems to apply and needs immediate attention for better validity of decisions.

This chapter also highlighted the importance for SM to consider all areas that may benefit from its services. Although SM work tends to particularly focus on remediating and treating a particularly dire social situation, it is important to remember that SM can be particularly helpful when trying to prevent a problematic situation from occurring. Finally, it is worth noting that SM is only limited by human imagination. It is therefore important to not overlook the possibilities that SM can offer in bringing people together and instilling a sense of *joie de vivre*, which could represent the best antidote against conflicts (these being mainly a symptom of weaknesses in the earlier aims).

6 The Socio-Economic Dimension of Behaviour

> The social logic that locks people into materialistic consumerism as the basis for participating in the life of society is extremely powerful, but detrimental ecologically and psychologically [...] An essential prerequisite for a lasting prosperity is to free people from this damaging dynamic and provide opportunities for sustainable and fulfilling lives.
>
> (Jackson, 2009, p. 104)

As argued earlier, it is difficult to find a completely pure dimension that influences consumer behaviour. Just like we had social-psychological influences, we also have socio-economic influences. In this respect we will consider Professor Tim Jackson's position on the socio-economic approach to consumption and how it motivates sustainable/healthy consumption (Jackson, 2009; NESTA, 2008).

Jackson's report, *Prosperity without Growth?* (2009), released originally by the Sustainable Development Commission (SDC), argued that our economies are focused primarily on achieving growth irrespective of whether this is sustainable or beneficial to the majority of the world's population. He saw financial crises as opportunities for going back to the drawing board and identifying new ways of stabilizing our economies while reaping the social and economic rewards. In fact, he suggests differentiating 'prosperity' (the target of every nation) from 'economic wealth', a purely materialistic outcome.

The report looked at the connections/associations between sustainability, well-being and growth. It also analysed the links between growth, environmental crises and social recessions. The results showed that while the global economy has doubled in size, such an increase had an environmental price tag in the form of the degradation of 60 per cent of the world's ecosystems. Additionally it showed that while the wealth of a few had increased manifold, about a fifth of the world population shares only 2 per cent of global income. The disparities affected both 'rich' and 'poor' nations.

The report put forward 12 steps to help develop a sustainable economy, broadly summarized as follows:

1. Supporting the development of capabilities, with reliable tools, to help develop macroeconomics for sustainability. The tools would help estimate the interactions between the various macroeconomic factors (e.g., investment and effect on sustainability) so as to help inform actions.
2. Investment on infrastructural assets that support the development of sustainability (e.g., jobs, renewable energy, public transport).
3. Reforming the regulation of national and international markets to minimize the occurrence of global economic crises. Among these, one would include both irresponsible financial practice (short-selling) and protection against consumer debt.
4. Making macroeconomic accountability go beyond the simple output or consumption measures. For example, we may take into account unfair distribution of incomes, depletion of natural resources (through environmental pollution) as well as its social cost.
5. Sharing jobs and improving working practices that promote healthier work–life balance.
6. Tackling systemic inequality such as discrimination, providing better education, fairer taxes and addressing the causes of poverty.
7. As stated above, there is a need to develop better measures of prosperity that go beyond the simple economic output or level of consumption. These new measures would include variables such as improved life expectancy, more inclusive educational participation, better social well-being, better community integration, social capital, etc.
8. More focus on human and social capital would look at improving social participation, public services (e.g., social/cultural events), supporting social communities in difficult times and protecting the public spaces.
9. Addressing the destructive physical, social and psychological aspects of the culture of consumerism, materialism and unhealthy competition through, for example, more responsible marketing communication.
10. Restricting economic activity to limit ecological damage. Such restriction would target waste and emissions per capita.
11. The above point can be supported with adequate fiscal/taxation policies that support sustainability by not only focusing on income but also on resources use and emission.
12. Encouraging advanced economies to support poorer countries while ensuring that their development will help our global ecosystem.

Broadly speaking, the above-listed requirements produced by Jackson (2009) highlight the importance of looking beyond hard conventional economics that seem to have 'overtaken' their purpose, which is to create thriving communities within healthier environments. The elements he identified in tackling the unsustainable human consumption include both micro and macro dimensions. These dimensions highlight the complexity and interrelations between the factors involved. As argued later in Chapter 8, there is a need to make use of any tool that helps identify and estimate the relative weight of each factor of our constantly fluctuating and dynamic economic, social and ecological environment. This approach would help simulate the respective contributions and enable researchers to zoom in on the most effective and efficient approach.

In the UK, an important report was commissioned by the government to address health inequalities and look at ways of minimizing them. The work for the report was triggered by an earlier World Health Organization report from the Commission on Social Determinants of Health (2008). The UK's published report came to be known as the *Marmot Review* (2010) as it was chaired by Professor Marmot. This report was particularly interesting as it led to some work being undertaken to seek the implementation of the report's recommendations via SM (see NSMC, 2012). The report's aims and recommendations will be briefly presented below.

The reports' aims, which were prefaced by the apt quote from Pablo Neruda 'Rise up with me against the organisation of misery', were fourfold:

1. Identify the health inequalities challenges together with evidence that can be used as a basis for future policy and action.
2. Advice on how the evidence can be translated into action.
3. Advise on specific objectives and associated measures building on earlier work by the Health Inequalities Infant Mortality Public Services Agreement (2007) that reviewed some useful measures of health inequalities.
4. Publish a report that supports the development of a post-2010 health inequalities strategy.

The *Marmot Review* came up with some disturbing results demonstrating that people living in poor areas will, on average, die seven years earlier than those living in the richest neighbourhoods. This result was compounded by an even more unfair finding showing that people in poor neighbourhoods tend to struggle with disability for 17 years more (in their shorter lives) compared to those living in a rich neighbourhood.

In fact the expression 'richest neighbourhood' does not reflect access to nationally available amenities, including health care services. Rather they reflect what may be termed 'social class' or social position that is associated with a healthier standard of living. Disadvantaged individuals tend to lose out at the following levels:

• Inequalities occurring in early childhood including lack of educational preparation.
• Different employment/work conditions.
• Housing and neighbourhood conditions.
• Different standards of living.

According to the executive summary of the *Marmot Review*, the Commission on Social Determinants of Health (2008) concluded that the:

social and economic inequalities underpin the determinants of health: the range of interacting factors that shape health and well-being. These include: material circumstances, the social environment, psycho-social factors, behaviours, and biological factors. In turn, these factors are influenced by social position, itself shaped by education, occupation, income, gender, ethnicity and race. All these influences are affected by the socio-political and cultural and social context in which they sit.

(Marmot Review, 2010, p. 10)

Figure 6.1 reflects the argument of this statement.

Accordingly, the review concluded that simple economic growth is not a necessary determinant of a country's success if it means social inequalities in health and well-being and lack of environmental responsibilities. Hence social and environmental responsibilities must be targeted together. In terms of tackling health inequalities, the review recommended the following:

- Give all children the best start in life.
- Maximize all sections of society's capabilities and control over their lives.
- Maximize adequate employment for all.
- Ensure healthy standards of living.
- Provide healthy and sustainable places and communities.
- Ensure adequate mechanism are in place to prevent ill health.

The above aims focus on individual, social and environmental targets. It is difficult to imagine the success of these targets in isolation from a fair and just approach to our global community given the interrelation between local and global. Additionally, and as argued earlier, physical health and well-being

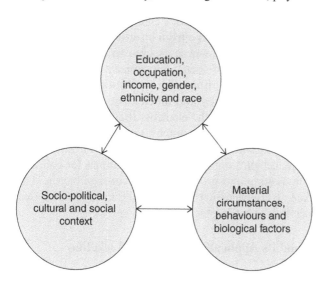

Figure 6.1 Determinants of social inequalities in health

may not necessarily mean psychological and social well-being. The above steps are important but may require a broader supportive environment whose values go beyond simple wealth accumulation.

Following the setting up of the above objectives, the NSMC (2012) project workers undertook to demonstrate the effectiveness of SM in achieving each of the six objectives. To do so they determined the underpinning factors of each objective. For instance, to ensure a best start to life means better physical, emotional, cognitive, linguistic and social development that, in turn, are affected by better maternity services and parenting programmes. Subsequently they identified projects that best achieve the objectives, and associated targets, and provide best value for money. Accordingly, they described 14 very successful SM projects that helped many thousands (in most cases, hundreds of thousands with a potential for millions of beneficiaries). The projects focused on improving communities' health at physical, social or economic levels. Examples ranged from dealing with addictions such as smoking, drug taking, alcohol or gambling, to turning around unhealthy lifestyles or setting up preventative measures to limit the occurrence of HIV, cancer, car accident casualties and increasing access to medicine or work. The projects' coverage ranged from specific towns to a whole country. Given the significant achievements of the projects, the NSMC advised that similar projects should be undertaken by government agencies responsible for achieving the *Marmot Review*'s six objectives.

Given the above arguments, the social marketer would start with the targeted aims and, after much consultation and research, would determine a strategy that should help implement them in an integrated manner. This would include creative communications to create a buzz as argued by Goodson (2012), who advises aligning with a powerful idea on the rise to define a culture. In line with Neil Smelser's view (1962), Goodson argues that a movement (and an SM project) stands a better chance of succeeding if it starts with a 'social strain', which may range from a sense of dissatisfaction or concern about the future to, in the extreme cases, oppression that may lead to a revolution. Ideally, if all elements of society recognize a problem then it would be better to talk about evolution rather than revolution. However, this evolution has to be transparently assessed and all elements of society have to be involved at different levels. Among the elements that Goodson advises to communicate a movement are: attractive content; targeting ready groups; selecting advocates; mass communication; search engine optimization; PR, social media and content placement; online and offline channels for continuing conversation; direct marketing and promotion to encourage buy-in. The issue of movement is taken up elsewhere in this book and the reader is advised to refer to the relevant sections (see Chapter 2).

Social Capital Theory and its Application to Social Marketing

According to Glenane-Antoniadis et al. (2003), there are broadly two trends within SM. The first trend reflects the 'traditionalists' who simply aim to apply conventional marketing principles such as the marketing mix and may feel that this approach is largely sufficient to address their needs. The second trend reflects the 'convergent' group, who adopt an interdisciplinary approach to the study of social marketing. This second trend argues that the traditionalist approach is no longer sufficient and should be extended to include the concept of social capital theory. The latter is seen as more encompassing as it takes into account behavioural and social issues. Such a view has already been partly addressed by Jackson above. However, in the light of the importance of the social capital dimension, perhaps it makes sense to dwell a bit more on this perspective.

Social capital theory (SCT) is increasingly referred to by various disciplines, such as organizational, political and organizational studies, that only a short while ago tended to be very reductionist and excluded important social dimensions from their respective disciplines, believing that it is important to keep their field 'pure' even if less relevant to the reality (Adler and Kwon, 2002). As its name indicates, SCT has its roots in sociology (e.g., Bourdieu, 1986; Portes, 1998; Lin, 1999). It focuses, among others, on the 'social wealth' dimension of groups that reflects aspects such as social support, social networks/exchange, relational embeddedness, culture, social/community resources, formal/contractual and informal links, goodwill, trust, multi-organizational networks (Adler and Kwon, 2002; Hirsch and Levin, 1999).

Some underpinning principles of SCT have been identified by social psychological studies such as those on persuasion. For example, Cialdini (1984; Goldstein et al., 2008) highlighted the importance of the 'goodwill' or 'reciprocity' that encourages individuals to feel obliged to others if they have been helped in some way and therefore feel bound to return the favour. This is also highlighted in the work of Bagozzi (1975) who stressed the importance of the concept of 'exchange' in marketing. An association can therefore be made between social capital and social marketing, in terms of the reciprocity and exchange principles. Accordingly, the argument is that social marketers should make more use of such principles as well as exploiting the opportunities that social networking (and its link to individual identities and positioning) provides in furthering the social aims of a healthier and yet still happy society. SM should also be aware of the dangers of restrictive and perhaps self- and socially destructive 'social norms' that are resistant to change. Hence, fostering trust in exchange relationships appears to be key to the success of SM projects supported by development of understanding of individual and social incentives.

This last point about using or countering the effects of group conformity is very much an issue associated with that of culture as discussed in Figure 4.1 reflecting an individual's embeddedness in increasingly larger social circles that contribute to the definition, explanation and influence of human behaviour (family, class and culture). It is crucial that marketers capitalize on the dimensions that help promote the socially good aims. Having said that, any project to gain the trust of an increasingly globally aware population has to reflect local and global arguments for the necessity of the changes it promotes with a view to be as inclusive as possible in its perspective.

Why are the Socio-Economic Dimensions Important?

This chapter demonstrated that behaviour is influenced by factors beyond the here-and-now biological/physical, social and psychological determinants. It particularly highlighted the influence of socio-economic factors on life chances. The chapter provided examples of the socio-economic determinants of life-chances that included what society values (e.g., economic growth at any price) together with the 'instituted' economic and social structures that may adversely affect health and economic chances of certain groups within our communities.

All studies referred to (Jackson's report, the Commission on Social Determinants of Health and the *Marmot Review*) tended to agree that many of the causes of disadvantage have their origin in earlier unequal chances that may go back to early childhood influences such as being born into the 'right' socio-cultural and social-class environment that not only leads to better health opportunities than other environments but also provides educational and work opportunities and better standards of living that, ultimately, provide more chances for happier lives. It is no surprise that time and again research shows that successful parents tend to produce successful children.

SM starts where the research on disadvantage finishes. If the research produces clear insights about what causes social ills or inequalities, SM would then consider how to address those social problems effectively and efficiently.

The chapter illustrated how SM can effectively address socio-economic targets if provided with adequate resources. All the studies quoted by NSMC (2012) showed that the success of the projects meant less human pain and more economic success for the country. Indeed, a project that leads to many thousands of recoveries from smoking or drug addiction means that the beneficiaries will break free from crippling habits and start leading productive and worthwhile lives. Economically, this means not only less spending by the national health service to look after the suffering populations but also a transformation into an economically productive population that helps create more wealth, thereby creating more resources for the country. SM therefore provides a cost-effective solution for social ills that pay dividends well into the long term.

7 The Marketing Dimension

Leading Social Marketing Projects Strategically

As argued in earlier chapters, marketing by itself is generally seen as insufficient to address the needs of social marketing (e.g., Glenane-Antoniadis et al., 2003). Nevertheless, both the title and the history of SM reflect the importance of this discipline on SM. Having said that, there seems to be a modernist flavour to the social marketing title (with its clearly delineated two fields of focus) and which also may suggest that it is an exact science that can induce people to undertake any behaviour irrespective of whether they want it or not. Clearly the reality is that this is a very complex science and art that generally works but is far from exact. Hence the idea of adopting an alternative name to signal the coming of age of this multilevel, multidisciplinary field is progressively becoming more forceful. Perhaps another way of looking at this field is from a management perspective. In such a perspective, marketing becomes one of several disciplines that 'managers' need to take into account to help develop healthier societies. Nowadays the business of marketing, just like that of other disciplines associated with commercial contexts (such as entrepreneurship), is no longer automatically associated with commercial businesses (e.g. consider causal marketing). Nevertheless, the word 'marketing' may not be readily associated with continuous, long-term, follow-up and review to make adjustments as and when required. Additionally, the word 'marketing' may be perceived as reductionist in the types and scope of activities or disciplines that may contribute to it. Perhaps a new title focusing more on the broader management dimension may be considered as an alternative. As stated earlier, a possible and more readily recognizable or self-explanatory title that comes to mind may be 'social cause management'. This point, together with alternative names, will be further discussed later.

Irrespective of the popularity of the title of the field, marketing still remains at the heart of SM procedure and therefore deserves a separate treatment. We have already looked above at how the concept of marketing developed from being a primarily commercial activity to expanding to include social responsibility dimensions. In this chapter we will look at some key strategic aspects of marketing and see how they have been expanded to cover the concerns of SM. In this process we will refer to a number of established SM frameworks.

From Marketing Strategy to SM Strategy

It may be argued that any systematic science tends to provide what constitutes good practice based on the latest advance of its knowledge. Such
good practice would include how to conceptualize, plan for and address a
problem based on its field's 'wisdom'. Hence a mechanic (or an analytic
software based on an algorithm), working backwards from what constitutes a good engine, may systematically review and disregard all potential
problems that may interfere with the good running of an engine. Marketing
is no different. In fact, there is an argument that what differentiates a 'fact'-
based science from other fields of knowledge, is the possibility of capitalizing on its empirically derived knowledge to help develop 'products'
or situations that reflect what science considers (at various points of history) to be the healthiest option. Marketing – and SM for that matter – is
no different. The fact that many people and organizations still overlook
the application of such knowledge does not preclude its existence. Indeed,
some marketing writers (e.g., Bowman, 1990; French and Gordon, 2015)
have advanced several reasons regarding why individuals or organizations
may miss the opportunity to adopt a strategic perspective that capitalizes
on the latest 'state-of-the-art' of a discipline. Such reasons include ignorance (of the field that may enlighten best practice or, alternatively, igno-
rance/lack of understanding of the needs of an organization); self-delusion
(or wishful thinking) about reality; self-interest (generally short-term);
interference of operational micro-management (and missing the wood for
the trees); overconfidence (links to the 'self-delusion' earlier point); lack of
humility to recognize past mistakes; lack of understanding of the causes of
success (which links up to the first point on ignorance).

Marketing is a strategic approach to business that has its own process/plan
that enables it to justify and maximize the chance of achieving its objectives.
There have been a number of models suggested for designing a marketing
strategic approach in profit and not-for-profit contexts. These include Paul
Smith's SOSTAC, McDonald's marketing planning and Dibb et al.'s (2006)
ASP process, to mention just a few.

The following presentation will aim to integrate key marketing strategic
dimensions of interest to social marketers.

When considering strategic dimensions, one needs to reflect on the broader
plan as well as the tactical dimensions. In terms of the broader dimensions,
there have been already a few attempts at reflecting an SM strategic perspective. For instance Andreasen (1995) presents six stages that may make up the
SM strategic perspective. These came under the banners of listening, planning, structuring (organizing steps and procedures), pre-testing, implementing and, finally, monitoring.

Another approach to SM strategy worth mentioning is that provided by
French and Gordon (2015). The authors advise the adoption of the following
four stages to maximize the relevance of policy formulation:

1. Insight into citizens' views, needs and behaviour.
2. Development of behavioural objectives informed by theory and situation analysis (e.g., using behavioural modelling that includes competing 'offers' encouraging alternative behaviours) that should give an idea about whether the suggested 'exchange offer' will prove attractive.
3. Development of targeted interventions based on optimal mix of interventions (according to effectiveness and efficiency principles).
4. Impact evaluation of the targeted interventions and feeding into strategic review and performance management.

Depending on the result obtained at stage 4, another cycle of actions may be undertaken.

The above models are useful broad steps that an SM researcher may find helpful as a quick bird's-eye view of key dimensions that need including in an SM strategy. However, it should be useful to review in more details the dimensions of an SM strategy, which perhaps may combine the characteristics of most strategic approaches.

What we may notice whenever issues of strategy (marketing or otherwise) are being discussed is that there are recurrent steps moving from broad project goals, to situation analysis, to strategy selection, strategy implementation and, finally, impact evaluation and control. In what follows, we will review each of these steps in turn, with the aim of identifying specific aspects that may need particular adjustment in the context of SM. Here they are:

Broad Organizational/Policy/Project Goals

These goals are the justifiers of the marketing initiatives. They are generally reflected in the vision and mission of any company. For instance, a global cancer charity's mission could be 'the complete eradication of cancer in any country in the world'. Accordingly, and as with other departments of an organization (e.g., finance, operations, etc.), the marketing department translates those aims strategically, tactically and operationally to help achieve them. To do that it would generally go through the subsequent steps listed below.

Carrying Out a Thorough Situation Analysis

At this level, the aim of the marketer is to understand as closely as possible the environment within which s/he operates. They may, for instance, invoke a number of conceptual tools such as PESTLE (political, economic, social, technological, legal and environmental dimensions) for identifying key influential contextual variables and SWOT (strength, weaknesses, opportunities and threats) to help capitalize on this understanding and take decisions about the best way forward for the business (marketing gaps/segments, offer, optimal portfolio, etc.). In a SM context, such PESTLE may be adjusted to focus on social initiatives. Figure 7.1 has been adapted from a standard marketing

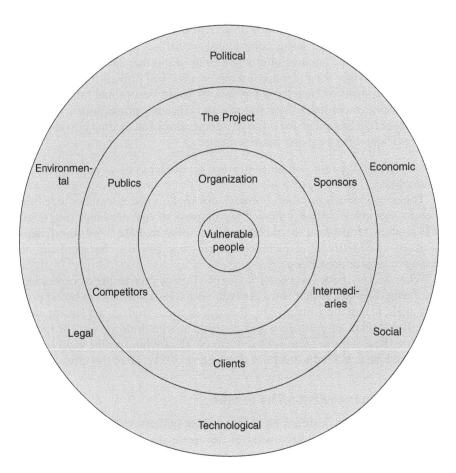

Figure 7.1 A SM contextual reflection of micro and macro environmental forces acting on project (adapted from Dibb et al., 2006)

environment audit (Dibb et al., 2006) and translated into an SM context. Thus, instead of talking about customers we may talk about 'vulnerable people' (e.g., with obesity, drug problems, etc.). Instead of a company, which suggests a commercial perspective, we may talk about an organization (e.g., a government department, an NGO, etc.). Similarly we may also just talk about 'intermediaries' to highlight the importance of those people/channels that may be called upon to help reach the target audience. In terms of competitors, we may consider the organizations (and activities) whose interest is to achieve the opposite of the aim of the organization running a social marketing project.

During this marketing analysis stage, the researcher may identify not only the population group targets that should benefit most from the programme but also their level of readiness. At the same time they need to identify obstacles to maximizing the benefits of the programmes (cultural, competition from other commercial programmes that may, for example, encourage more eating/drinking, etc.). The SWOT analysis is generally seen as a good balancing tool that takes into account opportunities based on the resources available to the SM programme.

As part of the analysis stage, it is also important to remind ourselves that each SM issue has a number of stakeholders associated with it. One might consider the general view about stakeholders being any group of people affected directly or indirectly by the work of an organization irrespective of the fact that some stakeholders are considered more important depending on power, legitimacy or urgency (Cornelissen, 2014). If we consider what contributes to a problem as a way of classifying stakeholders then one tool that marketers may use is the harm chain analysis. Such analysis investigates all those involved in the target problem at different stages of the problem development. The chronological/developmental stages are: pre-production, production, consumption and post-consumption. In this scheme, the stakeholders become: (1) those that contribute to harm; (2) those being harmed and, finally, (3) the regulatory bodies associated with the problem. This creates a four-by-three matrix that would make it easier to identify the aspects to target and coordinate efforts in effectively addressing the problem (Noble, 2006; Polonsky, et al., 2003). Nevertheless, recent work on the contribution by customers to product/service value, as implied by service dominant logic (Vargo and Lusch, 2004), suggests that the 'customer' is an active contributor to the creation of value whether at commercial or social cause levels. The customer, by using and experiencing a 'product', contributes to its value (Previte and Fry, 2006). Hence, such thinking should be taken into account when analysing the value of a 'product' produced by a social marketing project. This is quite an important concept as it helps understand how customers contribute to the success, adoption and diffusion/promotion of an initiative.

SM Strategy

Although the general understanding of a strategy tends to be seen in terms of 'how do I achieve what I want?', in reality such a question does not usually come without the preliminaries of 'where am I?' and 'where do I want to be?', as reflected in the above situation analysis. Only after clarifying these two questions could a strategic question of 'how do I get there?' become more fruitful. This question is about achieving objectives. In the case of SM, the objectives are usually in behavioural terms since they are about turning around self-destructive habits/lifestyles. The question has both strategic and tactical dimensions. The strategic dimensions would decide on where and on whom to focus the attention (segments of the population), how to differentiate between the initiatives (USPs or 'exchange offers') and competing messages including those about brand positioning; and, finally, what clear, realistic and measurable objectives to go for. Subsequently, the tactical dimension of the strategy or implementation stage will focus on what form the implementation will take. This usually takes the form of designing and implementing a valid marketing mix, based on a number of optional marketing mixes (i.e., the 4 or 7 Ps), so that it is most attractive to the target population, as shown in the next step.

SM Strategy Implementation

Marketers have traditionally looked at the 4 or 7 Ps to transform the strategy into reality. As stated previously, a number of marketing concepts need adjusting to the needs and context of SM. This is particularly important in the light of the adjustment of the broader aims of marketing itself. As seen earlier, the key aim of marketing is, broadly, about satisfying current and future needs of customers in a profitable manner. However, there is no explicit reference to long-term broader needs (the expression 'future needs' may be quite restrictive as it may primarily refer to extending current transactions to the future), including social and environmental responsibilities. For instance, in commercial marketing a beverage business would be very happy for each family to buy a case-load of bottles of alcohol each week for the next 20 years (killing themselves slowly in the process). Apart from the general social and environmental disregards (or, at best, secondary consideration) by commercial marketing, the marketing mix itself needs a closer look since the ultimate aims of SM will affect the very focus of the mix. As a minimum, the 4 Ps may need adjusting (e.g., see Kotler and Lee, 2008; French and Gordon, 2015) as follows:

- **'Product':** Like in marketing, this has a core, an actual and an augmented dimension with the main focus being on behaviour change. Hence the inverted commas (see Figure 7.2). These may also be tangible (e.g., vaccination, nicotine patches, condoms) or intangible (services, an idea or value).
- **Price:** The price may be either monetary (e.g., how expensive is it to adopt a healthy lifestyle considering joining a gym, buying healthy food, etc.) or non-monetary (psychological/emotional 'costs', physical efforts, pain, time, frustration, tolerance, etc., for example, how 'embarrassing' will it be to order a non-alcoholic drink?) taking into consideration both incentives and disincentives.
- **Place:** Refers to the channels used for accessing and promoting services and products. Proximity and time flexibility are key dimensions of 'place'.
- **Promotion:** This refers to the communication means that are used to communicate the benefits of the suggested change. Such communication may focus on both content and delivery of messages using the communication mix (ads, exhibitions, emails, etc.) and media mix (radio, newspaper, etc.). Note that the so-called 'SM campaigns' that exclusively use only this 'P', are not technically classified as SM projects. Rather they may be seen simply as 'social advertising'.

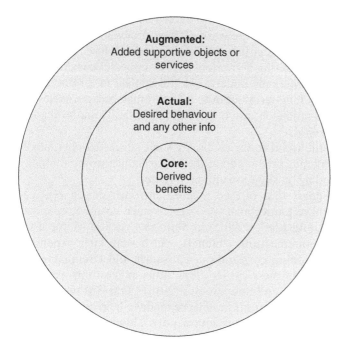

Figure 7.2 An SM reflection of a product's dimensions

Despite the above-suggested adjustments, a number of SM writers consider that the marketing mix is obsolete and need replacing by a more relevant SM 'mix'. One of the main criticisms directed against it is that the mix is designed from the perspective of the marketing planner rather than the client (Dev and Schultz, 2005). In other words, the mix is something 'done to' the target segments (O'Malley and Patterson, 2002) rather than consultatively derived in a spirit of trust and optimal offer. Such criticism may be seen as a key weakness given that the approach of SM must be consultative and voluntary. Additionally, it was argued that the 4 Ps may not consider wider influences, such as social, economic and environmental factors (French and Gordon, 2015). This is not optional for SM, as the context of an SM project is generally much wider and complex than the more commercial perspective. It seems that the first criticism would only be valid if the so-called 'marketer', with the responsibility of designing the marketing mix, decides to sacrifice the principle at the heart of the marketing philosophy (being customer-centric). If not, then it may not be necessary to adopt other models as long as the marketer is confident that the marketing philosophy is being adhered to.

The second criticism, again, may not represent the reality as several marketers who are still happy talking about traditional 4 or 7 Ps, tend to consider macro, meso and micro contextual dimensions when developing a marketing strategy. These arguments are by no means meant to disregard the good work produced by concerned marketers who offered new schemes to improve the effectiveness and efficiency of the work of their professional colleagues. Rather they are simply a reminder that any scheme may still lose relevance if the key philosophy of marketing is overlooked. As argued elsewhere, if the concept of marketing is routinely understood and applied in a responsible, inclusive manner, with a long-term outlook, then SM may become irrelevant as all 'products' should ultimately aim to serve the short- and long-term good of customers and stakeholders.

Nevertheless it is still useful to review briefly some suggested alternatives to the traditional marketing mix to add to the SM armamentarium that may come in handy depending on situation and preferences.

Among the contenders that offered a more customer-driven replacement of the 4 Ps we have Lauterborn's 4 C's (consumer, cost, communication, convenience) (Lauterborn, 1990) and Shimizu's version of the 4 Cs (commodity, cost, communication, channel), which were later expanded to produce his 7 Cs (adding corporation, consumer and circumstances) (Shizumu, 2003). Based on these earlier ideas, other suggestions were put forward. For instance, Tapp and Spotswood's (2013) COM-SM model that argued that three key considerations need to be made to help determine the likelihood of an SM offer being taken up (or not). These are the levels of motivation, opportunity and capability. It is advised that these three considerations should be made throughout an SM programme and especially when addressing promotion, nudge techniques, rewards and exchanges, service and support, and, more broadly, relationships and community. French (2011) offers a variation of this model, called the Behavioural Intervention Matrix (BIM). This model builds on his value/cost exchange matrix presented earlier, which resulted in four optional types of 'encouragements' (hugging, smacking, nudging and shoving). These options are contrasted with a number of aims of interventions (control, inform, design, educate, support) to produce the BIM (see ECDC, 2014; French and Gordon, 2015). Another model worth mentioning put forward, in response to views relating to arguments of obsolescence of the traditional 4 Ps, is that of Gordon (2012; French and Gordon, 2015). Like the others, this model advises the adoption of a consumer-centric decision model informed by research and supported through consultation with participants. The consultation would need to review five elements of an SM programme: circumstances (of the situation being faced), organizational and competition issues (stakeholder relations and challenges to the programme), cost (of behavioural change or status quo), process issues (including theoretical and programme design considerations) and, finally, channels and (implementation) strategies. Gordon (2011; French and Gordon, 2015) also suggested another, broader model, a more inclusive 'strategic social marketing mix' that reflected six levels of considerations presented in concentric circles covering: benchmark (target achievements), mass-media advertising, (other) communications, consumer marketing, macro-media and, finally, wider social norms. In our view, this later model could do with a more systematic link between the various levels together with some degree of rationalization (for example, it could be sounder to put together all communication-related concepts).

Clearly the above list of 'new 4 Ps' shows that despite some agreement about the lack of relevance (or misapplication) of traditional 4 Ps, there is no lack of alternatives. These range from a simple one-to-one readjustment to the existing 4 Ps to the more complex bird's-eye picture that increasingly moves between levels of considerations, from the consumer-level target benchmarks to broader, macro-level factors.

Given that the above alternative models were mainly suggested to highlight the need for customer-focused decisions derived through consultation with target groups and with a view to developing effective relationships, one may argue that all the above models may be considered for use. Indeed even the so-called traditional marketing mix (4 Ps) may be worth considering, as long as the criteria of inclusion, transparency, trust and relationship-building are weaved into the application of each model. Any model's primary principle is to consider the customer a partner in finding effective solutions rather than a person that receives them after some 'internal deliberations' have taken place behind some obscure closed doors. When a new model is put forward, even though it may be useful, there may be the danger that it becomes a de facto silver bullet that, with time, may overlook the very reasons why the new model was adopted. It seems best to encourage SM workers to consider each of the available models and determine which one/s (i.e., a combination) may be useful to them. Like with research models, it may become incumbent on the user to justify the selected mix so that other workers may take into consideration the specific circumstances that led to the adoption of a model or combination of models.

Monitoring and Control

Once a programme has been implemented, the next key question is 'how do I know when/if I get there (and therefore stop making adjustments to the strategy)?' This question shows that any credible strategy should take contingencies into consideration and plan possible responses to them. In order to do so there has to be clear time-tables in place, with associated resources such as budgets, responsibilities and the details of the monitoring process. The monitoring needs to agree on certain benchmarks that will be referred to, to decide on the level of success achieved in the pursuit of the objectives (e.g., awareness, conviction, change of behaviour, time, number of people affected, etc.).

Frameworks of the Social Marketing Process

The above strategic steps have generally been followed with different degrees of details by different social marketing professionals. Tables 7.1, 7.2 and 7.3 were adapted from Lefebvre (2013b) with the main difference being that the tables include one more model (in the first column). This model, which is based on Fourali (2010), has been added to the framework for comparative purposes. The tables represent an attempt at comparing the levels of foci reflected in different SM process frameworks. The three tables could have been amalgamated into one table (as done by Lefebvre) but, for simplification purposes, were presented in three steps. Hence all three tables add up to represent each of the SM process frameworks suggested by the selected authors. The steps are designed to focus in turn, and in a chronological manner, on all the dimensions that an SM approach should cover (in the case of French and Blair-Stevens model, we referred to two sources).

Initially an SM project would need to address the first four preliminary steps reflected in identifying the problem, defining it, determining the mission and investigating its context (broadly, the 'where are we now?' dimension) as summarized in Table 7.1. In the second stage, the focus is also threefold: to determine the objectives of the project, selecting the target groups and offering them an attractive proposition (broadly corresponding to 'what do we need to do?'). Finally, in the last stage, the focus is on the implementation of the objectives and monitoring the results (broadly corresponding to the question 'are we getting there?'). It is worth noting that whenever a step or dimension was not represented in one of the selected frameworks, the tables show 'NS' (i.e., 'not specified'). This is simply to denote that the step was not specified – it does not mean it was not covered. The only exception to this specification rule is the first stage, problem identification, which has been reported as 'tacit' as it is difficult to imagine the occurrence of an SM project without the existence of a problem. The purpose behind highlighting (specifying) the steps is to facilitate comparisons between different models with a purpose of encouraging SM reporters to be more comprehensive in reporting their work so that other workers can benefit from the details reported. The various steps shown in each model were not presented in the order in which they appeared in the Lefebvre presentation (2013b) but rather according to the level of matching with the SM framework derived by Fourali (2010), which attempted to represent several perspectives including the first world-class standards of SM as well as one of the later models offered by Kotler and Lee (2008) for the purpose of inclusivity. Finally, and as implied above, it is worth noting that since the publication of some of the models referred to by Lefebvre (2013b), there have been several modifications by some of the authors of the models referred to in the tables. In particular, the table refers to Kotler and Zaltman's publication, dated 1971, although since then Kotler has produced other models in cooperation with other writers (e.g., Kotler and Lee, 2008). In fact the Fourali model referred to in the table has benefitted from later ideas of Kotler and colleagues. Another example of later developed models is the one advocated recently by Jeff French that was published by the European Centre for Disease Prevention and Control and written by Jeff French and Franklin Apfel (ECDC, 2014). Incidentally, this publication is worth consulting as it has received the seal of approval from the EU and has a wealth of supporting material that a practitioner may find very handy. Kotler and Lee's (2008) and French and Apfel's (ECDC, 2014) later models were, unsurprisingly, much more comprehensive than their earlier versions. Hence the purpose of the tables is partly heuristic as it helps identify some missing dimensions from the original attempts. Most importantly, perhaps, is that the framework could offer a way of standardizing the variety of SM approaches, which can be very daunting to the 'uninitiated' who may still need straight advice on how to design and implement an SM project. A broader aim of this approach is to encourage SM techniques to become widely available to marketers so

Table 7.1 Stage 1 of selected SM frameworks: determining the problem, positioning the mission and undertaking fact-finding research

SM planning steps (Based on Fourali (2010))	Kotler and Zaltman (1971)	Lefebvre and Flora (1988)	Walsh et al. (1993)	Donovan and Henley (2010)	French and Blair-Stevens (2005, 2010)
Problem identification	Tacit	Tacit	Tacit	Tacit	Tacit
Planning	NS	Marketing management	Planning	NS	Theory-based
Purpose/mission	NS	Consumer orientation	NS	Consumer orientation	Customer orientation
Situation analysis/ market research	Environmental analysis	Formative research	Consumer analysis	NS	Insight/ competition
	Market research	NS	Market analysis	Use of market research	NS

NS: not specified.
The problem identification step shows the word 'tacit' throughout all models as it is prerequisite to any SM project.

Table 7.2 Stage 2 of selected SM frameworks: setting the objectives, targeting and providing an attractive customer proposition

SM planning steps (Based on Fourali (2010))	Kotler and Zaltman (1971)	Lefebvre and Flora (1988)	Walsh et al. (1993)	Donovan and Henley (2010)	French and Blair-Stevens (2005)
Objectives	Define the change	Voluntary exchange	NS	Exchange	Behavioural goals/ exchange
Target groups and obstacles	Segment the market	Audience: analysis and segmentation	NS	Selectivity and concentration	Segmentation
The customer proposition	Define the change	Voluntary exchange	NS	Customer value	Behavioural goals

NS: not specified.

that, eventually, many policymakers, marketers and managers – to mention a few – may become acquainted with its philosophy, theory and practice and develop a degree of confidence in applying it. Perhaps this may be the best way of ensuring this discipline is disseminated as widely as it deserves to be. Accordingly, it is felt that the SM practitioner would find it useful to identify a general 'standard' structure that helps identify, systematically, key dimensions of SM best practice. Clearly as the field develops, such best practice may need adjusting.

The above framework adopted the traditional 7 Ps to demonstrate the comparative advantage of the framework. However, as stated in Table 7.3, the practitioner could use any other of the adjusted or new marketing mixes including Lauterborn's 4 Cs, Shizumu's 7 Cs, COM-SM, the Behavioural Intervention Matrix or Gordon's marketing mix, depending on the perceived advantages associated with the selected alternative approach, for their particular purposes or contexts.

Depending on the needs (e.g., clarity or comprehensiveness), some elements have been repeated in the framework if they apply to more than one area (e.g., 'promotion' as one of the 4/7 Ps but also at 'implementation' or campaign stage). As stated above, some of the dimensions were not listed if the model referred to does not specifically mention the stage in the steps. Instead an NS, or 'not specified' is recorded. This simply means that the relevant stage hasn't been stated explicitly and does not necessarily mean it hasn't been covered by the authors of the concerned models. For instance covering the 'marketing mix' as a whole may reflect 4 Ps or more. In most cases, the 'missing dimensions' are presumed to have been tacit in the other dimensions. Their absence may mean, however, that more specific information may be needed.

In some cases, a word can be all-encompassing. However, its positioning may have been restricted to the most relevant of the above steps. For example, 'marketing management' in the Lefebvre and Flora (1988) model has been associated with the monitoring stage as it is assumed that all the above models adopt a 'marketing management' approach. Nevertheless, in this example this aspect has also been adopted for the general framework that appears in the left-hand side of the table.

The above reference framework, which mostly appeared in Fourali (2010), has also been adjusted for the purposes of this comparison to ensure as many elements mentioned in the reviewed models are covered to help with the comparisons. For instance 'problem identification' and 'planning' have been added at the outset together with the specification of both 'process' and 'outcomes' at the monitoring stage.

Although the tables above may be subject to various iterations during the life of a project, they do, however, have the advantage of guiding the SM project manager through a chronology of steps, at least in the initial stages, to ensure systematic coverage of the key SM stages.

Table 7.3 Stage 3 of selected SM frameworks: the details of the offer, its implementation and result monitoring

SM planning steps (Based on Fourali (2010))	Kotler and Zaltman (1971)	Lefebvre and Flora (1988)	Walsh et al. (1993)	Donovan and Henley (2010)	French and Blair-Stevens (2005, 2010)
Selecting a marketing mix (see below)	Marketing mix	Marketing mix	Marketing mix strategy	Differential advantage	Methods or marketing mix
May adopt any version of the marketing mixes offered, new or traditional ones. Options include Lauterborn's 4 Cs, Shizumu's 7 Cs, COM-SM, Behavioural Intervention Matrix or Gordon's marketing mix. In this table/example we are using the traditional 7 Ps as illustration.	Product planning	NS	NS	NS	NS
	Pricing/cost	NS	NS	NS	NS
	Promotion / communication	NS	Communication	NS	NS
	Place/distribution/ channels	Channel analysis	Channel analysis	NS	NS
	People	NS	NS	NS	NS
	Processes	NS	NS	NS	NS
	Physical evidence	NS	NS	NS	NS
	Promotion/ communication	NS	NS	NS	NS
Implementation (the campaign)	Promotion/ communication	NS	Implementation	Integrated approach to implementation	NS
Resources	NS	NS	NS	NS	NS
Monitoring and evaluation (process and outcomes)	Monitoring effectiveness	Marketing management/ process tracking	Process evaluation	Monitoring and influencing the environment	NS

NS: not specified.

The Value of Leadership

Although this chapter primarily concentrated on the marketing management dimension, it is important not to mistake management with leadership. Indeed, researchers have drawn our attention to the value of leadership in helping bring a project to a successful end. In order to counter any tacit assumption by the reader that the success of an SM initiative may overlook the value that the right leader may contribute to an SM project, it has been decided to put an argument, albeit briefly, at this stage about the importance of leadership. So what characteristics of leadership would an SM project leader need to possess?

Research literature highlights three broad dimensions of leadership, covering leadership traits, techniques and style (see Figure 7.3) (Northouse, 2013). From our perspective, a leader that reflects a style and approach that matches the aims and philosophy of SM and the associated project challenges may make a huge difference to the project outcome.

Considering Figure 7.3, one might argue that each of the leadership dimensions need addressing in the light of an SM context as follows:

- **Effects of characteristics of the leader:** The trait/psychology of a leader is very important in the light of the philosophy of SM that encourages transparency, consultation and respect for the human other. Hence a trait that encourages authoritarianism may not achieve those aims as it appears to be incompatible with such a philosophy and principles. Indeed, consider our earlier discussion on behavioural economics, where it was argued by some authors that it is perfectly acceptable to adopt the heuristics derived through psychological research to 'induce' people to change. Such an approach was considered inappropriate as it was paternalistic and, as such, did not always consider the importance of transparency about aims and techniques.
- **Effects of characteristics of the process:** As argued above, the design of a clear process for planning and implementing an SM project can be very helpful to advise on steps to follow that maximize systematic coverage of the key relevant actions that need undertaking. What's more, such 'standardization' may help further developments of the form or details of the procedure. So it is very important for a leader to offer clear guidance about the process to be followed to minimize errors. Nevertheless, a leader should also allow expressions of creativity so that a process can be adapted or adjusted as one sees fit to help optimize the results.
- **Effects of focusing on the needs of followers:** Focusing on needs of 'customers' is very much the philosophy of both marketing and SM, even though in this case the focus is the need of the followers. In fact, if we adopt the broader definition of 'customers' (i.e., stakeholders) then there is a valid argument to focus on all stakeholders who support an initiative. Addressing their needs would help enlist or keep the support of such stakeholders.

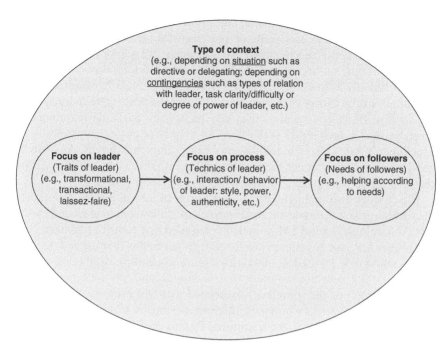

Figure 7.3 Key dimensions of leadership (adapted from Northouse, 2013)

Indeed, the above arguments suggest that as part of the aim of maximizing the success of an SM project, it is important that both process and nature of leadership are considered. Failing in either of these dimensions may lead to failure (or, with some luck, partial success) in fulfilling the aims of the projects.

Lessons to be Drawn from this Chapter

This chapter looked at the importance and contribution of the field of marketing to SM. While it stressed the need to differentiate marketing from SM given that the latter is more concerned with addressing a social issue as opposed to making a profit, which is the primary interest of marketing, it nevertheless not only shares a history but also a number of procedures that contributed to the field of SM.

Both approaches focus, at least theoretically, on short- and long-term needs of customers or, more accurately, stakeholders. So much so that it was argued that if marketing's aim is to truly meet the needs of customers, in both the short and long term, a significant amount of SM concerns would be allayed. Unfortunately this is not the case and many marketers see their aim as to make a profit first and foremost. Consequently SM is now a primary tool of policymakers who aim to address social ills.

The shared history is also reflected in the strategic approach to business since marketing is a way of managing a business to maximize commercial benefits. Similarly SM uses some of the powerful techniques of marketing to maximize benefits and minimize harm. Hence, like marketing, SM moves from vision, mission and policies to find the most optimal way of achieving them. It broadly follows the marketing strategic approach that capitalizes on insight about the causes of a particular problem, backed up by theories, and develops worthwhile objectives that may focus on a particularly vulnerable target group. Subsequently it develops an attractive customer proposition, which it translates into a marketing mix before implementing it. As with all good strategies, the planner needs to keep an eye on the results and impacts of the programme and make adjustments as and when necessary.

The chapter also highlighted the need to not blindly apply the techniques of marketing as it is important to keep track of differences in aims and methods. Accordingly, several SM workers have argued that some of the marketing techniques may not be appropriate for SM. In particular they argued that the traditional 4 or 7 Ps used in marketing are no longer appropriate as, on the one hand, they were not customer-centric enough and, on the other, do not seem to account of the complexity associated with SM projects.

As a result there was a flurry of alternatives ranging from a simple one to one translation of each of the traditional Ps into the SM context, to increasingly complex diagrams that purport to be more representative of the SM conditions. There was a counter-view to the argument that seemed to necessitate the adoption of new SM mixes. It was argued that although the new models were welcome and helpful, it was still left to the user to decide which, if any, of the new models to follow, with a provision of a helpful rationale to help advance the development of more SM-focused models. Indeed, even if a practitioner judges that such models are not necessary for adoption, they represent a stark warning against heedless adoption of concepts that may not be relevant to an SM purpose. Instead, whatever concept is used should be compatible with an SM philosophy that values transparency, trust, partnership and respect of the humans that it is trying to serve.

Finally the chapter considered the general issue of leadership and its importance for maximizing the chances of project success. It identified three dimensions that may contribute to a project's success depending on the characteristics that the leader decides to adopt. It argued that while focusing on the process (in our case, the marketing process) is important, SM projects still require characteristics of project leadership that do not overlook the philosophical and needs dimensions that make up the SM philosophy and purpose.

8 Methodological Tools for Changing the World

When discussing the rigour of a research methodology, a number of principles may occur to any researcher – especially one dealing with a social phenomenon such as 'consumer' behaviour. Already the so-called objectivity aim of research may be questionable in the light of the fact that SM aims to change human behaviour and can only hope to do so by being heavily involved in all dimensions that affect human behaviour.

The aim of this chapter is to review the research methodology in the light of SM aims and try to determine what research approach, if any, is most relevant to those aims.

When addressing research that is interested in the determinants of human behaviour a number of levels need considering (see Table 8.1). Such levels include 'upstream' issues such as ontological and epistemological assumptions as well as 'downstream' areas such as research methodology and techniques. In a way, the two opposite ends of the upstream core beliefs about the world are very much another representation of the old idealism–materialism debate. Table 8.1 summarizes the dilemmas facing researchers.

Despite the expected logical link between world perceptions and adapted methodology, we still find that some researchers, for various reasons, adopt 'accepted methodologies' irrespective of whether these methodologies match the diagnosed issue/problem or not. Such approach has been criticized under the label of 'methodolatry' (Chamberlain, 2000; Reicher, 2000).

It is clear that the nature of social phenomena makes them difficult to study/research neutrally as they are about interpretations of interpretations of social 'reality' (i.e., a meta interpretation). Such a position makes it impossible to avoid the subjective dimension including the value-laden nature of human undertaking. In fact such subjectivity is sought in SM studies, as the idea is to get to the perceptions, reasons behind the perceptions, resulting value judgements and behaviours.

A Journey Towards the Relevance of Social Research

There have been several criticisms about the aims of research throughout the past few decades reflecting views covering philosophical, political as well as

Table 8.1 Worldviews and the research approach (adapted from Burrell and Morgan, 1979; Gray, 2014; Fourali, in press)

Worldview	Key dilemma	Interpretation of dilemma
Ontology	Realism versus nominalism	The world (including ourselves) is externally structured and exists independently from our perceived reality versus the world 'reality' is structured in terms of our created concepts and language based on subjective and social conventions.
Human nature	Determinism versus voluntarism	We are victims of our own environment versus we are free agents who can decide what to do independently of any environmental influence.
Epistemology	Objectivism versus constructivism/ subjectivism	There is a reality that is separate from our conscious perceptions versus 'reality' is relative and constructed/created through a person's interactions with the world.
Theoretical perspective	Positivism versus interpretivism (with variations such as critical enquiry, post-structuralism, post-modernism, post-colonialism, feminism, etc.)	The phenomenon being studied exists independently and should be studied via disinterested observation versus phenomena are different things to different people and the aim of research is to reflect these subjective interpretations.
Methodology	Nomothetic versus ideographic	The event/subjects should be studied objectively by adopting systematic protocols that minimize subjective contamination of the reality versus the need to get as close as possible to the interpretation of the realities by adopting an 'insider' perspective so as to understand as closely as possible the 'reality' being studied.
Research approach	Deductive versus inductive	The research approach should aim to test different principles and associated hypotheses through experimentation versus gathering as much data as possible about the reality and work at determining patterns and principles that help to explain the phenomenon being studied.

Method	Experimental versus grounded theorization (with variations including survey, ethnography, phenomenology, heuristic enquiry, discourse analysis, action research, etc.)	The method is either theoretically-driven *versus* the attempt to discover the reality or realities.
Techniques	Quantitative versus qualitative (including sampling, statistical, fuzzy logic, questionnaire, observation, interview, focus group, document/ content analysis, etc.)	The technique adopted will aim to produce evidence in terms of quantitative support (backed up by probabilities and possibilities) *versus* building arguments reflecting the patterns being derived from observed phenomena to back up different interpretations.
Evaluation criteria	Validity/reliability versus generalizability	The acceptability of an argument will depend on whether the theory/hypothesis can be verified in different situations (thus generalized) *versus* triangulating the evidence to support arguments that may apply to a specific/unique situation thereby making generalizability unnecessary.

educational positions (e.g., Elliot, 2013). In particular, one of the claims levelled against 'conventional approaches' has been that they are removed from the real social issues that social research should target (e.g., Levin and Greenwood, 2013). These issues of criticizing research aims have even filtered through to criticism of the system of academic journal publications that, according to David Collinson, professor of leadership at Lancaster University, has become a proxy for quality that 'erodes diversity, innovation, critical evaluation and creativity' and this led to a 'journal fetishism' that 'not only reduces complex matters of quality assessment to quantified and simplistic measures, but also has a homogenizing effect on article content, while rendering the careers of business school academics ever more dependent on publishing in those journals that are deemed to "count"' (Collinson, 2014, p. 1).

These views are not new. Indeed the author (Fourali, 2014a) shared with his audience an anecdote about a French discussion that took place during his student days when the theme seemed to revolve around what would be a good solution for making educational institutions (or any institution for that matter) more relevant and responsible. Some more radical colleagues ventured a confrontational approach in the form of 'L'assaut de la cité corrompue par le "savoir"' (the assault/attack on the city corrupted by 'knowledge'). In this case, the word 'city' referred to higher education (or any institution claiming final authority on credible knowledge). The view behind the radical approach was that the institutions' irrelevance has become self-sustaining, thereby making it very difficult to attempt to change it by working with it. This discussion leads us to ask: can social research be made more relevant?

When addressing such an important question, one needs to perhaps borrow the strategic concepts so routinely used in business studies to understand the current level of health of any enterprise before determining the actions that need undertaking (McDonald, 2007; Kotler, 2013; Dibb and Simkin, 2008). Such a perspective has long been directly or indirectly advocated by academics in various areas who recognized that a narrow application of so-called research-derived best practice may miss the bigger picture about the intervening factors in the life of the subjects being studied (Fox and Prilleltensky, 1997; Kusiak, 2007).

Indeed an SM enterprise may be seen exactly as just that (i.e., as an enterprise) in the business sense. This chapter highlights both the need for a utilitarian as well as a more inclusive perspective that should help make research more relevant and useful to humans (which supports the deontological argument). It is clear there have been a backlash against such a perspective (e.g., Laing and Brabazon, 2007), with concerns raised about diverting research from its ('original'?) more fundamental science purpose. However, in the view of this author, the criticism tended to derive into an either/or positioning that restricts both practice-based *and* fundamental research-based perspectives. Notwithstanding the diversity of views, we consider pursuing the idea of SM as an enterprise. This considers the twin purpose of understanding phenomena and capitalizing on this understanding to help develop healthy and responsible citizens with the view to alleviating the human suffering. Bearing this purpose in mind, we favour a strategic perspective that would urge a researcher to ask the following questions: where are we? Where do we want to be? How do we get there? How do we know when/if we get there?

Fourali (2014a) argued that these questions match very nicely an action research (AR) perspective. Hence, in line with Elliot (2013) and Levin and Greenwood (2013), this author believes that AR should be more broadly adopted and valued in academic circles. This state of affairs will be realized when more people are aware of the relevance of AR to social research in general and SM research in particular and apply it more. Fourali (2014a) has already demonstrated the relevance of AR to social marketing. SM has a stated aim to use the marketing techniques for the good of society – hence all SM research activities are underpinned by this aim to ultimately make a difference. We believe that AR, like SM, exists to help understand and develop our societies with the ultimate aim to improve the quality of our lives.

In trying to achieve this aim, we argue that SM should adopt multimodal, democratic, top-down and bottom-up considerations that may help better understand the phenomenon at hand so that better and more efficient/effective decisions and subsequent changes can be made. Since its approach is no longer restricted by superficial demarcations such as university departments, its attempt will bring as many perspectives as necessary to bring to bear on the issues at hand. Triangulation of evidence should very much be the rule rather than the exception.

In the following section we demonstrate in more detail the relevance of the AR perspective and the characteristics that make it an ideal approach in the social sciences.

What is AR and How is it Relevant to SM?

At a recent conference, McNiff (2013) stated that there are around 30 versions of AR. The following three definitions should provide the key dimensions of what AR involves. In one of the most quoted definitions for AR, Rapoport states that:

> Action research aims to contribute both to the practical concerns of people in an immediate problematic situation and to the goals of social science by joint collaboration within a mutually acceptable ethical framework.
>
> (Rapoport, 1970)

McNiff and Whitehead (2011, p. 7) state: 'Action research is a form of enquiry that enables practitioners in every job and walk of life to investigate and evaluate their work'. Another definition describes AR as a:

> deliberate, solution-oriented investigation that is group or personally owned and conducted. It is characterized by spiraling cycles of problem

identification, systematic data collection, reflection, analysis, data-driven action taken, and, finally, problem redefinition. The linking of the terms 'action' and 'research' highlights the essential features of this method: trying out ideas in practice as a means of increasing knowledge about or improving curriculum, teaching, and learning.

(Kemmis and McTaggart, 1988)

Note that though the last definition is primarily focusing on the educational context, its utility is fairly broad. Based on the above definitions, one might derive the following characteristics associated with AR (Reason and Bradbury, 2007):

- improving education;
- spiral of circles/iterative model;
- participatory;
- testing own ideas, practice, assumptions;
- evidence-based;
- critical analysis (social/historical constructions);
- political (effect on social life/practice);
- ethical framework.

The last dimension, ethical framework, is perhaps a key element that differentiates AR. Despite the importance of this dimension, it is not always overtly stated as done in the first of the above three definitions.

Various authors identified a number of writers – such as Lewin (1946), Revans (1971) and Kolb (1984) – as key initiators/promoters of action-led research and learning. It may be argued that it is a common-sense, reality-based approach that has the purpose to improve the human condition. Accordingly, its origins can be much older than is usually argued by researchers. Perhaps Gibran (another AR instigator?) reflected the approach nicely when he stated in his masterpiece, *The Prophet*, almost a century ago:

> And I say that life is indeed darkness save when there is urge,
> And all urge is blind save when there is knowledge,
> And all knowledge is vain save when there is work,
> And all work is empty save when there is love;
> And when you work with love you bind yourself to yourself, and to one another, and to God.

(Gibran, 2011)

In this little poetical statement, Gibran beautifully combined desire (or solution-orientation), knowledge, action, ethics, collaboration and spiritual purpose.

The above-mentioned spiral of circles/iterative model usually comes in the form of reflecting, planning, acting and observing (Lewin, 1946; Kemmis and McTaggart, 1988). An alternative, slightly modified model, is the one offered

Table 8.2 Comparison between two perspectives on the AR stages

Lewin (1946)/Kemmis and McTaggart (1988)	Susman (1983)
Reflecting	Diagnosing
Planning	Action planning
Acting	Taking action
Observing	Evaluating
	Specifying learning

by Susman's action research model (1983): diagnosing a problem, action planning (looking for alternative courses of actions), taking action (selecting one option), evaluating (the consequences) and specifying the learning/findings.

Both these models are iterative in that the researcher will keep going around the steps of the models until satisfied with the outcome. Perhaps the difference between these two models is primarily the fact that Susman specifies the acquired learning (final step of each round of iteration). Susman's model also starts with a problem identification stage, which is also quite important if we are to argue about the practicality of AR. However, both models seem to assume that reflection tends to primarily take place at the first stage of the process. Given that reflection is pervasive to all these stages, one possible improvement would be the model shown in Figure 8.1. We also feel it reflects nicely the likely iterations between steps that, following the last step, may lead to new cycles (or spirals to stress that a new direction may be undertaken).

We feel that this later model may provide a more realistic representation of the 'problem-solving steps' reflected in an AR perspective. Clearly AR is not just about problem-solving here and now and overlooking existing theories and best practice. However, the latter should be put at the service of solving the problem at hand, even though the outcome may be a learning that may benefit others or can help develop a broader model/theory that may be applied elsewhere. We feel that reflection should be ongoing and does not only belong to either just the reflection stage or problem-identification stage. Even during implementation of action there has to be a parallel monitoring that ensures things are taking place as planned and that if there is a need for adjustment then this will be made. For instance, if an educational programme that includes showing an advert for the reduction of teenage smoking shows in the early stages that it has some adverse effects then the organizers will not wait until the end of the programme to start making changes.

Figure 8.1 also shows the need for iteration as well as showing the possibility that it can retrace each step. It also can go back to the problem identification stage and see whether the problem has been resolved or the obtained outcome may need more work or the questions need to be re/defined. Finally, it also includes the cyclical idea that if the researcher decides to reformulate the questions or the focus of the research s/he can restart from the beginning, initiating a second or more stages as required by the research.

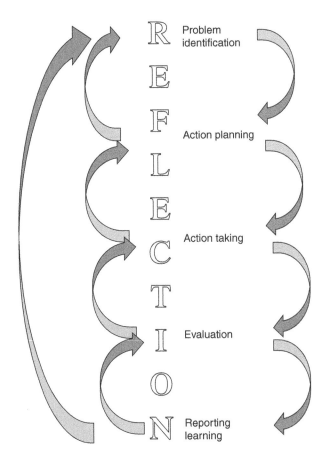

Figure 8.1 Steps of action research (adapted from Lewin (1946), Kemmis and McTaggart (1988) and Susman (1983))

If we refer to the argument above regarding choosing a method to fit the aim of a project, one may feel that advocating the above AR procedure goes against such advice. Additionally one may feel that any preliminary chosen approach may go against adopting a flexible pluralistic approach that befits the aims of SM. This is a valid criticism. However, like many procedures in several disciplines, one may find it useful to consider a tested approach whose aim and flexibility seem to match the purposes of SM. If for any reason there may be an argument either against using AR (in any of its existing forms) or for developing a new version, then this should be perfectly possible. The above arguments in a way are no different from those put forward by current social marketers who advocate an action-based methodology. In fact, it would be very hard not to see the parallels between SM methodologies and those of AR, even if they are not presented as such. For instance, consider French and colleagues' definition of SM method (see ECDC, 2014; French and Gordon, 2015), where they argue that SM:

> Like commercial marketing it is a fusion of science, practical 'know how' and reflective practice focused on continuously improving the effectiveness and efficiency of programmes.
>
> (ECDC, 2014, p. 4)

The authors clarify this statement further by presenting a four-step 'social marketing action framework', which includes: scoping (analysis), testing (pre-testing and piloting), enacting (planning and implementing) and, finally, learning and acting (reviewing).

These stages are very similar to the examples of AR shown in Table 8.2. This is no surprise because the authors have opted for an action framework and one would expect such steps in any AR framework.

The next section will present the varieties of AR and argues why AR seems to offer a 'paradigm' that is most compatible with SM purposes.

How Well Does AR Fit with the Aims of SM?

It is hard to overestimate the value of research methodology in guiding the researcher to help find the practical answer he or she needs. Any enterprise needs to adopt research procedures that match the aim of its mission and SM is no different.

SM by its very nature is a discipline that aims to make use of advances in knowledge and skills (including those in marketing) to induce changes for the good of society. In other words, the purpose of its research is to take action on a current unsatisfactory state of affairs. Fortunately there has been a lot of improvement in the action research methodology, which should help the work of action researchers. The aim of this chapter is to introduce and describe the relevance of action research to social marketing so that it is considered routinely by the SM practitioner.

AR is seen as a family of approaches/orientations rather than a method or technique. This perspective includes the following approaches:

- **Action science**, advanced by Argyris and colleagues (1985, Argyris and Schon; 1978). This approach focuses on the interplay of intention and environmental variables (single loop/defensive reasoning) versus the open discussion of problems and their origin and the possibility of changing/reframing of the variables (double loop/productive reasoning). They particularly differentiate between researchers (officially) espoused theories and their theories of action (or theories that actually guide their actions).
- **Cooperative/collaborative enquiry** suggested by Heron and Reason (1997). This approach advocates working *with* people (not *on*) people. This involves moving through the stages of (1) propositional knowing,

(2) practical knowing (testing within the researcher group), (3) experiential knowing (testing with external stakeholders) and (4) creating new knowledge and ways of acting. If this fourth stage, reflecting the end of the first-cycle research, is unsatisfactory, then the researchers will move onto another four-stage cycle. Such an approach very much reflects an SM philosophy.

- **Participatory action research** – this approach usually refers to critical pedagogy promoted by Paulo Freire (1970). However, it has developed a pluralistic perspective whose key aim is knowledge-making and social change (Chambers, 2000). Its 'participatory' dimension focuses on daily social life with a view to promoting democratic principles; the 'action' dimension highlights the importance of engaging with daily experience and historical factors; and, finally, the research dimension purports to develop sound knowledge that makes a difference (Chevalier and Buckles, 2013a, 2013b).
- **Developmental action research/enquiry** – this approach focuses on the mutual transformation value of research. It directs the researcher to focus on many levels as argued by Torbert and Taylor (2007):

  > it is a form of research that is conducted simultaneously on oneself, the first-person action inquirer, on the second-person relationships in which one engages, and on the third-person institutions of which one is an observant participant ... it generates not just single-loop feed-back that incrementally improves a stock of knowledge, but also double-and triple-loop transformations of structure, culture, and consciousness that influence ongoing interaction.
  >
  > (Torbert and Taylor, 2007, p. 239)

- **Living educational theories** (Carson and Summara, 1997; McNiff and Whitehead, 2011) – the authors of this approach argue that action research, by its very nature, is a lived practice that requires that the researcher highlights how both the researcher and the research process influence the subject at hand. The primary aim here was to promote transparency and honesty about our biases reflecting any aspect of our lives (including spiritual, existential and emotional). Note here the link with Torbert approach.

Other classifications have been suggested. For instance Bob Dick (2004) identifies four broad trends covering appreciative inquiry (Sorensen et al., 2003), action science (Argyris, 2004), systems approaches (Jackson, 2003) and action learning (Raelin, 2000). Others identify a separate 'canonical/classical/traditional' action research, which is based on Lewin's approach that argued that traditional science is not helping address our social problems (Davison et al., 2004). Lewin's (1946) AR is seen as more relevant to researching the conditions and effects of various forms of social action.

Despite the varieties of categorizations, there seems to be a general convergence about viewing action research as an integrative investigation that sees action as a form of enquiry and enquiry as a form of action (Torbert and Taylor, 2007). AR is also seen as a 'philosophy' that does not make previous assumptions about what research technique is most effective but rather is happy to promote a mixed design approach with a purpose of reaching genuine, long-term solutions to any type of problem (McNiff and Whitehead, 2011; Torbert and Taylor, 2007; Fourali, 2014a).

SM, AR and the Paradigm Revolutions

At this stage it may be worth mentioning that this author does not view AR as just another method to be contrasted with other research methods. Rather, and as stated above, AR is portrayed here as a paradigm or, better still, a philosophy that may make use of any research method/tool (qualitative, quantitative or mixed methods) to achieve its aim of inclusivity and social improvement (McNiff and Whitehead, 2011; Creswell, 2007; Galt, 2008). Consequently, the perspective adopted here is more about relevance and adequacy of fit of other paradigms for helping resolve societal issues. According to some AR researchers (e.g., McNiff and Whitehead, 2006), social research paradigms developed according to a number of steps:

Stage 1 – Positivistic approach (technical/rational): 'Researcher stays outside the research field to maintain objectivity and ensure knowledge is not contaminated by human contact'. Use of quantitative analysis.

Stage 2 – Interpretative: Observation of people in their natural settings and explain and describe what they are doing. Use qualitative analysis.

Stage 3 – Critical Theoretic Research: 'Research is never neutral. Social situations are created by people. They can be deconstructed and reconstructed'. Power relationships.

Stage 4 – Action research: 'How can the unsatisfactory situation be understood and be changed?' AR emphasizes both understanding and action.

Fourali (in-press) argued that a fifth stage can be added as follows:

Stage 5 – Inclusive AR with self-knowledge stage: taking into account global and local ('glocal') and short and long-term perspectives.

There are some differences between different authors regarding the above stages. For example Denzin and Lincoln (1994) or Guba and Lincoln (1994) add 'constructivism' or 'feminist theory' dimensions that, arguably, may be considered as part of the critical theoretic stage 3.

The above stage 5 focuses on both improving the social situation and changing the person (insight and attitudes) through developing self-awareness and knowledge. This dimension focuses on the transformative dimension of AR while viewing the best possible solutions as ones that take into account long-term and inclusive solutions. Arguably this is the most difficult stage of

←		→
Location of researcher		
Outsider (Externally focused)	Participating researcher (One of the stakeholders/subjects)	Insider (fully implicated)
Function of researcher		
Observer/reporter	Reflection on own practice	Self-critical analysis/transformational
Scope/purpose of research (focus of the lens)		
Only here and now (without the bigger picture)	Contextual (Light touch)	Contextual (full blown) Full embeddedness

Figure 8.2 Action Research as a point of confluence of continuums: Location, function and scope

AR because of this continuous challenge to personal values and how they match a more inclusive long-term approach. Such an approach goes beyond simplistic attempts at rationalizations but would rather tend to address the question of 'how can I live a meaningful and satisfactory life that if adopted by all would maximize human long-term happiness?' Such an approach would resist the tendency to align oneself with partisan camps that, although originally reflecting a thought through decision by those who adopt a particular camp, in the long term may be counterproductive as there is the danger of trying to prove one's position rather than finding solutions that may borrow from any perspective.

Fourali (2014a) identified three dimensions that also positioned the type of AR we may be dealing with as shown in Figure 8.2. According to this figure, it may be fair to portray AR as the outcome of an evolution of the research paradigm through various steps and adjustments to its methodology to address the issues at hand (either qualitative or practical aspects). Obviously one might argue that the neo-positivistic approach did identify and attempt to improve on the weaknesses (including the *reductio ad absurdum*) of the 'hard' positivistic model. Nevertheless, in the context of the social sciences in general and SM in particular, the neo-positivistic approach falls still short of the aims of AR and SM.

Criticism of AR and Response

AR has been criticized for being too subjective, yet AR actually sees this as a strength rather than a weakness. It recognizes that researchers are humans who as well as being unique are clearly affected by their respective social backgrounds (see Figure 4.2).

AR also encourages the interbreeding of ideas that help understand a particular problem with a view to resolving it. Accordingly, concepts such as triangulation, practicality, multidisciplinary and multimodality are very much 'up the AR street'. Such a perspective avoids the label of 'methodolatry' as argued by Chamberlain (2000) since it is no longer the acceptable tradition within a journal or university that determines the choice of method for understanding and trying to resolve the problem at hand. Indeed it would be very difficult to imagine any social issue that does not require the adoption of all these concepts to maximize the understanding with the view of providing robust answers and solutions. Imagine Sherlock Holmes, Poirot or Columbo trying to resolve a crime allegation with the restriction 'you can only use one type of evidence or sources'.

AR – and by extension SM – can capitalize on any new development in research methodology and add it to the armamentarium of the researcher if relevant. For example, facet theory (Brown and Sleath, 2015; Borg, 2005) may offer a promising approach that can help identify certain target individuals either because of their particular link to a particular programme or simply because they may be 'at risk' and may therefore benefit from educational and psychological programmes, among others, to remedy a particular situation. Facet theory may make use of three levels of characterization/description of individuals as follows:

- A background facet (gender, age, ethnic group).
- A domain facet (that is the focus of the research such as predisposition/ motivation to commit a crime).
- A range facet (reflecting the possible options that an individual may select in relation to the domain facet).

Statistical procedures may then be used to help determine the similarity/ closeness between facets and build a picture and associated arguments about likelihood of outcomes. This approach may facilitate the well-established 'segmentation' process used in social marketing and help make it more effective. However, this approach still depends on a significant amount of subjectivity in interpretation (Brown, 2011) and can only be used as an extra tool of information to be supplemented from other sources for more reliability.

In the light of the above, we feel AR provides an ideal flexible approach that is very well suited to SM's complex concerns with a view to maximize the benefits of the outcomes. In fact, AR seems to have become the de facto preferred approach to addressing SM issues as shown in many SM projects (see also Chapter 9).

From Hard Logic to Soft Logic

As argued above, any tool that helps understand and solve a problem is 'game' from an SM perspective irrespective of whether it is a tool that favours quantitative, qualitative or both analyses (i.e., mixed model AR design). In terms of quantitative analyses, there has been plenty of models arguing for ever-more sophisticated techniques currently including multimodal/level dimensions (e.g., Rudolph, 2013; Goldstein, 2003). Such approaches are very welcome if they help to shed light on the problem at hand. However, and as argued above, it is always worth remembering that tools also reflect assumptions and histories of practice that may become too entrenched to reconsider and look at alternative approaches. This brings one to the argument put forward by a branch of quantitative analysis that argues that most current statistical analysis are based on binary thinking.

Fourali (1997, 2009b) argued that researchers make assumptions that positions tend to be either 'black' or 'white' reflecting a dichotomous thinking well reported in recent psychological research. He advised for the uptake of the principles and methodology of fuzzy logic (FL), as they take into account uncertainties between assessors/judges therefore attracting different ratings that reflect more the grey-area judgements than the extreme 'either/or' thinking. He argued that most world phenomena and associated human judgements are not of a probability type but rather are of a fuzzy type reflecting opinions between two extremes. Smithson (1988) described the following event to clarify the relevance of FL. He argued that if we assume that the probability that it will rain tomorrow is $P(A) = 1/2$ this could mean that we know A and B are equally likely, or it could mean that we are utterly ignorant of the likelihood of A or B. In addition, probability is incapable of capturing any ambiguity or vagueness about the event. In the rain example, there still remains some ambiguity about whether the rain is a mist, drizzle, moderate or heavy. These are fuzzy uncertainties of a qualitative nature that can be dealt with by FL.

Fourali (2009b) used the concept to determine the likelihood and seriousness of emotional difficulties. Indeed, psychologists are not only interested in whether a person is unhappy but how serious that unhappiness is (e.g., are they sad? Depressed? Suicidal?). Subsequently, FL was demonstrated as a helpful tool in organizing the various factors that influence behaviour rated according to their degree of influence on an individual. Fourali argued that as the size of effects change, the general outcome will change. Such monitoring of effect can be easily carried out as estimates of changes are added to the algorithms reflecting the most relevant factors to each individual. Indeed, the factors that affect individuals are not only affecting individuals differentially in a tangible way, but semantically as well. For instance, if poverty or childhood abuse are factors that may lead to drinking, clearly their effect depends on how important these are perceived by each individual.

Fourali (2009b) argued that fuzzy logic offers great promise in developing dynamic understanding of a complex situation especially when combined with neural network thereby helping to determine a more accurate estimate of factors influencing a particular situation (see as an example Figure 8.3, borrowed from Fourali (2009b) showing how different selected factors interact and influence the ability of a person to change a self-destructing drinking behaviour).

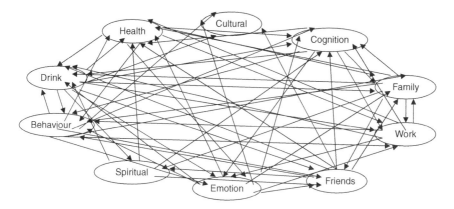

Figure 8.3 Interaction between different factors affecting drinking (from Fourali, 2009b)

Note: Depending on achieved insight, more contributory factors may be included in the diagram. Additionally each new contributing factor will iteratively react to all other factors and produce a new picture.

In the light of the above, we believe that FL offers a huge potential to marketers and, more particularly, social marketers as they deal routinely with very complex situations. FL helps take into account both uncertainties and qualitative views. Like many tools, it will not be a silver-bullet as it very much depends on assumptions made about contributory factors. Nevertheless it can be usefully added to the SM armamentarium.

FL is an established methodology that has been successfully implemented in several engineering fields. However, there still remains huge opportunities for its adaptation to the social sciences despite some promising demonstrations reflected in some work (e.g., Bassey, 1999; Fourali, 1997; 2009b).

What Advice Can We Derive from this Chapter?

Broadly speaking, the chapter argued for the need to encourage the SM community to be more aware about the type of research that is compatible with SM purposes. The chapter argued that, given that SM is an action-based discipline, it seems that the best possible research methodology for it would be AR. SM practitioners tend to work from the identification of a problem, to action planning and action taking, to evaluation of results and deriving new learning before taking any other actions or making adjustments. Such an approach is very much that of AR and, consequently, it may benefit the SM community to routinely consider AR methodology (with its many versions) before considering deriving a new method. Such an approach would help SM workers to determine which research methods may best help particular problems, thereby simplifying the work of the SM practitioners who may be lost among the various suggested methodologies.

We also believe that such an approach would help develop SM into a more rigorous science that can develop more accurate advice for both research and practice. In this respect, SM would develop more accurate procedures that match with its purpose and philosophy. It may decide to pick and mix any existing technique, in an eclectic manner, that may help its research, planning or action stages. In particular the above section introduced FL as a powerful potential tool that may be added to the SM researcher armamentarium.

What this chapter is not suggesting is to adopt right at the outset one type of research method in preference to all others without taking into account the purpose and principles of SM. It is advising SM researchers to consider the AR methodology while keeping their options open should there be other more suited approaches that maximize effectiveness and efficiency.

9 The Application of Social Marketing

An Illustration

As stated earlier, SM has been applied to numerous situations with significant amounts of success, and the field is expanding continuously. We will mention a few more areas of its applicability in Chapter 10. However, the purpose of this chapter is to select an example of the application of the SM approach with a view to help budding SM professionals gain some practical advice, at least in the early stages, before they proceed to develop their own personalized approach to their respective specific situations.

As shown in Chapter 7, there have been several proposed models that could be used to help implement the SM approach. As demonstrated in this chapter, although there are some differences between the various offered SM frameworks, they all generally seem to agree on the key marketing principles of understanding the customer and addressing the marketing mix when implementing the SM programme. In the following illustrative example we will refer to the model derived from Fourali (2010), and presented in Tables 7.1–7.3.

The example chosen to demonstrate our selected SM model is based on a report presented by Duane and Domegan (2014) that describes an initiative for fighting obesity in a particularly vulnerable group in Ireland: the truckers. In the following illustration we will refer to each of the steps presented in the adjusted Fourali (2010) model (see Chapter 7). The 'derived' information on the selected example may have been elicited either directly or indirectly from the report and at times simplified for purposes of demonstration. Readers who require more detailed analysis of this project may refer back to the original report.

Before proceeding further, it is useful to note that the example was primarily selected because of the richness of available information that can relate to the steps of our selected framework. It was not selected because of the level of success in achieving its objectives since, as will be seen later, the project had mixed results.

Step 1: Problem Identification

The SM project was undertaken to help address obesity among truck drivers in the isle of Ireland (combining Northern and Southern Ireland), hereafter

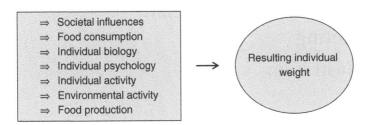

Figure 9.1 Factors contributing to obesity (adapted from Duane and Domegan, 2014)

referred to as Ireland. The problem of obesity had shown steady increase among the Irish population despite several initiatives, including multiple collaborations and use of mass-media approaches. At the time of the study, 39 per cent of adults in Ireland were classified as being overweight, with 18 per cent considered obese. The situation particularly affected the adult male population (46 per cent, as opposed to 33 per cent female), who in many cases were not even aware of the problem (Wardle and Johnson, 2002) putting them at the lowest level in terms of readiness for action as argued by Prochaska and colleagues (1992). The situation for truck drivers was even more dire given their generally unhealthy eating habits (e.g., irregular snacking) and sedentary lifestyle that minimizes opportunities for exercise. Subsequently an SM project, known as Get Your Life in Gear (GYLIG), was undertaken to focus on this particularly vulnerable group of male truck drivers. The SM approach was seen as particularly relevant after early indication showed that the factors contributing to obesity were systemic and multilevel as reflected in Figure 9.1. Additionally, it was found that gender-neutral messages were not very effective and there was a need for better targeting.

Step 2: Planning

Background research on health status of truck drivers suggested that overweight behaviour is induced by a multitude of systemic and multilevel factors and, accordingly, requires an integrated multipronged approach that combines individual, organizational, community and general population level strategies (Wilson et al., 1996; Makrides et al., 2006). A stakeholders' analysis was undertaken with a view to adopting a multilevel and multidisciplinary strategy that elicits the contribution of all key stakeholders.

Step 3: Purpose/Mission

The project's purpose was to raise awareness about the destructive effects of being overweight and initiate healthy lifestyle changes to stop and reverse the trend of weight-inducing behaviour.

Step 4: Situation Analysis/Market Research

A preliminary analysis considered several obesity-vulnerable groups. These included construction workers, taxi drivers and truck drivers. This led to selecting these categories given their perceived lack of healthy eating and exercise. The study subsequently focused on truck drivers as they had less access to facilities for access to healthy food. The literature review confirmed the vulnerability of this group and the difficulty in reaching them (Jack et al., 1998; Gill and Wijk, 2004; Krugar et al., 2007; Whitfield-Jacobson et al., 2007, Apostolopoulos et al., 2011). Their continuous snacking and lack of regular healthy meals combined with a sedentary lifestyle contributed significantly to their unhealthy weight conditions. Consequently this group was selected as the target for the project.

Subsequently this target group was selected for further analysis using the PESTLE framework, which suggested the following:

Political

A number of international bodies recommended health promotion in the workplace. Among these are: the 1986 Ottawa Charter for Health Promotion; the 1997 Luxembourg Declaration on Workplace Health Promotion in the European Union; the 1997 Jakarta Declaration on Leading Health Promotion into the 21st Century; the 2001 Lisbon Statement on Workplace Health in Small and Medium-Sized Enterprises; the 2002 Barcelona Declaration on Developing Good Workplace Health Practice in Europe; the 2005 Bangkok Charter for Health Promotion in a Globalised World; the 2004 WHO Global Strategy on Diet, Physical Activity and Health.

Economic

The economic downturn and loss of employment means there is a need to provide a strong rationale to convince employers to support the initiative. The argument can take the form of 'healthier staff means more sustainable businesses and higher return on investment derived from encouraging healthier lifestyles'.

Social

This has several dimensions that have been linked to a person's weight:

- Social norms of masculinity and transport industry tend to see weight gain as a normal work side-effect.
- Social class and geo-demographics (e.g., there may not be any social or professional demand to look good).
- Family life.

- Ethnicity and social network (e.g., type of food).
- Occupational demands/management (e.g., type of working hours).

Technical

The following 'technical' aspects may influence the implementation of the initiative:

- Facilities provided by the organization (e.g., canteen, gym, vending machines).
- The cost incurred in supporting the initiative.
- The variety of communication means (e.g., internet, intranet, Facebook page) that the organization makes available to its employees.
- Transport facilities to or from work may affect the level of access and 'free' time for health-promoting activities.

Legal

- How much time the employment law stipulates in terms of time off for employees.

Environmental

- Environment that normalizes and promotes obesity (obesogenic).
- Type of organizational culture and support from organization/management.
- Availability of facilities to support the initiative (also links to above 'technical' dimension).
- Staff turnover that may influence commitment to the initiative.
- Type of staff commitment to organizational initiatives (e.g., union).

Following this early assessment a SWOT analysis was undertaken as summarized in Table 9.1.

The above preliminary investigations suggested a number of gaps in knowledge that required further research in the form of primary research targeting the following:

- Gain a deeper understanding of attitude, lifestyles and behaviours of truck drivers with a view to clarify their health needs and concerns.
- Understand the likely effect of a health and lifestyle change initiative facilitated by the workplace.

Two data-gathering approaches, in the form of interviews and focus groups, were carried out throughout Ireland to elicit this information as follows:

Table 9.1 SWOT analysis of Get Your Life in Gear campaign

Strengths	Weaknesses
• Several national and international reports support this initiative. • Peer support may be provided in the workplace. • High media attention of some successful initiatives (e.g., Gut Busters). • Attractive benefits of initiative based on exchange theory. • Interest from stakeholders, especially employers, to improve health of employees.	• Restricted focus on male truck drivers (may attract criticism from non-targeted groups). • The initiative is new and has not benefitted from adequate background information. • SM is a new concept in Ireland with which the population is not familiar. • The initiative may target and show more effect on certain subgroups (e.g., health-conscious) and less on others.
Opportunities	**Threats**
• Involvement of relevant NGOs. • Involvement of relevant networks including online communities. • Opportunities for useful long-term advice. • The initiative may benefit other similar initiatives/work environments.	• Competition from unhealthy promotional messages (e.g., alcohol, unhealthy food, inactive lifestyles). • Possible adverse effect of social male norms and gender expectations. • Risk of lack of support at the workplace (e.g., long working hours). • Benefit may not be sustainable. • High turnover of the industry may be compounded by the initiative. • Scarcity of jobs may affect commitment to initiative. • Some job categories may be adversely affected (e.g., subcontracted staff).

- 14 interviews undertaken at a distribution depot in Northern Ireland; and
- six focus groups carried out across Ireland.

The obtained information highlighted the following key findings:

- The work conditions of truck drivers made it hard to accommodate a healthy lifestyle.
- Some older drivers managed to introduce changes in their lifestyle following doctor's advice.
- Those who more recently undertook to become more healthy demonstrated that this is possible when supported by wisdom (acquired with age or experience) or prompted by health scares suffered by oneself or significant others.
- Belief significantly affected readiness to make change (e.g., belief that work prevents any behavioural change).
- The inconsistency of work shifts presented a difficult challenge to manage food consumption.

- Other observed factors included impact of education, convenience, cost, support of partner/wife, comfort eating/sweet tooth and adherence to stereotypical image of truck driver.
- Findings that may become the basis for change included: general awareness that snacking was unhealthy; importance of demonstrating tangible benefits from weight-loss attempts and continuous motivational support until the new lifestyle has become routinized; importance of educating/advising about positive changes that can be made; importance about educating about healthy eating and food for energy as well as addressing misguided attitudes towards food.

As a result of these findings the campaign 'Get Your Life in Gear' (GYLIG) was initiated. This title resonated well with the male truck driver who wanted to make healthier changes in their lives and develop better quality time with their significant others.

Step 5: Objectives

To be considered successful the initiative was to ensure that the truck drivers achieved the following, SMART objectives by the end of the 12-week period:

- Physical activity to increase to at least 30 minutes per day, five days per week.
- Fatty and sugary foods and drinks to be reduced by 10 per cent.
- Increase truck drivers' fruit and vegetable consumption by at least one portion per day.
- Healthy weight and/or reduce weight by 10 per cent for truck drivers with a BMI over 25.

Step 6: Target Groups and Obstacles

The target group was male truck drivers. The obstacles were shown above following PESTLE and summarized in SWOT analyses (see 'Weaknesses' and 'Threats' in Table 9.1).

Step 7: The Customer Proposition

This should reflect the exchange principle highlighted by an SM perspective. For the exchange to happen, the initiative should offer a feasible alternative that is of significant value to the target group to elicit the necessary behavioural changes. As stated by Duane and Domegan (2014), the proposition was presented in the form of 'highlighting the benefits of the proposed changes over the consequences of not adopting the changes'. These two facets of the same coin combined both reward and punishment that mutually support the same goal of a healthier lifestyle.

This proposition also provided support that helped move the target group from intention to change to taking action (as highlighted in the stages of change model discussed earlier). The support will be described below in the form of the marketing mix. Hence the customer proposition combined both awareness-raising (building conviction) and action supporting.

Step 8: The Marketing Mix

> In this example the marketing mix is based on traditional 4 P's. However, as the 'standard' model presented earlier suggests, other types of SM-linked marketing mixes may be used depending on relevance and perceived advantages.

As in all marketing initiatives, the marketing mix needed to take into account the background research on challenges, restrictions and need and concerns of the target group to produce a very attractive offer that can keep other competing offers at bay. This meant that a great idea for inducing change that may have been attractive to the general population may not apply to the target group if it did not take full account of their work or social conditions. Even the positioning of the initiative had to be appealing to the target group. Accordingly it was found that positioning it as a whole package of positive lifestyle change is more attractive then positioning it as a simple weight-loss initiative, which conjures up ideas of dieting and ongoing pain.

The following marketing mix will focus on the 4 Ps in their order of relevance starting with the creation of a 'product' and promoting it, so the audience knows about it, to estimating the monetary, physical and psychological costs of accessing it (price) to finding out about how to access it (place).

'Product' Considerations

If we consider the three dimensions of the 'product' (core, actual and augmented), one may envisage the following:

- The core product may be described as 'getting healthier by losing weight'.
- The actual product may be seen as 'engaging in healthy behaviour in line with the lifestyle change programme' (see below description of 12-week programme).
- The augmented product is reflected in the supporting toolkit components to help adopt and maintain the new healthier lifestyle.

The 12-week programme included two free professional checks (pre- and post-programme). The checks were primarily motivational in nature as it was found that generally men tended to decide to lose weight when prompted by evidence-based health concerns (De Souza and Ciclitiva, 2005). The health checks included waist, cholesterol and blood pressure measurements. The nurse doing the checks gave free and confidential advice and introduced them to the GYLIG programme to develop a healthier lifestyle through healthier food and more exercise.

The toolkit was introduced as a reinforcement tool to support the drivers' decision and act as a reminder of the need to maintain their commitment. It contained a booklet, cool bag (to keep fresh food on the road), pedometer, tape measure, safe food pen, bottle of water and information on how to sign up to receive free SMS motivational messages. Any queries about the toolkit were addressed by the nurses. The booklet was pre-tested for design and content to ensure all key issues were addressed but also with a view to strike the right tone between entertainment (through humour) and being informative to garner as much involvement as possible. In terms of steps followed, drivers were encouraged to set their own achievable goals for the 12-week period and keeping a diary every two or three days to keep track of their eating habit. Physical activity was measured and encouraged via a pedometer, as walking seemed to be the most likely activity drivers would be ready to engage in. The advice was to aim to walk at least 10,000 steps a day.

'Promotion' Considerations

Promotion is key to help reach and engage as many people of the target group as possible. However, given that the allocated budget was too small to afford use of mass-media, the fallback option was internal/word-of-mouth communication that in many ways can be more effective than broader communication strategies. As with the toolkit, the promotional material was also pre-tested for adequacy and effect. Again, the target group was more keen on engaging with a humorous approach than a patronizing one.

Each pilot site (see 'Place' below) used for reaching the target group also displayed the initiative's posters.

The promotion also included use of reminders through text, letters and phone calls as well as encouraging peer support.

Price

There was no monetary cost to be paid by participants as their involvement was on a voluntary basis. Nevertheless taking part in the programme required time and sustained effort and commitment, and the equivalent sacrifices that participants were willing to forego (e.g., ensuring regular walks could mean missing on some other more enjoyable activities the participants used to undertake). Investigations also threw up some other potential psychological costs, such as perceived source of embarrassment in taking part in the programme. The sacrifices were seen as worthwhile in the light of the long-term benefits that, arguably, allowed more comfort and enjoyment in the long term. Hence a pros and cons analysis would be as shown in Table 9.2.

Such clear listing of the pros and cons of the new lifestyle should prepare better the drivers for the change and minimize discouraging surprises.

Table 9.2 Pros and cons of Get Your Life in Gear campaign

Cons (loss)	*Pros (win) – short or long term*
• Efforts to carry out the new task • Embarrassment in undertaking in such an activity • Loss of free time • Missing out on the usual enjoyable activities (e.g., watching TV)	• More quality time with family • Increased energy • Being more in control • Peace of mind and less worries about health problems • Feel-good factor • Long-term/more lasting benefits • Reduced symptoms of ill health

Place

The place dimension needed particular preparation as it is important to reach the target group at a convenient place and time that made it possible to engage with them. The sites used for the campaign were:

• Dockland distribution centre in Belfast (Mondays and Tuesdays from 5am to 10pm).
• Service station of docklands area of Belfast (Wednesdays, Thursdays and Fridays from 6am to 3pm).
• Service station with restaurant outside Dublin (Tuesdays, Wednesdays and Thursdays from 5pm to 10pm).

The above sites were chosen as the preliminary investigation showed that they were most appropriate to engage with the target group. In particular, the site managers were happy to lend a helping hand in informing drivers about health checks. The sites also benefitted from a most welcome support from project champions in the form of employees who were committed to the project and were leading by example and offered an effective partner in persuading drivers about the importance of engaging in the initiative.

Step 9: Implementation (the Campaign)

The implementation of the campaign involved two main stages:

Stage one: At this stage, issues such as planning, recruitment of contributors to the project, setting up of committees as well as testing of material took place.

Stage two: Recruitment posters and leaflets were distributed two weeks before the launch. At the launch there was onsite recruitment supported by questionnaires, 30-minute health checks, lifestyle advice and an introduction to programme. Following the launch, those recruited were supported with motivational text messaging on a weekly basis; and six weeks later, a letter was sent to participants to motivate them, remind them about the follow-up 12-weeks health check, offer advice and provide a new lifestyle questionnaire.

These two stages involved some variations between implementation in Northern Ireland and the Republic of Ireland (ROI) depending on timing and available resources (e.g., in the ROI, a dietician was involved).

Step 10: Resources

The implementation required the support of several partners including:

- Safefood, the funding agency, which managed the coordination of all partnership activities supported by its internal advisory group.
- The Irish Heart Foundation.
- Truck drivers that advised on the project.
- Agency workers.
- Pilot site managers.
- Numerous representatives of organizations with expertise in in the areas of obesity, men's health, occupational health and communications. The role of these contributors was key in advising the project's steering group.

The programme also benefitted from several academic contributions that supported its development. Obviously the above statement is quite broad and any project would need to unpack the actual contributions from each supporter.

Step 11: Monitoring and Evaluation (Process and Outcomes)

As stated above, the monitoring was meant to be primarily undertaken via contrasting the results of the two evaluations undertaken, first, at the recruitment stage and, last, 12 weeks later to measure the effect of the change of lifestyle.

The results in terms of effectiveness were derived from Alves and Vázquez (2013) who at the onset highlighted the difficulty in undertaking a proper follow-up evaluation (i.e., 12 weeks later) given the heavy driving schedules that prevented the majority of the target group from returning for the follow-up check-up. Nevertheless, the project workers did what they could to follow up with phone calls and the following picture emerged:

- There was a clear positive behaviour change, although the responses indicated there was still some way to go before reaching desired physical activity guideline recommendations.
- The amount of snacking reduced as many drivers were reluctant to eat snacks three times a day and more drivers managed to avoid them completely.
- Despite the indefinite nature of the results, there were clear indications that drivers were intent to continue in their efforts to adopt healthier lifestyles despite significant challenges. As an example, a driver expressed regrets that he happened to be driving through an icy area that temporarily prevented him from pursuing his healthy lifestyle. He went for a second health check to help maintain his commitment to the programme.

As suggested in the last point, the second health check was also an opportunity to further motivate the drivers and even consider other measures in addition to the original aims. This was made possible given that this second time, drivers spent more than an hour with the nurse (double the time allowed for the initial health check). Among the extra advice provided to the drivers included referral to a GP if one or more cardiovascular symptoms were observed. Another area thrown up at the second evaluation was that of mental health. This should not be surprising, as any radical change to one's lifestyle is bound to bring up some mental and emotional issues that may explain some of the triggers or maintenance causes that contributed to the self-destructive lifestyle. Drivers at times broke down or even expressed suicidal tendencies. Such cases were not only given the opportunity to discuss their problems with the nurse but were also referred to relevant support services such as counselling. The mental health issues were not isolated cases as some of the project workers who made follow-up phone calls to invite drivers to carry out the second health check found out. Six lost their jobs and there were a number who were admitted for alcoholism and emotional problems.

General Comments

The above example was meant to provide a broad feel to the issue of adopting a systematic SM approach to a real problem, using the derived model in Chapter 7, while allowing flexibility that may be necessary depending on the context being dealt with. For example the above scheme seemed to focus on the restricted 'traditional' version of the marketing mix. So it overtly tackled the 4 Ps, although it also addressed the remaining 3 Ps indirectly. Hence adopting a 4 Ps as opposed to a 7 Ps perspective may be more based on presentational justifications than lack of information. To illustrate, in the above example the 'partner dimension' or 'social/family influences' could easily fit within the 'people' aspect of the 7 Ps, even though it was presented as part of the 'resources' dimension. Nevertheless, verifying systematically all elements of the 7 Ps may help ensure no significant dimension has been overlooked even if the report structure may decide to present the information in terms of just the 4 Ps. Additionally, and as highlighted in Step 8 above and, earlier, in Chapter 7, SM practitioners should consider adopting SM-specific marketing mix models. A number of such alternatives were listed. The SM practitioners may select among the models according to a set of principles that may include relevance, clarity, simplicity, comprehensiveness, etc. In line with the chosen principles, they may go for any of the following marketing mix options:

1. Select *one* of the existing SM marketing mix models.
2. Select a *composite model* that may combine more than one of the existing models or, alternatively, the derived model may be a combination of one or more existing models with adjustments introduced by the practitioners to serve their specific needs.

3. Create a *completely new* marketing mix to serve the specific purposes of the practitioner's project (suggesting that none of the other options are adequate).

It is clear that despite a well-established marketing tradition to monitor the outcome of any marketing initiative, usually based on SMART objectives, this example demonstrates that such monitoring may not always be easy to carry out. Indeed, the complexity of the problem and the multiplicity of factors affecting the beneficiaries of the programme, not to mention the ethical dimensions associated with trying to formally implement a rigorous marketing approach, may prevent an accurate, if not regular, monitoring. Of course this does not mean such projects should not be undertaken. Rather it means that social marketers should relentlessly look for new creative, unobtrusive measures that interfere as little as possible with the life of the beneficiaries of the programme while at the same time presenting a very rigorous strategy.

The above results have clearly highlighted the complexity of factors affecting the obesity issue and the dangers of oversimplification. Given the seriousness of some of the reactions (e.g., being admitted for serious mental and emotional problems including addiction) and the potential for lawsuit liabilities from taking part in the programme, it is important that such future programmes ensure adequate resources are available (to minimize 'adverse effect' or unforeseen reactions) as well as preventative measures to minimize lawsuits especially as, despite all the good intentions and, arguably, the predominant benefits over costs (financial, domestic, social, physical and emotional), one may never be sure about potential consequences. Actually the issue of lawsuits is a case in point since professional counsellors and psychotherapists are expected to prepare against possible lawsuits. Given the higher probability of these lawsuits in a discipline (SM) that potentially may reach millions of people, the issue becomes even more pressing.

As stated at the outset of this chapter, the selection of the truck driver example was not made because the example was particularly successful. Indeed, there are countless examples of SM projects that demonstrated more substantial, if not outstanding, results. Rather, it was selected partly because of the richness of the available information and to highlight the complexity of the intervening factors. Nevertheless, we feel that this project has been quite successful in its aims taking into consideration the limited amount of resources available to it. Clearly any other project with similar aims would benefit greatly from capitalising on the learning of this project. It is possible that another project may come up with some creative ideas to achieve wider and more involving reach through say "guerrilla marketing", more counselling support, more options associated with exercise activities or more availability of access to support.

Ultimately the effect of such programmes may never be adequately measured as they affect individuals who, in turn, affect others until such influence becomes so pervasive that it may affect society and its cultural make-up, thus reflecting another case of the butterfly effect.

10   The Way Forward

The Promise

We covered a lot of ground since introducing SM in Chapter 1. I hope, as a reader, you are by now convinced about the promise that such a discipline offers or, at least, have become enthused enough to find out more.

Perhaps if you are put off by the name then feel free to adopt another one ('a rose by any other name…'). A few have already been suggested, including 'social causal marketing', 'social healing and emancipation strategies', 'communities healing theory and practice'. Perhaps one of my favourites in terms of clarity and social focus is 'social cause marketing' (a slight variation from the one put forward by Kotler). It is clear that all may have restrictive associations. Other contenders, possibly with an entrepreneurial slant, could also include 'responsible entrepreneurship', 'value-based entrepreneurship', 'inclusive/360° entrepreneurship' or 'social cause entrepreneurship'. These titles drop altogether any reference to the word 'marketing' and replace it with 'entrepreneurship' (very loosely applied) as the latter is arguably not only broader in scope but also more result-focused. Indeed, as argued below, a marketing perspective, 'to serve the needs and wants of customers', may not always be helpful if those needs and wants are self-, socially or environmentally destructive. These titles are different from what has come to be known as 'social entrepreneurship' that generally refers to the initiatives of people who set up organizations with a particular social aim (Bornstein and Davis, 2010). The difference is clear: SM or, say, social value based entrepreneurship would not exclusively apply to the task of developing enterprises that serve a social cause. Rather it refers to any initiative or project, irrespective of how small it is, with the overriding purpose to address a social ill (current or potential). It also assumes that such initiatives are informed by the latest wisdom of the supporting social disciplines, including best (social) marketing practice. As suggested earlier, if you have other ideas, feel free to share them (see my email address at the end of this chapter).

Although we mentioned many areas that may benefit from adopting the principles of SM, those areas are by no means exhaustive. In principle, any social ill may benefit from this young discipline. Despite the good work of many pioneers of the field, many of whom are mentioned in this book, we feel that there are still many areas yet to be tackled by SM, including corruption, lack of confidence in one's culture, social integration (local or global level), social responsibility or social entrepreneurship, to mention just a few. Theoretically, all issues tackled by psychology or sociology have the potential to be addressed or supported by social marketing.

As argued earlier, many of the social ills cannot be tackled unilaterally and simplistically as such a perspective would be, at best, misguided if it undermines legitimate demands of disadvantaged groups. We already mentioned the example based on the recent 'Je suis Charlie' ('I am Charlie') event following a terrorist attack on a French magazine (*Charlie Hebdo*) that took place in early 2015. The event led to tragic consequences condemned by most nations from all parties and beliefs. There was a lot of grief and with a view to strengthening the unity of the French people, a day of protest was organized with an unfortunate rallying motto ('Je suis Charlie'). As argued earlier, this motto tacitly assumes winners and losers rather than aiming to create a genuine solidarity that strengthens the ties between all parts of society. Commenting on the motto, a friend stated 'I may be *Le Figaro*, *Le Monde* or any other newspaper but definitely not *Charlie Hebdo*. So how can they expect me to ally myself to a magazine that continuously insulted me or my culture for many years?'. Yes of course there will be people who still support this approach as they say it is about the principle of free speech rather than forced conversion to a worldview. Nevertheless, many who had been hurt over the years by unbridled 'free speech' thought otherwise and although they were completely against the terrorist act, they nevertheless thought they were victims too. For those who invoke the famous adage 'I do not agree with what you have to say, but I'll defend to the death your right to say it', such a statement does not imply taking part in a march that chants 'Je suis Charlie'. If anything, the use of such an example is a plea not to alienate further groups of a community who could be strong partners in finding a solution.

The attitude portrayed above is not new, as reflected by some politicians and newspaper when commenting on the later terrible and tragic events in Paris in November 2015. Some politicians stated that this was the 'worst massacre since World War II' (e.g., Mallett-Outtrim, 2015), when actually it was the worst massacre since 1961, when more than 200 Algerians were brutally murdered in Paris for protesting against French colonialism and abuse in Algeria and supporting Algeria's independence movement.

Rightly, politicians have been talking about soft power and fighting erroneous ideology and misrepresentation of religions, but how can they claim the high ground if they are themselves unwilling to question their deeply ingrained discriminatory ideologies and core beliefs about the respective values of different human beings? If they don't change, they will simply be seen as confirming the view that yet here is another case of dominant powers using self-serving narratives to suit their strategic neo-colonial aims, rather than genuine egalitarian, fraternal ideology leading to genuine liberty, to borrow the three principles proclaimed by French revolutionaries. Mallett-Outtrim (2015) summarized the core beliefs as follows:

When comparing reactions to the 1961 and 2015 massacres, it's hard to avoid few basic facts: one tragedy was about the West being attacked, the other was about Arabs being attacked. One massacre stopped the world, while the other remains almost forgotten in our collective psyche.

(Mallett-Outtrim, 2015)

Social and environmental responsibilities could also become targets of SM programmes. Take the fact that 50 per cent of Americans, the richest nation on earth, are poor (Klein, 2015) and we are not even talking about the less wealthy nations. Is there a surprise that there are conflicts in the world? Yes, everybody states publicly that they don't condone violence but what are they doing about it when clear injustice continues to be inflicted on the majority of people in the name of freedom? Summers and Balls – Emeritus Professor at Harvard University and former US Treasury Secretary, and Shadow Chancellor of the Exchequer respectively – were unequivocal about the consequences when considering the issue of democracy in the face of exclusive prosperity:

When democratic governments and market systems cannot deliver such prosperity to their citizens, the result is political alienation, a loss of social trust, and increasing conflict across the lines of race, class, and ethnicity. Inclusive prosperity nurtures tolerance, harmony, social generosity, optimism, and international cooperation. And these are essential for democracy itself.

(Summers and Balls, 2015)

Democracy has also to apply to all spheres of human endeavours and not just at economic levels if it is to be successful because, as we have seen, these spheres are interrelated. Indeed what is institutional racism if not racism that may be legally banned but still pervasive because of entrenched attitudes within society that remain unchallenged by the leaders of that society bar some tokenistic gesturing for the cameras?

SM teaches us that like all other sciences, we have to consider the events as symptoms that can be addressed systematically and effectively by considering all their contributing dimensions and when problems take place in a society it usually means that everybody contributed to that situation and everybody has a responsibility to do something about it. We stated that an event generally is affected by and in turns affects economic, social, political (including geopolitical), psychological, historical and legal dimensions, to mention just a few. We know that generally people do not want to be lumbered with complex situations and want simple answers. Although this type of attitude is patronizing, it can also be very damaging to the integration of society creating a 'them and us'. It is ironic that this same society is on a daily basis subjected to Hollywood-style plots that certainly do not lack in complexity. SM teaches us that whether we are dealing with dieting, domestic violence or terrorism, the approach should be as inclusive as possible. Anybody that tries to provide a simpler picture is either deluded or has some irresponsible, at least in the long-term, invested interests they are trying to serve.

We mentioned above that any social ill may benefit from SM. However, SM can also be supported by proactive (as opposed to reactive) human-condition-enhancing enterprises. Such enterprises may include encouraging social entrepreneurship or simply developing a 'happier yet inclusive society'.

Marketing, and by extension capitalism, when adopted responsibly, seems to offer a better model at serving human nature (and the economy) than perhaps offered by other disciplines, as long as its primary focus is 'enlightened self-interest' that takes into account social needs rather than exclusively focusing on short-term profit. Indeed, the very existence of a sustainable capitalistic society depends on supporting the consumers by ensuring they have the means to continue consuming the products provided by the capitalistic system (Kotler, 2015). Marketing focus is human purpose. Marketers ask 'what are the needs of my clients and what makes them tick?' They then proceed to identify through research what attracts them and aim to set up a programme for fulfilling those needs profitably. Even the word 'profitably' can assume different meanings. If we talk about 'enlightened marketing' we may not even talk about SM since all marketing initiatives will assume benign and constructive aims. Nevertheless, social marketing would relegate the 'commercial profitability' to a lower degree of importance as its aim and recurrent associated question is 'how can we help people change for the better?'. The aim is simply unadulterated 'social good'. The question still remains 'who will pay for the social good?' The response is 'everyone'. Just like looking after the environment should be part of any enlightened company, as the destruction of the environment would ultimately affect us all, social responsibility affects us all in the long term, but in many cases in the short term too. In this era of global consequences, it is becoming increasingly clear to all why good business is responsible business for reputational (Cornelissen, 2014) and survival reasons.

We spoke at the start of this book about certain issues such as Arab Spring, WikiLeaks, Big Society and Occupy Wall Street. SM could become a source of philosophical, practical and social change. It offers a less brutal, yet more effective modern-day way of producing revolutionary changes in human societies where what is right or wrong is soberly researched and painstakingly scrutinized through involvement of all stakeholders with the view to maximize benefits to all parts of society.

The revolutionary changes can be initiated by a government that wants to be effective or a people who feel that government is not effective. Ideally, a responsible government should proactively look for opportunities for improvement to the lot of its people. Unfortunately this is rarely done, as somehow those in authority tend to naively ignore the legitimate demands of the people for the benefit of short-term expediency and run the risk of insurgency that may lead to civil wars, as demonstrated over the past few years

in several parts of the Middle East, where what started with peaceful pro-
tests ended in all-out civil war and destruction for all concerned. SM, wisely
applied, can offer a valuable tool for pre-empting such destruction. However,
this is not about taking sides with tyrant regimes that have yet another 'card'
in their hands to 'control the people' and continue running the show. In this
day of free information flows, people can easily see through such stratagems
and the consequences can be dire if trust is lost, as there may be no second
chance for the abuser of power.

There is a point of convergence where individual, national and international aims meet. Part of the aims of SM is to assess an 'unhealthy' situation and identify alternative scenarios and means to achieve the most healthy
alternative. In trying to do so, it looks for enticing options or at least enticing arguments that can galvanize people for life and offer them pleasure and
worthwhile reasons in the most challenging circumstances.

As demonstrated in this book, one of the great gurus of marketing (and
social marketing), Philip Kotler, considered ways in which the principles of
SM can help address the causes of wars and terrorism. Arguments have been
put forward about existence of knowledge and procedures not only in marketing but other disciplines that may provide valuable information about causes
of wars. This is a long way from using marketing to sell toothpaste. It moved
on to applying these techniques to help with hygiene and social responsibility
but now it seems to be moving to a much higher purpose: bringing humanity together to provide a healthier peaceful future. At this stage we may not
have reached the level of marketing as a tool to help sell 'brotherhood of
men', but at least we're promoting mutual respect. As a marketer would do,
Kotler recommends working closely with all stakeholders ('customers') to
understand the various perspectives and act accordingly. So it may be time
to bury the 'them against us' arguments, as we all live in one world and the
consequences of such an approach are all too obvious to see. Perhaps it is
high time to aim for a genuine 'them *with* us'. Is there any sustainable option
but to work together at times when any missed opportunity can bring closer a
bigger humanitarian disaster?

Perhaps another key thread that runs throughout the SM enterprise is
ethical consciousness. Indeed, although marketing is a key dimension of
the SM approach, its commercial philosophy (maximizing profit) is a far
cry from the tacit SM value of social responsibility, even if targets of a programme may insist that they are happy with their condition and they do not
want any help. To do anything directly or indirectly against the 'will' of the
people would be anathema to a liberal democratic outlook. This is a tough
and sensitive issue that is not easy to address. Consider somebody who
clearly has an alcohol dependency problem and would not consider giving
up alcohol because they do not see it as a problem or because it makes them
happy. They would 'rather live a short life with alcohol [or any addictive life-
style] than a long but "unhappy" life'. Obviously such rationalizations have
not only been observed when dealing with clinical psychological settings but

are actually used daily by people with huge responsibilities (e.g., country leaders) for the sake of expediency. To address such dilemmas, we could refer to philosophical principles of freedom and refrain from doing anything, or we could refer to a philosophy of basic rights and capabilities (e.g., Sen, 1999; Haq, 1995; Nussbaum, 2000; Adolf, 2009), which would clearly require among its first precepts life and bodily health (Nussbaum, 2000). Sticking with the alcoholic example, the latter approach would also be supported by psychotherapeutic clinical experience that shows that those who manage to recover after sustained therapy mostly report a more worthwhile and fulfilled life than those who remain addicted. This is why the adage that 'the aim of business is to meet the expressed needs of clients' may not always be adequate, as we know that some of those 'needs' are self-destructive or, at best, unhealthy.

There is also a broader perspective to this argument. At an organizational level or even country level, such 'needs' may be developed through the use of well-developed marketing communication strategies. Communication is at the heart of developing our identities. With enough resources being thrown at a particular worldview, it would be possible to create a 'them and us' type of view that can have disastrous effects for us and our children. At the simplest level, such outcome can be the result of repeated messages expressed by influential people either under duress (economic, social or otherwise) or ignorance regarding alternatives to current plight. Indeed, the media proffers daily insults on people's intelligence by offering truncated points of view on history (or general events) that may be decontextualized and devoid of evidence; yet its owners expect – and, unfortunately, tend to get – 'converted' voices because of the laws of probability, if nothing else. This is perhaps one of the biggest anomalies of the power of marketing communications that can make a farce of the concept of democracy.

There is no lack of examples of the disastrous results reflected in the 'them and us' ideology as demonstrated in many places around the world over recent human history, ranging from the 'killing fields' of Cambodia, Rwanda, Auschwitz, Katyń, French Algeria, the Gulags, Iraq, Syria, Bosnia, Grozny, to the more recent wanton destruction of homes and ruthless killing of children in Gaza or the inhuman bomb destructions caused by senseless killings in heavily populated areas as seen throughout the Middle East. If we extend the list to earlier periods then it could include decimations of whole communities such as native populations in the Americas, Africa or Australia. Such crimes were perpetrated by humans against other humans under all sorts of manufactured pretences and definite broad-brush tarnishing of entire populations. Despite the obvious destruction endured by the victims, one must not forget the well-documented argument that when a human being humiliates or abuses another human being, this also leaves an indelible mark in the abuser.

There is nothing new about highlighting the power of marketing and its methods of persuasion in the light of both anecdotal and factual evidence including its harmful effects in creating materialistic overconsuming societies that equate happiness with material wealth. The good news, as has been argued throughout this book, is that such power can be harnessed for the good of man to help break the spirals of violence and counter-violence and develop happier societies. If nothing else, responsible societies should routinely expose the stealth community-integration destructive communication in all contexts, and certainly through enlisting our educational institutions, to guard against its short- or long-term destructive effects and, consequently, encourage more genuine democracy that minimizes cynical crowd manipulation. As a starter, it would be akin to blatant irresponsibility if any programme of business education did not include integrating ethical considerations as part of evaluating the value of any business model irrespective of how creative it may be. Given that success is a socially constructed concept, the leaders of our society should assume their responsibilities in 'educating' our communities to value success not only in terms of the size of bank accounts, but also in terms of how much contribution has been made to bringing our communities together (despite historical differences) and promoting their happiness. Our global world is here to stay. This calls for a global approach to values, ethics and mutual relationships. In this sense, SM offers a 'science' with a soul that puts values before profit. So far our institutions have tended to be reactive and only act if the effects are clear. As a case in point, witness the increasing number of international agreements associated with reducing global pollution, thereby slowing global warming. If, in the first place, our societies and communities supported each other to avoid global 'human values pollution', perhaps the actual environmental pollution would have been reduced much earlier and well before the witnessing of disasters.

Clearly it may take a long time for many communities to learn to trust each other but the sooner one starts the earlier one may get to the 'promised land'. Perhaps in the first instance, international organizations such as the EU, UNESCO or World Bank could multiply efforts in supporting projects to help develop bridges across communities so as to allow them to see the possibilities for healing and mutual support. Such an approach should benefit all parties, oppressed (Freire, 1970; Redeker, 2007; Bandura et al., 1975) and oppressors (Wing Sue and Rivera, 2011), and help heal them internally and externally.

Right at the beginning of this book we highlighted the USP of SM and, consequently, this book, arguing that many people talk about problems with our societies such as greed, abuse, obesity, discrimination, persecutions, terrorism, etc. without offering any practical way forward. This book goes beyond the identification of the problems but presents a developing discipline with tested tools for providing solutions to human ills. As demonstrated throughout history, effective tools can be used for 'selling' bad products, services or ideas etc. But they also can be used for making a difference to millions of people around the world. The tools have been developed through deriving insights from several sciences. They are presented here to be made available to as many people as possible to help make the world a better place.

Finally, and especially if you managed to go through the whole book, I would like to thank you for sharing this journey with me. I know different people go through a book differently. Some may dip in and out depending on the need, while others can read it from cover to cover in a single sitting. Whatever your approach is, I hope you found it useful and, with some luck, it may even have helped inspire you to pursue some of the ideas therein. If you would like to share your views about how to develop or further the ideas discussed in this book I would very much like to hear them. Feel free to address them to chahidfourali@learning4good.co.uk. I will aim to address as many as possible.

References

Adler, P.S. and Kwon, S.W. (2002) Social capital: prospects for a new concept, *Academy of Management Review*, 27, 17–40.

Adolf, A. (2009) *Peace: A World History*, Cambridge: Polity Press.

Ainslie, G. and Monterosso, J. (2003) Hyperbolic discounting as a factor in addiction: a critical analysis, in R.E. Vuchinich and N. Heather (eds.), *Choice, Behavioural Economics and Addiction*, Amsterdam: Pergamon, pp. 35–48.

Ajzen, I. (1991) The theory of planned behaviour, *Organizational Behavior and Human Decision Processes*, 50, 179–211.

Alves, H. and Vázquez, J.L. (2013) *Best Practices in Marketing and their Impact on Quality of Life*, Berlin: Springer-Verlag.

Andreasen, A. (1972) *Improving Inner City Marketing*, Chicago: American Marketing Association.

Andreasen, A. (1995) *Marketing Social Change: Changing Behavior to Promote Health, Social Development, and the Environment*, San Francisco, CA: Jossey-Bass.

Andreasen, A. (2002) Marketing social marketing in the social change marketplace, *Journal of Public Policy Marketing*, 21(1), 3–13.

Andreasen, A. (2006) *Social Marketing in the 21st Century*, Thousand Oaks, CA: Sage.

Andreotti, V. (2011) *Actionable Postcolonial Theory in Education*, New York and London: Palgrave Macmillan.

AMA (2013) *Statement of Ethics*, www.marketingpower.com/AboutAMA/Pages/Statement%20of%20Ethics.aspx (accessed 3 January 2014).

AMA (2016) *About Marketing*, www.ama.org/AboutAMA/Pages/Definition-of-Marketing.aspx (accessed 20 March 2016).

Apostolopoulos, Y., Sönmez, S., Shattell, M., Strack, R., Haldeman, L. and Jones, V. (2011) Barriers to truck drivers' healthy eating: environmental influences and health promotion strategies, *Journal of Workplace Behavioral Health*, 26(2), 122–147.

Argyris, C. (2004) *Reasons and Rationalizations: The Limits to Organizational Knowledge*, Oxford: Oxford University Press.

Argyris, C. and Schon, D. (1978) *Organisational Learning: A Theory of Action Perspective*, Reading, MA: Addison Wesley.

Argyris, C., Putnam, R. and McLain Smith, D. (1985) *Action Science, Concepts, Methods, and Skills for Research and Intervention*, San Francisco: Jossey-Bass.

Armenakis, A.A. and Harris, S.G. (2009) Reflections: our journey in organizational change research and practice, *Journal of Change Management*, 9, 127–142.

Bagozzi, R. (1975) Marketing and exchange, *Journal of Marketing*, 39, 32–39.

Bagozzi, R. (1978) Marketing as exchange, *American Behavioural Scientist*, 21, 535–536.

Baines, P., Fill, C. and Page, K. (2008) *Marketing*, Oxford: Oxford University Press.

Baker, T.E., Stockwell, T., Barnes, G. and Holroyd, C.B. (2011) Individual differences in substance dependence: at the intersection of brain, behaviour and cognition, *Addiction Biology*, 16, 458–466.

Bandura, A. (1977) Self-efficacy: toward a unifying theory of behavioral change, *Psychological Review*, 84, 191–215.

Bandura, A., Underwood, B. and Fromson, M.E. (1975) Disinhibition of aggression through diffusion of responsibility and dehumanization of victims, *Journal of Research in Personality*, 9(4), 253–269.

Barratt, R. (2006) *Building a Values-Driven Organization: A Whole System Approach to Cultural Transformation*, Oxford: Butterworth-Heinemann.

Bassey, M. (1999) *Case Study Research in Educational Settings*, Buckingham: Open University Press.

Bate, P., Bevan, H. and Robert, G. (2004) *Towards a Million Change Agents: A Review of the Social Movements Literature: Implications for Large Scale Change in the NHS*, London: NHS Modernisation Agency, http://discovery.ucl.ac.uk/1133/1/million.pdf (accessed 8 March 2016).

Beck, U. (2001) *Individualization*, London: Sage.

Bentall, R.P. (2003) *Madness Explained: Psychosis and Human Nature*, London: Penguin.

Berridge, K.C., Robinson, T.E. and Aldridge, J.W. (2009) Dissecting components of reward: 'liking', 'wanting', and learning, *Current Opinion in Pharmacology*, 9, 65–73.

Blaszczynski, A. and Nower, L. (2002) A pathways model of problem and pathological gambling, *Addiction*, 97, 487–499.

Bloom, P.N. and Novelli, W.D. (1981) Problems and challenges in social marketing, *Journal of Marketing*, 45, 79–88.

Blume, A.W. and Schmaling, K.B. (1996) Loss and readiness to change substance abuse, *Addictive Behaviors*, 21, 527–530.

Blumer, H. (1969) *Symbolic Interactionism*, Englewood Cliffs, NJ: Transition.

Borg, I. (2005) *Facet Theory: Encyclopedia of Statistics in Behavioral Science*, Chichester: Wiley.

Borland, R., Young, D., Coghill, K. and Zhang, J.Y. (2010) The tobacco use management system: analyzing tobacco control from a systems perspective, *American Journal of Public Health*, 100, 1229–1236.

Bornstein, D. and Davis, S. (2010) *Social Entrepreneurship: What Everyone Needs to Know*, London: Oxford University Press.

Bourdieu, P. (1986) The forms of capital, in J.G. Richardson (ed.), *Handbook of Theory and Research for the Sociology of Education*, New York: Greenwood.

Bowman, C. (1990) *The Essence of Strategic Management*, London: Prentice Hall.

Brassington, F. and Pettitt, S. (2006) *Principles of Marketing*, 4th edn, Harlow: Prentice Hall.

Brewer, J.A. and Potenza, M.N. (2008) The neurobiology and genetics of impulse control disorders: relationships to drug addictions, *Biochemical Pharmacology*, 75, 63–75.

Bronfenbrenner, U. (1979) *The Ecology of Human Development*, Cambridge, MA: Harvard University Press.

Brown, D.E. (1991) *Human Universals*, New York: McGraw-Hill.

Brown, J.M. (2011) Facet theory and multi-dimensional scaling methods, in K. Sheldon, J. Davies and K. Howells (eds.), *Research in Practice for Forensic Professionals*, London: Sage, pp. 60–85.

Brown, S. and Sleath, E. (2015) *Research Methods for Forensic Psychologists: A Guide to Completing Your Research Project*, London: Routledge.

Buci-Glucksmann, C. (1985) La Postmodernité: In Dix ans de Philosophie en France, *Magazine Littéraire*, 225 (December).

Burrell, G. and Morgan, G. (1979) *Sociological Paradigms and Organizational Analysis: Elements of the Sociology of Corporate Life*, London: Heinemann.

Butler, A.C., Chapman, J.E., Forman, E.M. and Beck, A.T. (2006) The empirical status of cognitive-behavioral therapy: a review of meta-analyses, *Clinical Psychology Review*, 26, 17–31.

Campbell, D.J. and Campbell, K.M. (2009) Embracing change: further examination of a 'capabilities and benevolence' beliefs model in a military sample, *Military Psychology*, 21, 351–364.

Carson, T. and Sumara, D. (1997) *Action Research as a Living Practice*, New York: Peter Lang.

Cawley, J., Markowitz, S. and Tauras, J. (2004) Lighting up and slimming down: the effects of body weight and cigarette prices on adolescent smoking initiation, *Journal of Health Economics*, 23, 293–311.

CDC (2013) www.cdc.gov/nccdphp/dnpao/socialmarketing/index.html (accessed 13 April 2013).

Chaffey, D., Chadwick, E., Mayer R. and Johnston, K. (2009) *Internet Marketing: Strategy, Implementation and Practice*, 4th edn, Harlow: Pearson.

Chamberlain, K. (2000) Methodolatry and qualitative health research, *Journal of Health Psychology*, 5(3), 285–296.

Chambers, R. (2000) Us and them: finding a new paradigm for professionals in sustainable development, in D. Warburton (ed.), *Community and Sustainable Development*, London: Earthscan, pp. 116–147.

Chapman, S. (2015) *Social Marketing and a Total Market Approach: Performance Measures*, http://tcp-events.co.uk/wsmc/downloads/breakouts/Tuesday/1200/Assessment%20&%20SM%20Theory/S%20Chapman.pdf (accessed on 16 May 2015).

Chartrand, T.L. and Bargh, J.A. (1999) The chameleon effect: the perception–behavior link and social interaction, *Journal of Personality and Social Psychology*, 76(6), 893–910.

Chassany, A.-S. (2015) Lunch with the FT: Thomas Piketty, *Financial Times*, www.ft.com/cms/s/0/7ca6cfc2-1b39-11e5-a130-2e7db721f996.html (accessed 8 July 2015).

Cheng, H., Kotler, P. and Lee, N. (2011) *Social Marketing for Public Health: Global Trends and Success Stories*, London: Jones and Bartlett.

Chevalier, J.M. and Buckles, D.J. (2013a) *Participatory Action Research: Theory and Methods for Engaged Inquiry*, London: Routledge.

Chevalier, J.M. and Buckles, D.J. (2013b) *Handbook for Participatory Action Research, Planning and Evaluation*, Ottawa: SAS2 Dialogue.

Cialdini, R.B. (1984) *Influence: The Psychology of Persuasion*, New York: Morrow.

CIM (2016) *What is Marketing?*, www.cim.co.uk/more/getin2marketing/what-is-marketing (accessed 20 March 2016).

Cirksena, M.K. and Flora, J. (1995) Audience segmentation in workplace health promotion: a procedure using social marketing, *Health Education Research*, 10, 211–224.

Cochrane, F. (2008) *Ending Wars*, Cambridge: Polity.

Colby, A. and Kohlberg, L. (1987) *The Measurement of Moral Judgment Vol. 2: Standard Issue Scoring Manual*, Cambridge: Cambridge University Press.

Collinson, D. (2012) Prozac leadership and the limits of positive thinking, *Leadership*, 8(2), 87–107.

Collinson, D. (2014) US ideas have a disproportionate influence on business schools, *Financial Times*, www.ft.com/cms/s/2/50709c4c-f7a6-11e3-90fa-00144feabdc0.html (accessed 7 July 2014).

Commission on Social Determinants of Health (2008) *CSDH Final Report: Closing the Gap in a Generation: Health Equity Through Action on the Social Determinants of Health*, Geneva: World Health Organization.

Community Guide (2015) *Health Communication and Social Marketing: Health Communication Campaigns That Include Mass Media and Health-Related Product Distribution*, www.thecommunityguide.org/healthcommunication/campaigns.html (accessed 10 July 2015).

Cooper, M.L., Frone, M.R., Russell, M. and Mudar, P. (1995) Drinking to regulate positive and negative emotions: a motivational model of alcohol use, *Journal of Personality and Social Psychology*, 69, 990–1005.

Cornelissen, J. (2014) *Corporate Communication: A Guide to Theory and Practice*, 4th edn, Thousand Oaks, CA: Sage.

Creswell, J.W. (2007) *Qualitative Inquiry & Research: Choosing Among Five Traditions*, Thousand Oaks, CA: Sage.

Crompton, T. (2008) *Weathercocks and Signposts: The Environment Movement at a Crossroads*, http://wwf.org.uk/strategiesforchange (accessed 14 November 2009).

Dann, S. (2009) *Redefining Social Marketing*, First World Social Marketing Conference, Brighton, UK.

Davidson, H. (2002), *The Committed Enterprise: How to Make Vision and Values Work*, Oxford: Butterworth Heinemann.

Davison, R.M., Martinsons, M.G. and Kock, N. (2004) Principles of canonical action research, *Information Systems Journal*, 14(1), 65–86.

Dawkins, R. (2006) *The God Delusion*, New York: Bantam Press.

Day, L.A. (2006) *Ethics in Media Communications: Cases and Controversies*, 5th edn, Belmont, CA: Wadsworth/Thomson Learning.

Denzin, N. and Lincoln, Y. (1994) *Handbook of Qualitative Research*, London: Sage.

Derrida, J. (1988) Afterword, in *Limited, Inc.*, Evanston, IL: Northwestern University Press.

de Savigny, D. and Adam, T. (2009) *Systems Thinking for Health Systems*, Geneva: World Health Organization.

De Souza, P. and Ciclitiva, K.E. (2005) Men and dieting: a qualitative analysis, *Journal of Health Psychology*, 10(6): 794–804.

Dev, C.S. and Schultz, D.E. (2005) A customer focused approach can bring the current marketing mix into the 21st century, *Marketing Management*, 14(1), 18–24.

Devos, G., Buelens, M. and Bouckenooghe, D. (2007) Contribution of content, context, and process to understanding openness to organizational change: two experimental simulation studies, *Journal of Social Psychology*, 147, 607–629.

Dibb, S. and Simkin, L. (2008) *Marketing Planning: A Workbook for Marketing Managers*, London: Cengage Learning.

Dibb, S., Simkin, L., Pride, W.M. and Ferrell, O.C. (2006) *Marketing: Concepts and Strategies*, 5th edn, Boston: Houghton Mifflin.

Dick, B. (2004) Action research literature: themes and trends, *Action Research*, 2(4), 425–444.

DiClemente, C. and Prochaska, J. (1998) Toward a comprehensive, transtheoretical model of change, in W. Miller and N. Heather (eds.), *Treating Addictive Behaviours*, New York: Plenum Press.

Donovan, R. and Henley, N. (2010) *Principles and Practice of Social Marketing: An International Perspective*, Cambridge University Press: Cambridge.

Donovan, R. and Vlais, R. (2005). *VicHealth Review of Communication Components of Social Marketing Public Education Campaigns Focusing on Violence Against Women*, Melbourne: Victorian Health Promotion Foundation.

Dowrick, C. (2004) *Beyond Depression: A New Approach to Understanding and Management*, Oxford: Oxford University Press.

Duane, S. and Domegan, C. (2014) Get Your Life in Gear, in G. Hastings and C. Domegan (eds.), *Social Marketing: From Tunes to Symphonies*, Abingdon: Butterworth Heinemann/Elsevier.

ECDC (2014) *Social Marketing Guide for Public Health Managers and Practitioners*, Stockholm: European Centre for Disease Prevention and Control.

Edwards, W. (1961) Behavioral decision theory, *Annual Review of Psychology*, 12, 473–498.

Efron, N. (2013). The Real Reason Why Jews Win So Many Nobel Prizes. www.haaretz.com/opinion/.premium-1.553485 (accessed on 2 May 2016).

Elkington, J. (1998) *Cannibals with Forks: The Triple Bottom Line of 21st Century Business*, Oxford: Capstone.

Elliot, G., Fourali, C. and Issler, S. (2010) *Education and Social Change: Linking Local and Global Perspectives*, London: Continuum.

Elliott, J. (2009) Building educational theory through action research, in B. Somekh and S. Noffke (eds.), *The Sage Handbook of Educational Action Research*, Thousand Oaks, CA: Sage, pp. 28–38.

Ellis, A. (1962) *Reason and Emotion in Psychotherapy*, New York: Lyle Stuart.

Ellis, A. (1994) *Reason and Emotion in Psychotherapy*, revised and updated edition, New York: Birch Lane Press.

Evans, M. and Moutinho, L. (1999) *Contemporary Issues in Marketing*, London: Macmillan Press Ltd.

Everitt, B.J., Belin, D., Economidou, D., Pelloux, Y., Dalley, J.W. and Robbins, T.W. (2008) Neural mechanisms underlying the vulnerability to develop compulsive drug seeking habits and addiction, *Philosophical Transactions of the Royal Society B*, 363(1507), 3125–3135.

Fernandez-Serrano, M.J., Perez-Garcia, M., Perales, J.C. and Verdejo-Garcia, A. (2010) Prevalence of executive dysfunction in cocaine, heroin and alcohol users enrolled in therapeutic communities, *European Journal of Pharmacology*, 626, 104–112.

Fanon, F. (1963) *The Wretched of the Earth*, New York: Grove Press.

Ferrence, R. (2001) Diffusion theory and drug use, *Addiction*, 96, 165–173.

Festinger, L. (1957) *A Theory of Cognitive Dissonance*, Stanford: Stanford University Press.

Feyerabend, P. (1975) *Against Method*, London: Verso.

Field, M. and Cox, W.M. (2008) Attentional bias in addictive behaviors: a review of its development, causes, and consequences, *Drug and Alcohol Dependence*, 97, 1–20.

Flew, A. (2007) *There is a God: How the World's Most Notorious Atheist Changed His Mind*, New York: HarperOne.

Flores, P.J. (2004) *Addiction as an Attachment Disorder*, Lanham, MD: Jason Aronson.

Fourali, C. (1994) *Quality and Equality in Education: A Rejoinder to Anthony Flew*, Oxford: Review of Education.

Fourali, C. (1997) Using fuzzy logic in educational measurement, *Evaluation and Research in Education*, 11(3), 129–148.

Fourali, C. (2000) *Educational Rights: A Discussion Paper for the Research Group, City and Guilds*, unpublished paper.

Fourali, C. (2006) The responsibility of marketing leaders, *The Marketing Leaders*, October.

Fourali, C. (2008) *World-class National Occupational Standards in Social Marketing*. First International Conference on Social Marketing, 29–30 September. Brighton & Hove City, UK.

Fourali, C. (2009a) Developing world-class social marketing standards: a step in the right direction for a more socially responsible marketing profession, *Social Marketing Quarterly*, 15(2), 14–24.

Fourali, C. (2009b) Tackling conflict: a beyond opposites approach, *Counselling Psychology Quarterly*, 22(2), 147–169.

Fourali, C. (2010) Social marketing, in G. Elliot, C. Fourali and S. Issler (eds.), *Education and Social Change: Linking Local and Global Perspectives*, London: Continuum.

Fourali, C. (2014a) *'Traditional' Versus 'Non-Traditional' Research in (Post-Compulsory) Education: A False Dichotomy?* Paper presented at Conference on Post-compulsory research, Oxford University, Manchester Harris College.

Fourali, C. (2014b) Review of 'Human Development and Capabilities – Re-imagining the university of the twenty-first century. Aleyandra Boni and Melanie Walker'. *Widening Participation and Lifelong Learning*, spring.

Fourali, C. (forthcoming) Qualitative research methods: elements of a good design, in R. Benzo, C. Fourali and M. Gad Mohsen (eds.), *Marketing Research Planning and Practice*, London: Sage.

Fox, D. (2008) *Palestinians Under Siege: A Critical Psychology Perspective on Mental Health and Justice*, conference presentation, Siege and Mental Health... Bridges vs. Walls, Gaza Community Mental Health Center's 5th International Conference, Gaza and Ramallah Palestinian National Authority, www.dennisfox.net/papers/siege.html (accessed 10 August 2013).

Fox, D. and Prilleltensky, I. (1997) Introducing critical psychology: values, assumptions, and the status quo, in D. Fox and I. Prilleltensky (eds.), *Critical Psychology: An Introduction*, London: Sage.

Fox, K.F.A. and Kotler, P. (1980) The marketing of social causes: the first ten years, *Journal of Marketing*, 44, 24–33.

Freeman, A., Felgoise, S.H., Nezu, A.M., Nezu, C.M. and Reinecke, M.A. (eds.) (2005) *Encyclopedia of Cognitive Behavior Therapy*, New York: Springer.

Freire, P. (1970) *Pedagogy of the Oppressed*, New York: Herder & Herder.

French, J. (2011) 'Why nudging is not enough'. *Journal of Social Marketing*, 1 (2): 154–162.

French, J. and Blair-Stevens, C. (2005) *Social Marketing Pocket Guide*, London: National Consumer Council.

French, J. and Blair-Stevens, C. (2010) Using social marketing to develop policy, strategy and operational synergy. In J. French, C. Blair-Stevens, R. Merritt and D. McVey (eds.), *Social Marketing and Public Health: Theory and Practice*, Oxford: Oxford University Press.

French, J. and Gordon, R. (2015) *Strategic Social Marketing*, London: Sage.

French, J. and Russell-Bennett, R. (2015) A hierarchical of social marketing, *Journal of Social Marketing*, 5(2), 139–159.

French, M.T., BrownTaylor, D. and Bluthenthal, R.N. (2006) Price elasticity of demand for malt liquor beer: findings from a US pilot study, *Social Science & Medicine*, 62, 2101–2111.

Frey, R.G. and Wellman, C.H. (2005) *A Companion to Applied Ethics*, Oxford: Blackwell Publishing Ltd.

Fukuyama, F. (1992) *The End of History and the Last Man*, New York: Free Press.

Futrell, C. (2010) *Fundamentals of Selling: Customers for Life Through Service*, London: Irwin/McGraw-Hill.

Galt, K. (2008) *An Introduction to Mixed Methods Research*, Creighton University, http://spahp2.creighton.edu/OfficeOfResearch/share/sharedfiles/UserFiles/file/Galt_MM_slides_CU_092309.pdf (accessed 29 June 2013).

Gardner, H. (2004) *Changing Minds: The Art and Science of Changing Our Own and Other People's Minds*, Cambridge, MA: Harvard Business School Press.

Gardner, H., Csikszentmihalyi, M. and Damon, W. (2001) *Good Work: When Excellence and Ethics Meet*, New York: Basic Books.

Gibbons, F.X., Gerrard, M. and Lane, D.J. (2003) A social-reaction model of adolescent health risk, in J.M. Suls and K.A. Wallston (eds.), *Social Psychological Foundations of Health and Illness*, Oxford: Blackwell, pp. 107–136.

Gibran, K. (2011) *The Prophet*, London: Collectors' Library.

Gill, P.E. and Wijk, K. (2004) Case study of healthy eating interventions for Swedish lorry drivers, *Health Education Research: Theory and Practice*, 19(3), 306–315.

Glenane-Antoniadis, A., Whitwell, G., Bell, S.J. and Menguc, B. (2003) Extending the vision of social marketing through social capital theory: marketing in the context of intricate exchange and market failure, *Marketing Theory*, 3(3), 323–343.

Goldstein, H. (2003) *Multilevel Statistical Models*, 3rd edn, London: Edward Arnold.

Goldstein, N.J., Martin, S.J. and Cialdini, R.B. (2008) *Yes! 50 Secrets from the Science of Persuasion*, New York: Free Press.

Goldstein, R.Z., Volkow, N.D., Wang, G.J., Fowler, J.S. and Rajaram, S. (2001) Addiction changes orbitofrontal gyrus function: involvement in response inhibition, *Neuroreport*, 12, 2595–2599.

Gollwitzer, P.M. (1999) Implementation intentions: strong effects of simple plans, *American Psychologist*, 54, 493–503.

Goodson, S. (2012) *Uprising: How to Build a Brand – and Change the World – by Sparking Cultural Movements*, London: McGraw-Hill.

Gordon, R. (2011) *Critical Social Marketing: Assessing the Cumulative Impact of Alcohol Marketing on Youth Drinking*, PhD thesis, University of Stirling.

Gordon, R. (2012) Re-thinking and re-tooling the social marketing mix, *Australasian Marketing Journal*, 20, 122–126.

Gould, S.J. (1977) *Ontogeny and Phylogeny*, Cambridge MA: Belknap Press of Harvard University Press.

Govier, T. (2002) *A Delicate Balance. What Philosophy Can Tell Us about Terrorism*, Oxford: Westview Press.

Gray D. (2014) *Doing Research in the Real World*, London: Sage.

Gray, M. (1992) *A Dictionary of Literary Terms*, Beirut: York Press.

Guardian (2013) www.guardian.co.uk/world/2013/may/10/noam-chomsky-stephen-hawking-israel-boycott (accessed 21 July 2013).

Guba, E.G. and Lincoln, Y.S. (1994) Competing paradigms in qualitative research, in N.K. Denzin and Y.S. Lincoln (eds.), *Handbook of Qualitative Research*, London: Sage, pp. 105–117.

Habermas, J. (1987) *The Theory of Communicative Action: Volume 2: The Critique of Functionalist Reason*, Oxford: Polity.

Haq, M. (1995) *Reflections on Human Development*, Oxford: Oxford University Press.

Harford, T. (2014) Behavioral economics and public policy, *The Financial Times*, 21 March, www.ft.com/cms/s/2/9d7d31a4-aea8-11e3-aaa6-00144feab7de.html#axzz30 po3p6lE (accessed 8 March 2016).

Harris, P.R., Mayle, K., Mabbott, L. and Napper, L. (2007) Self-affirmation reduces smokers' defensiveness to graphic on-pack cigarette warning labels, *Health Psychology*, 26, 437–446.

Hart, W. (1987) *The Art of Living: Vipassana Meditation as Taught by S.N. Goenka*, New York: HarperCollins.

Hastings, G. (2007) *Social Marketing: Why Should the Devil Have All the Best Tunes?* Abingdon: Butterworth Heinemann.

Hastings, G. (2013) *The Marketing Matrix: How the Corporation Gets its Power – and How We Can Reclaim It*, London: Routledge.

Hastings, G. and Domegan, C. (2014) *Social Marketing: From Tunes to Symphonies*, Abingdon: Butterworth Heinemann/Elsevier.

Hastings, G. and Haywood, A. (1991) Social marketing and communication in health promotion, *Health Promotion International*, 6, 135–145.

Hayes, S.C., Strosahl, K.D. and Wilson, K.G. (1999) *Acceptance and Commitment Therapy: An Experiential Approach to Behavior Change*, New York: Guilford Press.

Health Inequalities Infant Mortality Public Services Agreement (2007) London Department of Health.

Hendershot, C.S., Witkiewitz, K., George, W.H. and Marlatt, G.A. (2011) Relapse prevention for addictive behaviors, *Substance Abuse Treatment, Prevention, and Policy*, 6, 17.

Heron, J. and Reason, P. (1997) A participatory inquiry paradigm, *Qualitative Inquiry*, 3(3), 274–294.

Herscovitch, L. and Meyer, J.P. (2002) Commitment to organizational change: extension of a three-component model, *Journal of Applied Psychology*, 87, 474–487.

Heyes, C. (2011) Automatic imitation, *Psychological Bulletin*, 137, 463–483.

Hill, C. (2011) *Global Business Today*, 6th edn, New York: McGraw-Hill.

Hill, L., O'Sullivan, C. and O'Sullivan, T. (2003) *Creative Arts Marketing*, Abingdon: Butterworth Heinemann.

Hirsch, P.M. and Levin, D.Z. (1999) Umbrella advocates versus validity police: a life cycle model, *Organization Science*, 10(2), 199–212.

Heron, J. and Reason, P. (1997) A participatory inquiry paradigm, *Qualitative Inquiry*, 3(3), 274–294.

Hofmann, S.G., Asnaani, A., Vonk, I.J.J., Sawyer, A.T. and Fang, A. (2012) The efficacy of cognitive behavioral therapy: a review of meta-analyses, *Cognitive Therapy and Research*, 36(5), 427–440.

Hofstede, G. (1984) *Culture's Consequences: International Differences in Work-Related Values*, Beverly Hills, CA: Sage.

Hollensen, S. (2011) *A Decision-Oriented Approach*, Edinburgh: Pearson.

Holt, D.T., Armenakis, A.A., Harris, S.G. and Feild, H. S. (2007) Toward a comprehensive definition of readiness for change: a review of research and instrumentation, *Research in Organizational Change and Development*, 16, 289–336.

Horwitt, S.D. (1989) *Let Them Call Me Rebel: Saul Alinsky, His Life and Legacy*, New York: Knopf.

Horwitz, A.V. and Wakefield, J.C. (2007) *The Loss of Sadness: How Psychiatry Transformed Normal Sorrow into Depressive Disorder*, Oxford: Oxford University Press.

Howe, K.R. (1999) Equality of educational opportunity: philosophical issues, in P. Keeves and G. Lakomski (eds.), *Issues in Educational Research*, Oxford: Pergamon.

Hunt, S. (1981) Macromarketing as a multidimensional concept, *Journal of Macromarketing*, 1(1), 7–8.

Hussong, A.M., Jones, D.J., Stein, G.L., Baucom, D.H. and Boeding, S. (2011) An internalizing pathway to alcohol use and disorder, *Psychology of Addictive Behaviors*, 25, 390–404.

Hustad, J.T., Carey, K.B., Carey, M.P. and Maisto, S.A. (2009) Self-regulation, alcohol consumption, and consequences in college student heavy drinkers: a simultaneous latent growth analysis, *Journal of Studies on Alcohol and Drugs*, 70, 373–382.

Jack, F.R., Piacentini, M.G. and Schroder, M. (1998) Perception and role of fruit in the workday of Scottish lorry drivers, *Appetite*, 30, 139–149.

Jackson, M.C. (2003). *Systems Thinking: Creative Holism for Managers*, Chichester: Wiley.

Jackson, T. (2005) *Motivating Sustainable Consumption: A Review of Evidence on Consumer Behaviour and Behavioural Change*, Guildford: Centre for Environmental Strategy, University of Surrey.

Jackson, T. (2009) *Prosperity Without Growth: The Transition to a Sustainable Economy*, London: Sustainable Development Commission, www.sd-commission. org.uk/publications/downloads/prosperity_without_growth_report.pdf (accessed 24 March 2016).

Jain, A. (2009) *Principles of Marketing*, 3rd edn, Delhi: FK Publication.

James, O. (2007) *Affluenza: How to Be Successful and Stay Sane*, London: Vermilion.

James, O. (2008) *The Selfish Capitalist*, London: Vermilion.

Janis, I.L. and Mann, L. (1977) *Decision Making: A Psychological Analysis of Conflict, Choice and Commitment*, New York: The Free Press.

Jellinek, E.M. (1960) *The Disease Concept of Alcoholism*, New Brunswick, NJ: Hillhouse Press.

Jobber, D. (2003) *Principles and Practice of Marketing*, 4th edn, Maidenhead: McGraw-Hill.

Johnson, C.E. (2012) *Meeting the Ethical Challenges of Leadership: Casting Light or Shadow*, Thousand Oaks, CA: Sage.

Justin, M. (2002) *Nader: Crusader, Spoiler, Icon*, Cambridge, MA: Perseus Publishing.

Kahneman, D. (2003) A perspective on judgment and choice: mapping bounded rationality, *American Psychologist*, 58(9), 697–720.

Kahneman, D. and Tversky, A. (1979) Prospect theory: an analysis of decision under risk, *Econometrica*, 47, 263–292.

Kahneman, D., Diener, E. and Schwarz, N. (1999) *Well-Being: The Foundations of Hedonic Psychology*, New York: Russell Sage Foundation.

Kanayama, G., Brower, K.J., Wood, R.I., Hudson, J.I. and Pope, H.G. (2009) Anabolic-androgenic steroid dependence: an emerging disorder, *Addiction*, 104, 1966–1978.

Kandel, D.B., Yamaguchi, K. and Chen, K. (1992) Stages of progression in drug involvement from adolescence to adulthood: further evidence for the gateway theory, *Journal of Studies on Alcohol*, 53, 447–457.

Kavanagh, D. (1995) *Election Campaigning: The New Marketing of Politics*, Oxford: Blackwell.

Kearney, M.H. and O'Sullivan, J. (2003) Identity shifts as turning points in health behavior change, *Western Journal of Nursing Research*, 25, 134–152.

Keeney, R.L. and Raiffa, H. (1976) *Decisions with Multiple Objectives: Preferences and Value Tradeoffs*, New York: Wiley.

Keller, K.L. (2012) *Strategic Brand Management, Building, Measuring and Managing Brand Equity*, New Jersey: Pearson.

Kemmis, S. and McTaggart, R. (1988) *The Action Research Planner*, 3rd edn, Victoria, Australia: Deakin University Press.

Kennedy, A.-M. and Parsons, A. (2012) Macro-social marketing and social engineering: a systems approach, *Journal of Social Marketing*, 2(1), 37–51.

Khantzian, E.J. (1997) The self-medication hypothesis of substance use disorders: a reconsideration and recent applications, *Harvard Review of Psychiatry*, 4, 231–244.

Kidder, R.M. (1995) *How Good People Make Tough Choices: Resolving the Dilemmas of Ethical Living*, New York: Fireside.

Kinnier, T.R., Kernes, L.J. and Doutheribes, T.M. (2000) A short list of universal moral values, *Counseling & Values*, 45(1), 4–17.

Klandermans, B. (2004) The demand and supply of participation: social-psychological correlates of participation in social movements, in D.A. Snow, S.A. Soule and H. Kriesi (eds.), *The Blackwell Companion to Social Movements*, Oxford: Blackwell.

Klein, R. (2015) More than half of American schoolchildren now live in poverty, *The Huffington Post*, www.huffingtonpost.com/2015/01/16/southern-education-foundation-children-poverty_n_6489970.html (accessed 16 January 2015).

Kohlberg, L.A. (1971) *From Is to Ought: How to Commit the Naturalistic Fallacy and Get Away with It in the Study of Moral Development*, New York: Academic Press.

Kohlberg, L.A. (1986) A current statement on some theoretical issues, in S. Modgil and C. Modgil (eds.), *Lawrence Kohlberg: Consensus and Controversy*, Philadelphia: Palmer, pp. 485–546.

Kohlberg, L.A. and Lickona, T. (eds.) (1976) Moral stages and moralization: the cognitive-developmental approach, in *Moral Development and Behavior: Theory, Research and Social Issues*, Holt, NY: Rinehart and Winston.

Kolah, A. (2013) *Essential Law for Marketers*, 2nd edn, London: Kogan Page.

Kolb, D. (1984) *Experiential Learning*, Englewood Cliffs, NJ: Prentice-Hall.

Koob, G.F. and Le Moal, M. (2008) Addiction and the brain antireward system, *Annual Review of Psychology*, 59, 29–53.

Koob, G.F., Maldonado, R. and Stinus, L. (1992) Neural substrates of opiate withdrawal, *Trends in Neurosciences*, 15, 186–191.

Kotler, P. (2013) *World Social Marketing Conference (WSMC)*, www.youtube.com/watch?v=aLHgyxW1WD8 (accessed 29 November 2014).

Kotler, P. (2015) *Confronting Capitalism: Real Solutions for a Troubled Economic System*, New York: Amacom.

Kotler, P. and Lee, N. (2008) *Social Marketing: Influencing Behaviours for Good*, London: Sage.

Kotler P. and Levy, S.J. (1969) Broadening the concept of marketing, *Journal of Marketing*, 33(1), 10–15.

Kotler, P. and Roberto, E.L. (1989) *Social Marketing Strategies for Changing Public Behavior*, New York: The Free Press.

Kotler, P. and Zaltman, G. (1971) Social marketing: an approach to planned social change, *Journal of Marketing*, 35, 3–12.

Kotler, P., Armstrong, G., Brown, L. and Chandler, S.A. (1998) *Marketing*, 4th edn, Sydney: Prentice Hall.

Kotler, P., Armstrong, G., Saunders, J. and Wong, V. (2001) *Principles of Marketing*, 3rd edn, Harlow: Prentice Hall.

Kotler, P., Roberto, N. and Lee, N. (2002) *Social Marketing: Improving the Quality of Life*, Thousand Oaks, CA: Sage.

Kotler, P., Kartajaya, H. and Setiawan, I. (2010) *Marketing 3.0: From Products to Customers to the Human Spirit*, New Jersey: John Wiley and Sons.

Krugar, G.P., Brewster, R.M., Dick, V., Inderbitzen, R. and Staplin, L. (2007) *Health and Wellness Programs for Commercial Drivers: A Synthesis of Safety Practice, Federation Motor Carrier Safety Administration*, Washington, DC: Transport Research Board.

Kuhn, T. (1962) *The Structure of Scientific Revolutions*, Chicago: University of Chicago Press.

Kusiak, A. (2007) Innovation: the Living Laboratory perspective, *Computer-Aided Design and Applications*, 4(6), 863–876.

Laczniak, G.R., Lusch, R.F. and Murphy, P.E. (1979) Social marketing: its ethical dimensions, *Journal of Marketing*, 43, 29–36.

LaFollette, H. (ed.) (2007) *Ethics in Practice: An Anthology*, 3rd edn, Oxford: Blackwell.

Laing, S. and Brabazon, T. (2007) Creative doctorates, creative education? Aligning universities with the creative economy, *Nebula*, 4(2), 253–267.

Land, R., Meyer, J.H.F. and Smith, J. (2008) *Threshold Concepts Within the Disciplines*, Rotterdam and Taipei: Sense Publishers.

Lannon, J. (2008) *How Public Service Advertising Works*, London: World Advertising Research Center.

Lauterborn, B. (1990) New marketing litany: four Ps passé: C-words take over, *Advertising Age*, 61(41), 26.

Layard, R., Clark, D., Knapp, M. and Mayraz, G. (2007) Cost–benefit analysis of psychological therapy, *National Institute Economic Review*, 202, 90–98.

Lefebvre, R.C. (2013a) *A Consensus Definition of Social Marketing*, http:// socialmarketing.blogs.com/r_craiig_lefebvres_social/2013/10/a-consensus-definition-of-social-marketing.html#sthash.uKlH6J9k.dpuf (accessed 9 July 2015).

Lefebvre, R.C. (2013b) *Social Marketing and Social Change: Strategies and Tools to Improve Health, Well-Being and the Environment*, San Francisco: Jossey-Bass.

Lefebvre, R.C. and Flora, J.A. (1988) Social marketing and public health intervention, *Health Education Quarterly*, 15(3), 299–315.

Lennick, D. and Kiel, F. (2007) *Moral Intelligence: Enhancing Business Performance & Leadership Success*, Upper Saddle River, NJ: Wharton School Publishing.

Levenstein, M. (2013) A third way? Unifying two long-opposed philosophical schools could have far-reaching practical implications, *RSA*, 4, 26–29.

Levin, M. and Greenwood, D. (2013) Revitalising universities by reinventing the social and action research, in N. Denzin and L. Yvonna (eds.), *The Landscape of Qualitative Research*, Thousand Oaks, CA: Sage.

Levitt, T. (1960) Marketing myopia, *Harvard Business Review*, 38(4), 45–56.

Lewin, K. (1946) Action research and minority problems, *Journal of Social Issues*, 2(4), 34–46.

Lin, N. (1999) Building a network theory of social capital, *Connections*, 22(1), 28–51.

Loomba, A. (2005) *Colonialism/Postcolonialism*, London and New York: Routledge.

Lubman, D.I., Yucel, M. and Pantelis, C. (2004) Addiction, a condition of compulsive behaviour? Neuroimaging and neuropsychological evidence of inhibitory dysregulation, *Addiction*, 99, 1491–1502.

Luck, D.J. (1974) Social marketing: confusion compounded, *Journal of Marketing*, 38, 70–72.

Lyotard, J. (1979) *La Condition postmoderne: rapport sur le savoir*, Paris: Minuit.

Lyotard, J. (1985) Retour au Postmoderne. In Dix ans de Philosophie en France, *Magazine Littéraire*, 225 (December).

MacFadyen, L., Stead, M. and Hastings, G. (1999) *A Synopsis of Social Marketing*, Stirling: Institute for Social Marketing, http://staff.stir.ac.uk/w.m.thompson/ Social%20Enterprise/Library/Synopsis%20of%20Social%20Marketing.pdf (accessed 20 March 2016).

Madoz-Gurpide, A., Blasco-Fontecilla, H., Baca-Garcia, E. and Ochoa-Mangado, E. (2011) Executive dysfunction in chronic cocaine users: an exploratory study, *Drug and Alcohol Dependence*, 117, 55–58.

Maina, F. (2013) Le français, ce 'butin de guerre' aujourd'hui rejeté par l'Algérie www.algerie-focus.com/blog/2013/06/le-francais-ce-butin-de-guerre-aujour dhui-rejete-par-lalgerie (accessed 27 July 2014).

Makrides, L., Heath, S., Farquharson, J. and Veinot, P.L. (2006) Perceptions of workplace health: building community partnerships, *Clinical Governance: An International Journal*, 12(3), 178–187.

Mallett-Outtrim, R. (2015) *No, This Wasn't the Worst Massacre in Paris Since WWII*, www.telesurtv.net/english/analysis/No-This-Wasnt-the-Worst-Massacre-in-Paris-Since-WWII-20151116-0041.html (accessed 24 November 2015).

Mansfield, B. and Mitchell, L. (1997) *Towards a Competent Workforce*, Aldershot: Gower.

Manoff, R.K. (1985). *Social Marketing: New Imperative for Public Health*, New York: Praeger.

Marlatt, G.A. and George, W.H. (1984) Relapse prevention-introduction and overview of the model, *British Journal of Addiction*, 79, 261–273.

Marmot Review (2010) *Fair Society, Healthy Lives*, www.instituteofhealthequity.org/ projects/fair-society-healthy-lives-the-marmot-review (accessed 24 March 2016).

Marzillier, J. and Hall, J. (2009) The challenge of the Layard initiative, *The Psychologist*, 22, 396–399, https://thepsychologist.bps.org.uk/volume-22/edition-5/ challenge-layard-initiative (accessed 30 April 2015).

McCowan, T. and Unterhalter, E. (2015) *Education and International Development: An Introduction*, London: Bloomsbury.

McDonald, M. (2007) *Marketing Plans: How to Prepare Them, How to Use Them*, Oxford: Heinemann.

McNiff, J. (2013) *Comments on Action Research*, The Value and Virtue in Practice-Based Research conference, York St John conference.

McNiff, J. and Whitehead, J. (2011) *All You Need to Know About Action Research*, 2nd edn, London: Sage.

Mezirow, J.E. (1995) Transformative learning: theory to practice, in M.R. Welton (ed.), *In Defense of the Lifeworld*, New York: SUNY Press, pp 36–70.

Miller, E.K. and Cohen, J.D. (2001) An integrative theory of prefrontal cortex function, *Annual Review of Neuroscience*, 24, 167–202.

Morris, D. and Gilchrist, A. (2011) *Communities Connected: Inclusion, Participation and Common Purpose*, www.thersa.org/__data/assets/pdf_file/0011/518924/RSA_Communities-Connected-AW_181011.pdf (accessed on 26 February 2013).

MRS (2013) *MRS Code of Conduct*, www.mrs.org.uk/pdf/code_of_conduct.pdf (accessed 3 January 2013).

Murray, C. (2016) Craig Murray, former UK ambassador to Uzbekistan. https://www.youtube.com/watch?v=CIQ8VVn8AJA&feature=youtu.be (accessed on 4 May 2016).

Mytton, O., Clarke, D. and Rayner, M. (2012) Taxing unhealthy food and drinks to improve health, *British Medical Journal*, 344, e2931.

Nash, L.L. (1989) Ethics without the sermon, in K.R. Andrews (ed.), *Ethics in Practice: Managing the Moral Corporation*, Boston: Harvard Business School Press, pp. 243–257.

NESTA (2008) *Selling Sustainability: Seven Lessons from Advertising and Marketing to Sell Low-Carbon Living*, London: NESTA.

Nevin, J.A. and Grace, R.C. (2000) Behavioral momentum and the law of effect, *Behavioral and Brain Sciences*, 23, 73–90.

Noble, G. (2006) *Maintaining Social Marketing's Relevance: A Dualistic Approach*, ANZMAC Conference, Brisbane, Australia.

Northouse, P.G. (2013) *Leadership: Theory and Practice*, 6th edn., Thousand Oaks, CA: Sage.

NSMC (2006) *Social Marketing: Presentational Resource Material*, London: National Consumer Council.

NSMC (2012) *What Role Can Social Marketing Play in Tackling the Social Determinants of Health Inequalities?* London: NSMC.

Nussbaum, M.C. (2000) *Women and Human Development: the Capabilities Approach*, Cambridge: Cambridge University Press.

Oancea, A. (2012) Philosophy of education, in J. Arthur and A. Peterson (eds.), *The Routledge Companion to Education*, London: Routledge.

OECD (2001) *Citizens as Partners: Information, Consultation and Public Participation in Policy-making*, Paris: Organisation for Economic Co-operation and Development.

Oliver, A. (2013) *Behavioural Public Policy*, Cambridge: Cambridge University Press.

O'Malley, L. and Patterson, M. (2002) Vanishing point: the mix management paradigm reviewed (introspective retrospective), *The Marketing Review*, 3(1), 39–63.

Orford, J. (2001) Addiction as excessive appetite, *Addiction*, 96, 15–31.

Palmer, P. (1997) *The Courage to Teach: Exploring the Inner Landscape of a Teacher's Life*, San Francisco: Jossey-Bass.

Peattie, S. and Peattie, K. (2003) Ready to fly solo? Reducing social marketing's dependence on commercial marketing theory, *Marketing Theory*, 3(3), 365–385.

Peterson, C. (2006) *Primer in Positive Psychology*, New York: Oxford University Press.

Peterson, C. and Seligman, M.E.P. (2004) *Character Strengths and Virtues: A Handbook and Classification*, Oxford: Oxford University Press.

Petty, R.E., Baker, S.M. and Gleicher, F. (1991) Attitudes and drug-abuse prevention-implications of the elaboration likelihood model of persuasion, in

L. Donohew, H. Sypher and W. Buksoski (eds.), *Persuasive Communication and Drug Abuse Prevention*, London and New York: Routledge, pp. 71–90.

Philips, D.C. (2010) What is philosophy of education? in R. Bailey, R. Barrow, D. Carr and C. McCarty (eds.), *The Sage Handbook of Philosophy of Education*, London: Sage, pp. 3–19.

Piketty, T. (2013) *Le capital au 21e siècle*, Paris: Editions du Seuil.

Polonsky, M.J., Carlson, L. and Fry, M.-L. (2003) The harm chain: a public policy development and stakeholder perspective, *Marketing Theory*, 3(3), 345–364.

Popper, K. (1966 [1945]) *The Open Society and Its Enemies, Vol. 1*, 5th edn, Princeton: Princeton University Press.

Portes, A. (1998) Social capital: its origins and applications in modern sociology, *Annual Review of Sociology*, 98, 1320–1350.

Positive Psychology Centre (2014) *University of Pennsylvania: Frequently Asked Questions*, www.ppc.sas.upenn.edu/faqs.htm (accessed 8 March 2016).

Prayson, D. (2012). *Flew, Dawkins and God*, https://withalliamgod.wordpress.com/2012/11/02/flew-dawkins-and-god (accessed 3 May 2015).

Previte, J. and Fry, M.-L. (2006) *Conceptualising the Harm Chain in Social Marketing Strategy: A Drink-Drive Application*, ANZMAC 2006 Conference, 4–6 December, Brisbane, Queensland.

Prochaska, J.O., DiClemente, C.C. and Norcross, J.C. (1992) In search of how people change-applications to addictive behaviors, *American Psychologist*, 47, 1102–1114.

Raelin, J.A. (2000) *Work-Based Learning: The New Frontier of Management Development*, Upper Saddle, NJ: Prentice-Hall.

Rapoport, R. (1970) Three dilemmas of action research, *Human Relations*, 23, 499–513.

Rawls, J. (1972) *A Theory of Justice*, Oxford: Clarendon Press.

Reason, P. and Bradbury, H. (eds.) (2007) *The Sage Handbook of Action Research: Participative Inquiry and Practice*, Thousand Oaks, CA: Sage.

Redeker, R. (2007) *The New Face of Humanity*, Bethesda, MD: Academica Press.

Reicher, S. (2000) Against methodolatry: some comments on Elliott, Fischer, and Rennie, *British Journal of Clinical Psychology*, 39, 1–6.

Rende, R., Slomkowski, C., Lloyd-Richardson, E. and Niaura, R. (2005) Sibling effects on substance use in adolescence: social contagion and genetic relatedness, *Journal of Family Psychology*, 19, 611–618.

Rest, J.R. (1986) *Moral Development: Advances in Research and Theory*, New York: Praeger.

Rest, J.R., Narvaez, D., Thoma, S.J. and Bebeau, M.J. (1999) DIT2: devising and testing a revised instrument of moral judgment, *Journal of Educational Psychology*, 91(4), 644–659.

Rest, J.R., Narvaez, D., Thoma, S.J. and Bebeau, M.J. (2000) A neo-Kohlbergian approach to morality research, *Journal of Moral Education*, 29(4), 381–395.

Revans, R.W. (1971) *Developing Effective Managers: A New Approach to Business Education*, New York: Praeger.

Riley, W., Rivera, D., Atienza, A., Nilsen, W., Allison, S. and Mermelstein, R. (2011) Health behavior models in the age of mobile interventions: are our theories up to the task? *Translational Behavioral Medicine*, 1, 53–71.

Rice, R.E. and Atkin, C.K. (eds.) (1989) *Public Communication Campaigns*, Thousand Oaks, CA: Sage.

Robinson, M.N., Tansil, K.A., Elder, R.W., Soler, R.E., Labre, M.P., Mercer, S.L., Eroglu, D., Baur, C., Lyon-Daniel, K., Fridinger, F., Sokler, L.A., Green, L.W., Miller, T., Dearing, J.W., Evans, W.D., Snyder, L.B., Viswanath, K.K., Beistle, D.M., Chervin, D.D., Bernhardt, J.M., Rimer B.K. and the Community Preventive Services Task Force (2014) Mass media health communication campaigns combined with health-related product distribution: a Community Guide systematic review, *American Journal of Preventive Medicine*, 47(3), 360–371.

Robinson-Maynard, A., Meaton, J. and Lowry, R. (2013) Identifying key criteria as predictors of success in social marketing: establishing an evaluative template and grid (ETG), in *Contemporary Issues in Social Marketing*, Cambridge: Cambridge Scholars, pp. 41–58.

Rudolph, L. (2013) *Qualitative Mathematics for the Social Sciences: Mathematical Models for Research on Cultural Dynamics*, London: Routledge.

Ryan, R.M. and Deci, E.L. (2000) Self-determination theory and the facilitation of intrinsic motivation, social development, and well-being, *The American Psychologist*, 55, 68–78.

Said, E. (1979) *Orientalism*, New York: Vintage Books.

Said, E. (2001) The clash of ignorance, *The Nation*, 22 October.

Sajoo, E. (2015) Education, religion, and values, in E. Unterhalter and T. McCowan (ed.), *Education, Religion, and Development: Practice, Policy, and Research*, London: Bloomsbury Press.

Samson, A. (ed.) (2014) *The Behavioral Economics Guide 2014*, www.behavioraleconomics.com (accessed 8 March 2016).

Schiffman, L.G., Kanuk, L.L. and Hansen, H. (2012) *Consumer Behaviour: A European Outlook*, 2nd edn, Harlow: Pearson.

Schon D. (1987) *Educating the Reflective Practitioner*, San Francisco, CA: Jossey-Bass.

Seligman, M.E.P. (2002) *Authentic Happiness: Using the New Positive Psychology to Realize Your Potential for Lasting Fulfillment*, New York: Free Press/Simon and Schuster.

Seligman, M.E.P. and Csikszentmihalyi, M. (eds.) (2000) Positive psychology [Special issue] *American Psychologist*, 55(1).

Seligman, M.E.P. and Pawelski, J.O. (2003) Positive psychology: FAQs, *Psychological Inquiry*, 14, 159–163.

Sen, A.K. (1999) *Development As Freedom*, Oxford: Oxford University Press.

Sen, A.K. (2009) *The Idea of Justice*, London: Allen Lane, Penguin Books Ltd.

Shafir, E. (ed.) (2013) *The Behavioural Foundations of Public Policy*, Princeton and Oxford: Princeton University Press.

Shah, A.K and Oppenheimer, D.M. (2008) Heuristics made easy: an effort-reduction framework, *Psychological Bulletin*, 134(2), 207–222.

Sheard, M. (2013) *Mental Toughness: The Mindset Behind Sporting Achievement*, 2nd edn, London: Routledge.

Shizumu, K. (2003) *Symbiotic Marketing Strategy*, Japan: Souseisha Book Company.

Simon, H. (1979) *Models of Thought*, Vols. 1 and 2, New Heaven, CT: Yale University Press.

Skog, O.-J. (2003) Addiction: definitions and mechanisms, in R.E. Vuchinich and N. Heather (eds.), *Choice, Behavioural Economics and Addiction*, Amsterdam: Pergamon, pp. 157–175.

Slovic, P., Finucane, M., Peters, E. and MacGregor, D.G. (2002) The affect heuristic, in T. Gilovich, D. Griffin and D. Kahneman (eds.), *Intuitive Judgement: Heuristics and Biases*, New York: Cambridge University Press, pp. 397–420.

Smelser, N.J. (1962) *Theory of Collective Behavior*, London: Collier-Macmillan.

Smith, B. (2008) Save the crabs. Then eat 'em, in P. Kotler and N. Lee (eds.), *Social Marketing: Influencing Behaviors for Good*, London: Sage.

Smithson, M. (1988). Possibility theory, fuzzy logic, and psychological explanation, in T. Zetenyi (ed.), *Fuzzy Sets in Psychology*, North Holland: Elsevier Science Publishers.

Sober, E. and Wilson, D.S. (1998) *Unto Ohers: The Evolution and Psychology of Unselfish Behavior*, Cambridge, MA: Harvard University Press.

Sorensen, P.F., Yaeger, T.F. and Bengtsson, U. (2003) The promise of appreciative inquiry: a 20-year review, *OD Practitioner*, 35(4), 15–21.

Soumyaja, D., Kamalanabhan, T.J. and Bhattacharyya, S. (2011) Employee readiness to change and individual intelligence: the facilitating role of process and contextual factors, *International Journal of Business Insights and Transformation*, 4(2), 85–91.

Spivak, G. (1988) Can the subaltern speak? in C. Nelson and G. Lawrence (eds.), *Marxism and the Interpretation of Culture*, Chicago: Illinois University Press, pp. 271–313.

Stead, M., Gordon, R., Angus, K. and McDermott, L. (2006) A systematic review of social marketing effectiveness, *Health Education*, 17(2), 126–191.

Stearns, P. (1999) *Consumerism in World History: The Global Transformation of Desire*, London: Routledge.

Stevens, G.W. (2013) Toward a process-based approach to conceptualizing change readiness, *Journal of Applied Behavioural Science*, 49(3): 333–360.

Stokes, P. (2004) *Philosophy: 100 Essential Thinkers*, Kettering: Index Books.

Summers, L. and Balls, E. (2015) *How to Create Inclusive Prosperity – and Save Democracy*, www.huffingtonpost.com/larry-summers/how-to-save-democracy_b_6484320.html (accessed 18 January 2015).

Susman, G. (1983) Action research: a sociotechnical systems perspective, in G. Morgan (ed.), *Beyond Method*, Beverly Hills, CA: Sage.

Tapp, A. and Spotswood, F. (2013) From the 4 Ps to COM-SM: reconfiguring the social marketing mix, *Journal of Social Marketing*, 3(3), 206–222.

Terracciano, A., Abdel-Khalek, A.M., Ádám, N., Adamovová, L., Ahn, C.-K., Ahn, H.-N., et al. (2005) National character does not reflect mean personality trait levels in 49 cultures, *Science*, 310, 96–100.

Thaler, R. and Sunstein, C. (2008) *Nudge: Improving Decisions About Health, Wealth and Happiness*, New Haven, CT: Yale University Press.

Thomas, P. (2008) *Marxism and Scientific Socialism: From Engels to Althusser*, London: Routledge.

Thomas, R.K. (2008) *Health Service Marketing: A Practitioner's Guide*, New York: Springer.

Torbert, W.R. and Taylor, S.S. (2007) Action inquiry: interweaving multiple qualities of attention for timely action, in P. Reason and H. Bradbury (eds.), *The Sage Handbook of Action Research: Participative Inquiry and Practice*, Thousand Oaks, CA: Sage.

Tudge, J., Mokrova, I., Karnik, R.B. and Hatfield, B.E. (2011) Uses and misuses of Bronfenbrenner's bioecological theory of human development, *Journal of Family Theory & Review*, 1(4), 198–210.

Turkovich, M. (2014) Kateb Yacine, in *Voices, Compassion, Education*, http://voiceseducation.org/content/kateb-yacine#sthash.H0XP2wN5.dpuf (accessed 28 July 2014).

Tversky, A. and Kahneman, D. (1974) Judgment under uncertainty: heuristics and biases, *Science*, 185(4157), 1124–1131.

UKCES (2013) *National Occupational Standards (NOS): Social Marketing (Suite)*, http://nos.ukces.org.uk/Pages/results.aspx?u=http%3A%2F%2Fnos%2Eukces%2Eorg%2Euk&k=social%20marketing#k=social%20marketing (accessed 18 June 2013).

Uleman, J.S. and Bargh, J.A. (1989) *Unintended Thought*, New York: Guilford Press.

Vargo, S.L. and Lusch, R.F. (2004) Evolving to a new dominant logic for marketing, *Journal of Marketing*, 68, 1–17.

Wallensteen, P. (2007) *Understanding Conflict Resolution: War, Peace and the Global System*, 2nd edn, London: Sage.

Walsh, D.C., Rudd, R.E., Moeykens, B.A. and Moloney, T.W. (1993) Social marketing for public health, *Health Affairs*, 12(2), 104–119.

Wardle, J. and Johnson, F. (1996) Weight and diets: examining levels of weight concern in British adults, *International Journal of Obesity*, 26, 1144–1149.

Weinreich, N.K. (2013) www.social-marketing.com/Whatis.html (accessed 3 April 2013).

Wells, W.D., Burnett, J. and Moriarty, S. (2000) *Advertising: Principles and Practice*, Harlow: Prentice Hall.

West, R. (2013) *Models of Addiction. EMCDDA Insights. Number 14: European Monitoring Centre for Drugs and Drug Addiction*, Luxembourg: Publications Office of the European Union.

West, R. and Brown, J. (2013) *Theory of Addiction*, Chichester: John Wiley & Sons.

Whitfield-Jacobson, P.J., Prawitz, A.D. and Lukaszuk, J. M. (2007) Long-haul truck drivers want healthful meal options at truck-stop restaurants, *Journal of the American Dietetic Association*, 107(12), 2125–2129.

Whitelaw, S., Baldwin, S., Bunton, R. and Flynn, D. (2000) The status of evidence and outcomes in stages of change research, *Health Education Research*, 15(6), 707–718.

Widiger, T.A. and Sankis, L.M. (2000) Adult psychopathology: issues and controversies, *Annual Review of Psychology*, 51, 377–404.

Wiebe, G.D. (1952) Merchandising commodities and citizenship on television, *Public Opinion Quarterly*, 15, 679–691.

Wilkinson, R.G. and Pickett, K. (2009) *The Spirit Level: Why Greater Equality Makes Societies Stronger*, London: Bloomsbury.

Wilson, M., Holman, P. and Hammock, A. (1996) A comprehensive review of the effects of worksite health promotion on health-related outcomes, *American Journal of Health Promotion*, 10, 429–435.

Wing Sue, D. and Rivera, D. (2011) Microaggressions in everyday life: a new view on racism, sexism, and heterosexism, *Psychology Today*, www.psychologytoday.com/blog/microaggressions-in-everyday-life/201102/how-does-oppression-microaggressions-affect (accessed on 4 May 2015).

WSMC (2008) World Social Marketing Conference, Brighton and Hove City, 29–30 September, www.tcp-events.co.uk/wsmc/speakers.html (accessed 10 July 2015).

Young, D., Borland, R. and Coghill, K. (2011) An actor–network theory analysis of policy innovation for smoke-free places: understanding change in complex systems, *American Journal of Public Health*, 100, 1208–1217.

Zaltman, G. and Zaltman, L. (2008) *Marketing Metaphoria: What Deep Metaphors Reveal About the Minds of Consumers*, Cambridge, MA: Harvard Business School Press.

Index

Taylor & Francis eBooks

Helping you to choose the right eBooks for your Library

Add Routledge titles to your library's digital collection today. Taylor and Francis ebooks contains over 50,000 titles in the Humanities, Social Sciences, Behavioural Sciences, Built Environment and Law.

Choose from a range of subject packages or create your own!

Benefits for you

» Free MARC records
» COUNTER-compliant usage statistics
» Flexible purchase and pricing options
» All titles DRM-free.

Benefits for your user

» Off-site, anytime access via Athens or referring URL
» Print or copy pages or chapters
» Full content search
» Bookmark, highlight and annotate text
» Access to thousands of pages of quality research at the click of a button.

REQUEST YOUR FREE INSTITUTIONAL TRIAL TODAY

Free Trials Available
We offer free trials to qualifying academic, corporate and government customers.

eCollections – Choose from over 30 subject eCollections, including:

Archaeology	Language Learning
Architecture	Law
Asian Studies	Literature
Business & Management	Media & Communication
Classical Studies	Middle East Studies
Construction	Music
Creative & Media Arts	Philosophy
Criminology & Criminal Justice	Planning
Economics	Politics
Education	Psychology & Mental Health
Energy	Religion
Engineering	Security
English Language & Linguistics	Social Work
Environment & Sustainability	Sociology
Geography	Sport
Health Studies	Theatre & Performance
History	Tourism, Hospitality & Events

For more information, pricing enquiries or to order a free trial, please contact your local sales team:
www.tandfebooks.com/page/sales

Routledge
Taylor & Francis Group

The home of
Routledge books

www.tandfebooks.com

For Product Safety Concerns and Information please contact our EU representative GPSR@taylorandfrancis.com Taylor & Francis Verlag GmbH, Kaufingerstraße 24, 80331 München, Germany

Printed and bound by CPI Group (UK) Ltd, Croydon, CR0 4YY

01/05/2025

01858448-0001